HOW AMERICA LOST ITS MIND

THE JULIAN J. ROTHBAUM DISTINGUISHED LECTURE SERIES

HOW AMERICA LOST ITS MIND

The Assault on Reason
That's Crippling Our Democracy

THOMAS E. PATTERSON

UNIVERSITY OF OKLAHOMA PRESS : NORMAN

Library of Congress Cataloging-in-Publication Data

Names: Patterson, Thomas E., author.

Title: How America lost its mind : the assault on reason that's crippling our
    democracy / Thomas E. Patterson.

Description: Norman, OK : University of Oklahoma Press, [2019] | Series: The Julian J.
    Rothbaum distinguished lecture series ; volume 15 | Includes bibliographical
    references and index.

Identifiers: LCCN 2019005277 | ISBN 978-0-8061-6432-8 (hardcover : alk. paper)

Subjects: LCSH: Political culture—United States. | Polarization (Social sciences)—
    Political aspects—United States. | Mass media—Political aspects—United States. |
    United States—Politics and government—2017–

Classification: LCC JK1726 .P363 2019 | DDC 306.20973—dc23

LC record available at https://lccn.loc.gov/2019005277

How America Lost Its Mind: The Assault on Reason That's Crippling Our Democracy is
Volume 15 in The Julian J. Rothbaum Distinguished Lecture Series.

The paper in this book meets the guidelines for permanence and durability of the
Committee on Production Guidelines for Book Longevity of the Council on Library
Resources, Inc. ∞

2 3 4 5 6 7 8 9 10

To the memory of Wolfgang Donsbach,
a friend and colleague like no other

CONTENTS

FOREWORD

Among the many good things that have happened to me in my life, there is none in which I take more pride than the establishment of the Carl Albert Congressional Research and Studies Center at the University of Oklahoma, and none in which I take more satisfaction than the Center's presentation of the Julian J. Rothbaum Distinguished Lecture Series. The series is a perpetually endowed program of the University of Oklahoma, created in honor of Julian J. Rothbaum by his wife, Irene, and son, Joel Jankowsky.

Julian J. Rothbaum, my close friend since our childhood days in southeastern Oklahoma, has long been a leader in Oklahoma in civic affairs. He served as a Regent of the University of Oklahoma for two terms and as a State Regent for Higher Education. In 1974 he was awarded the University's highest honor, the Distinguished Service Citation, and in 1986 he was inducted into the Oklahoma Hall of Fame.

The Rothbaum Lecture Series is devoted to the themes of representative government, democracy and education, and citizen participation in public affairs, values to which Julian J. Rothbaum was committed throughout his life. His lifelong dedication to the University of Oklahoma, the state, and his country is a tribute to the ideals to which the Rothbaum Lecture Series is dedicated. The books in the series make an enduring contribution to an understanding of American democracy.

Carl B. Albert
Forty-Sixth Speaker of the
United States House of Representatives

PREFACE

Dystopian titles are often nothing more than marketing tools, but such a title is necessary for this book. *How America Lost Its Mind* describes the sorry state of our democracy at this early point in the twenty-first century. The corruption of thought, information, and common sense is eroding governing institutions and traditions that took more than two centuries and ten generations of Americans to build.

This book originated in the Julian J. Rothbaum Distinguished Lecture series that I gave at the University of Oklahoma. Sponsored by the Carl Albert Congressional Research and Studies Center, the series is held biennially and extends for a week. Its earlier speakers have included scholars whose work I admire: James MacGregor Burns, Steve Smith, Seymour Martin Lipset, Jennifer Hochschild, Morris Fiorina, Theda Skocpol, Chuck Jones, Dick Fenno, and Ted Lowi. It was easy to accept an invitation to join that list, but there was a problem. The lecturer is required to write a book derived from the lectures, and I didn't have one in mind, other than knowing that in one way or another it would address the topic of the media and public opinion. It was during the course of preparing the lectures—and even more while listening to those who came to my talks—that the core argument of the book began to take shape.

Americans have lost touch with reality. On virtually every issue, from climate change to immigration, tens of millions of Americans have opinions and beliefs wildly at odds with the facts. As I show in the first chapter, today's level of misinformation is unprecedented and is a far greater danger to our democracy than the long-standing problem of an uninformed citizenry. The uninformed know what they don't know, whereas the misinformed think they know something but don't know it, which leads them into senseless decisions. The second chapter examines the link between misinformation and partisanship. On almost every issue, misinformation is concentrated in the minds of either Republicans or Democrats. It has reached the point where, although Republicans and Democrats live in the same country, their minds reside in different ones, making it nearly impossible for them to understand each other, much less resolve their differences.

Age-old incentives—the lure of power, celebrity, and money—have corrupted the media system that is the source of our information. Media dysfunction began decades ago but is now careening out of control. One set of information corruptors, whom I call the "disruptors" and discuss in the third chapter, lust for power and have weaponized information, twisting it to serve their political and personal agendas. Another set, whom I call the "performers," lust after celebrity and thrive in a mutual-referential world of caricatures and inane chatter. Their role in misinforming us is explained in the fourth chapter. Then there are the "marketers," who are the subject of the fifth chapter. Their lust is money, and they peddle what sells, no matter how trivial, inaccurate, or distracting. Collectively, these media and political actors have scrambled our minds. We've reached a point where we think that nonsense is knowledge. It's a dangerous position for a democracy. As the philosopher Hannah Arendt noted decades ago, demagoguery is abetted by "people for whom the distinction between fact and fiction, true and false, no longer exists."

The forces that have brought us to this point are powerful and will not bend easily. But I discuss in the final chapter what could be done to bring about change. It would require us to wrest power from the ideologues and mind twisters and entrust it to level-headed leaders and reliable sources. It would also require us as citizens to accept our role in the misinformation crisis. We can't have a thriving citizen democracy if citizens fail to accept the responsibilities of citizenship.

———

I have many people to thank for their contributions to this book, including the kind and thoughtful folks at the University of Oklahoma. I talked with so many faculty in the political science and communication departments that I would inadvertently leave some off the list if I tried to name them. But I do want to single out and thank the principals at the Carl Albert Center who hosted my lecture series: Gary Copeland, Ron Peters, Cindy Rosenthal, and Ladonna Sullivan. During my week at Oklahoma, I also had the wise counsel of Joel Jankowsky, son of Julian and Irene Rothbaum, who endowed the Rothbaum Lecture series. Kent Calder was my acquisitions editor at the University of Oklahoma Press; I'm indebted to him for his insightful suggestions. I also want to thank in particular Keith Gaddie of Oklahoma's political science department. Keith served as a reviewer and provided thoughtful ideas for revising the manuscript, as did the second reviewer, Texas A&M's Kirby Goidel.

This book would be mighty thin if not for the hundreds of research scholars whose work has informed it. The footnotes testify to their contribution. As one of the book's reviewers noted, the book is a meta-study, although not written in the scholarly style of a meta-study. I'm sure that some of these scholars would take exception to some of my arguments, but their work nonetheless shaped my thinking. I've strived to cite their work fully and accurately, so that they get the credit that's due them.

Finally, I owe a special thanks to those at Harvard who had a hand in the book. I had the help of dedicated research assistants: Emily Roseman, Eric Singerman, and Adam Giorgi. I benefitted from the advice of superb colleagues who listened to my arguments and read early drafts: Matt Baum, Nancy Gibbs, Alex Jones, Nicco Mele, and Nancy Palmer. And then there was my constant and first reader, Lorie Conway, who is my wife. No chapter reached the eyes of another until she signaled that it was deserving of a second look.

Thomas E. Patterson
Cambridge, Massachusetts

HOW AMERICA LOST ITS MIND

CHAPTER 1

THE KNOW NOTHINGS

*I hate purity, I hate goodness. I don't want any virtue to
exist anywhere. I want everyone to be corrupt to the bones.*

Well then, I ought to suit you, dear. I'm corrupt to the bones.

George Orwell, *Nineteen Eighty-Four*

It was a bright Sunday afternoon in the nation's capital when Edgar
Maddison Welch walked into Comet Ping Pong and, after telling
customers to flee, searched the restaurant and opened fire. After
his arrest, police recovered a pistol and assault rifle at the scene and
another gun in his pickup truck. What prompted Welch to shoot
up a pizzeria? He didn't have a grudge against a former boss or fellow employee. Welch had driven his truck from North Carolina to
"self-investigate" a story he had seen online.[1] The fake story claimed
that coded emails on Hillary Clinton's private server revealed the
pizza shop was a front for a child sex ring in which she and other top
Democrats were involved. The victims were supposedly imprisoned
in vaults hidden below the shop.

Whatever fool Welch might have been, he was not alone in his thinking. A poll taken after Welch's arrest indicated that a third of American
adults thought the sex ring allegation was "definitely" or "probably"
true.[2] A third of adults is roughly eighty million people. If they could
somehow join hands, they would form six lines stretching all the way
from New York to Los Angeles.

Absurd ideas are nothing new. When fluoride was added to the
nation's water supply six decades ago, some Americans said it was a
communist plot to poison the nation's youth.[3] Fear of communism soon
led to other bizarre ideas, including the claim that President Eisenhower

and Martin Luther King were Soviet agents.[4] In a seminal 1964 *Harper's Magazine* article, the historian Richard Hofstadter described such thinking as "the paranoid style." "No other word," Hofstadter wrote, "adequately evokes the sense of heated exaggeration, suspiciousness, and conspiratorial fantasy that I have in mind."[5]

The crazed anti-communists of the cold war era have met their match in recent years. Nearly every major political development has sparked fanciful claims, even when the facts are right in front of our eyes. On September 11, 2001, Americans saw commercial airliners plow into the World Trade Center towers and the Pentagon. Within days, they saw footage of the terrorists going through security lines at Boston's Logan Airport and heard that they had taken flight training in Florida and Arizona. Nevertheless, conspiracy theorists claim it was an inside job orchestrated by the U.S. government. Rather than being piloted by hijackers, the airliners were said to be on autopilot. And rather than collapsing from intense heat, the World Trade Center towers were allegedly brought to earth by preset explosive devices triggered by government agents.[6]

If 9/11 sparked some of the more farfetched conspiracies, one doesn't have to search hard to find others. They number in the scores and have one thing in common—the belief that powerful actors secretly plotted a foul deed and are getting away with it.

It is nearly impossible to convince conspiracy theorists that they are out of their minds. They've woven a story so tightly knit that it can't be unwrapped. The logic of a conspiracy theory is its own defense. Powerful actors who are clever enough to pull off an evil deed are clever enough to cover their tracks with a plausible lie. Why did one of the hijacked airliners on 9/11 crash in a Pennsylvania field on its way to Washington? Conspiracy theorists would have us believe that the plane was shot down by a military jet, which officials covered up by saying that valiant passengers had attacked the hijackers, causing the plane to spin out of control.[7]

How about our crazed pizza shop shooter? How did conspiracy buffs deal with his fruitless search of Comet Ping Pong? After his arrest, they concluded that he was a plant—a "false flag," to use their term. They claimed that Clinton's agents had sent him to Washington to throw the police off track.[8]

———

Some conspiracy theories are harmful. A few are downright dangerous. Most are merely bizarre. They might even keep the paranoid among us from fixating on their neighbors. More harmful to our democracy is a cousin of conspiracy theories—misinformation. It also involves fanciful ideas about the actual state of the world, but it is far more widespread and a far greater threat. At times, it describes the thinking of a majority, as it did during the lead-up to the 2003 Iraq invasion. Polls showed that most Americans falsely believed that Iraq was aligned with al-Qaeda, the terrorist group behind the 9/11 attacks. Many Americans even falsely believed Iraqis were flying the planes that slammed into the World Trade Center towers and the Pentagon. Those with false beliefs were four times more likely than better-informed Americans to favor an invasion of Iraq.[9] Exclude them from the numbers and the George W. Bush administration would have been forced to invade Iraq against the wishes of a solid majority. Whether President Bush would then have pursued a different policy is impossible to know. But it's conceivable that he would have decided to rely on economic sanctions and UN weapons inspectors to contain Iraq, which would have limited the turmoil that ensued after the American invasion.

Misinformation has its comic side. In one poll, 10 percent of respondents thought Judith Sheindlin ("Judge Judy") holds a seat on the Supreme Court.[10] But the grim side is alarming. It is easy today to find policy issues on which millions of Americans are wildly misinformed. Never in the history of scientific opinion polls, which date to the 1930s, has misinformation clouded the minds of so many people.[11]

Some degree of political misinformation is to be expected. Politics is largely a secondhand experience—something we hear about from others. We would understand it better if we experienced it directly. A skier who has just smacked into a tree has a reality check denied to the citizen who is convinced that welfare recipients eat up half the federal budget.

But today's volume of misinformation is unprecedented. Some beliefs are so far off the mark as to raise doubts about our reasoning ability. A recent poll asked Americans for their "best guess" of the percentage of the federal budget spent on foreign aid. On average, respondents estimated it at 26 percent, which would make the foreign aid budget larger than that of the Pentagon or Social Security.[12] The actual number is less than 1 percent. At that, much of this spending is in the form of foodstuffs and military hardware produced by Americans and sent overseas.

Ironically, the misinformed think they're highly informed. "Cognoscenti of their own bamboozlement" is how sociologist Todd Gitlin describes them.[13] A study found, for example, that those who know the least about climate-change science are the ones who think they're the best informed on the issue.[14] Another study found that those who are the least knowledgeable about welfare benefits are the ones who claim to know the most about it.[15]

A full list of Americans' false beliefs would fill many pages. Here are some of the more prominent ones from recent years, along with the rough percentage of Americans who believed they were true at the time the poll was taken:

Crime has gone up in the past decade (70 percent).[16]

Donald Trump won the popular vote in the 2016 election (20 percent).[17]

The unemployment rate went up during Obama's presidency (40 percent).[18]

Iraqis used weapons of mass destruction against U.S. troops during the Iraq invasion (20 percent).[19]

The 2010 Affordable Care Act includes "death panels" (40 percent).[20]

Childhood vaccines cause autism (15 percent).[21]

The federal budget deficit could be eliminated by cutting government waste and fraud (70 percent).[22]

China owns more than half of U.S. debt (50 percent).[23]

The 2010 Affordable Care Act provides free medical care to illegal immigrants (55 percent).[24]

Millions of people cast illegal votes for Hillary Clinton in the 2016 election (30 percent).[25]

Barack Obama was definitely or probably born outside the United States (30 percent).[26]

Global warming is a hoax (35 percent).[27]

Genetically modified foods are unsafe to eat (40 percent).[28]

Russia didn't meddle in the 2016 presidential election (37 percent).[29]
The 2009 economic stimulus bill caused job losses (20 percent).[30]
U.S. military forces found weapons of mass destruction after
     invading Iraq (25 percent).[31]
Social Security will go totally broke in my lifetime (50 percent).[32]

There is substantial empirical evidence to show that each of these beliefs is false. Not that the individuals who hold such beliefs would agree. As the philosopher Ludwig Wittgenstein wrote, "If there were a verb meaning 'to believe falsely,' it would not have any significant first person, present indicative."[33]

————

Early scientific opinion polls revealed that Americans didn't know much about public affairs.[34] An alarming number of citizens couldn't answer simple questions like the name of their state's governor. Analysts questioned whether citizens were equipped to play the role that democracy asks of them.[35]

Since then, there has been a revolution in mass communication and a substantial increase in the number of people with a college education. Americans have never had so much information available or been better trained to handle it. Yet they are no better informed today than they were decades ago.[36] The high-school-educated public of the 1950s knew as much about the structure of America's government as does the media-saturated, college-educated public of today. When asked in a recent national survey to name the three branches of government, only a third of respondents could do so. Another third could name one or two. The final third couldn't name a single one.[37] Those ratios are nearly the same as when Americans were asked the question in 1952.[38] In poll after poll, Americans come up short in their factual information about politics, even when prompted. A recent Pew poll, for instance, asked respondents to pick the current Israeli prime minister from a list of four—Benjamin Netanyahu, David Cameron, Ariel Sharon, and Hosni Mubarak. A majority of the respondents—three in every five—picked someone other than Netanyahu or said they didn't know.[39]

Duke University's James David Barber wrote that the uninformed "are dangerously unready when the time comes for choice."[40] But whatever

risk the uninformed pose, it pales alongside the risk posed by the misinformed. The uninformed know what they don't know, whereas the
misinformed think they know something but don't know it. It is the
difference between ignorance and irrationality.[41]

Scholars argue over the question of whether the public behaves
rationally.[42] Some scholars, noting the large number of uninformed
citizens, say "no" while others, looking at the decisions of the public as
a whole, say "yes."[43] The second view acknowledges that many voters are
uninformed and make erratic choices but concludes that their selections
are random enough to cancel each other out, allowing better-informed
voters to decide the outcome.

I have long sided with the second view, which is similar to that of
James Surowiecki's notion of the "wisdom of crowds."[44] But I am now
less sure that the evidence supports a claim of collective rationality. If
vast numbers of citizens are misinformed and make policy and candidate choices on that basis, it becomes harder to assert that ignorance
is randomly distributed and that the public as a whole knows what it's
doing. Rationality goes out the window when citizens lose touch with
reality.[45] The problem of the misinformed voters is not their logic. Their
decisions make perfect sense given what they believe. The problem is
that they are living in an alternative world. It is a bit like going into a
store thinking you are buying half a dozen donuts and proudly walking
out with a six-pack of beer.

———

Anxiety can play tricks on the mind. It was anxiety stemming from
the threat of a nuclear-armed Soviet Union that spawned wild ideas
in the 1950s about the extent of the communist threat. My childhood
home was a rural Minnesota town of a thousand people. I heard some
townsfolk say—whether they were joking or serious I was too young to
know—that our local jeweler was a communist sympathizer. Mr. Kalle
was a small, frail man with tiny fingers, thinning hair, and translucent
skin. His solitary manner was a sign that he might be up to no good.
But his glasses were a dead giveaway. They were the only ones like it for
miles around. Wire frames with round lenses—the same type worn by
the alleged master spy Julius Rosenberg!

Anxiety is raging in today's America. The American Psychological Association conducts a yearly survey of Americans' level of stress over issues such as work and money. In the most recent survey, 80 percent of respondents reported a symptom of stress during the past month, such as feeling overwhelmed or depressed. Two-thirds of respondents expressed anxiety over the country's future.[46]

We don't have to look hard for reasons. The middle class has shrunk, despite the fact that dual-income households are now the norm.[47] The manufacturing sector with its high-paying union jobs has shrunk while the service sector, with its lower wages and smaller benefits, has grown dramatically.[48] Mechanized farming, smaller families, and flight to the cities have hollowed out many of our rural communities.

When anxiety is high, people look for someone or something to blame for why things are not going well.[49] Their identification with those who share their plight strengthens, as does their belief that other people are the cause of their problem. If that belief is dismissed by outsiders, it heightens their sense of injustice. It becomes easier for them to accept the notion that immigrants are the major cause of low wages or that free trade is the main reason for the loss of factory jobs, although neither belief is factually correct.

The need to cast blame outweighs the urge to discover the truth. In *Thinking Fast and Slow,* Nobel laureate Daniel Kahneman demonstrates that people are not driven by a desire for accuracy. What they seek instead are explanations that meet their psychological needs. We have, says Kahneman, an "almost unlimited ability to ignore our ignorance."[50]

Better-educated citizens would like to believe that misinformation is a problem of the less educated. That is generally true. Psychologists have found that individuals with weakly developed cognitive skills suffer from an inflated sense of what they know.[51] Nevertheless, when it comes to misinformation on more complicated issues, the better educated are often the most misinformed.[52] How can that be? What kind of world would place the better educated at the top of the delusional chart? It's known as the "smart idiot effect." On more complicated subjects, better-educated individuals with strong opinions find it easier to come up with reasons that support their thinking.[53] Better-educated Republicans, for example, are more likely than other Republicans to believe that the theory of climate change is a hoax.[54]

Changes in communication have fueled the rise in misinformation. The traditional guardians of information—our journalists, educators, and scientists—have been losing authority while less-reliable sources— our talk show hosts, bloggers, and ideologues—have been gaining our loyalty.[55] At the same time, faster modes of communication have supplanted slower ones. Before the internet, people had a harder time peddling crackpot ideas. When the John Birch Society in the late 1950s began touting the notion that fluoridation was a communist plot, it took a lengthy period for the claim to be widely known. Even the John Birch Society itself operated in relative obscurity until its founder, candy mogul Robert Welch, accused President Eisenhower of being a communist stooge, at which point the news media took an interest. As the negative publicity mounted, Welch begrudgingly recanted. "Eisenhower," he said, "may be too dumb to be a communist."[56]

With the internet, crackpots don't need the news media to spread their nonsense. The Comet Ping Pong allegation started on the internet and then was propelled by fake news sites and amplified by Twitter bots based in eastern Europe.[57] Within a few weeks, the claim was widely known.[58]

———

Although collective ignorance on the scale of recent years is rare, the casual way in which Americans arrive at their opinions is altogether ordinary. We are far too busy and the world is far too complex to be traversed without mental shortcuts—what the mathematician George Zipf called the "principle of least effort."[59] We routinely take shortcuts, as when we follow a store owner's advice on which coffee maker to buy rather than consulting *Consumer Reports*.

When it comes to politics, party loyalty is the typical shortcut.[60] In an experiment designed to demonstrate partisan cueing, Stanford psychologist Geoffrey Cohen exposed Democrats to two hypothetical news stories, one containing a proposal for a generous welfare program and the other containing a proposal for a less generous one. Half of the subjects read stories that presented the proposals without reference to a political party. Most of these Democrats chose the generous program— the more liberal of the two alternatives. The other half read stories that included an endorsement of the skimpy program by Democratic Party leaders. Most of these Democrats picked the skimpy program—the more conservative option.[61]

Party allegiance doesn't drive every opinion. Undeniable facts can override party loyalty. Opposition to sending U.S. troops to the Middle East increased among Republicans and Democrats alike as the human and financial costs of America's involvement in the region soared.[62] But when the issue is less clear-cut, party loyalty is typically our guide.[63] In 2015, Republicans had a more favorable view of free trade agreements than did Democrats. Nearly 60 percent of Republicans said that the agreements were good for the country. By 2017, with a Republican president opposed to free trade in the White House, Republicans had switched sides on the issue; less than 40 percent now felt that free trade agreements benefitted the country.[64]

Partisan bias is a powerful psychological defense.[65] During the 2016 presidential election, Donald Trump was heard saying on *Access Hollywood* tapes that he groped women at will: "When you're a star, they let you do it." Trump's opponents saw his behavior as sexual abuse. Trump's supporters accepted his explanation—"locker room talk."[66] When more than a dozen women then came forward to accuse Trump of sexual impropriety, the vast majority of non-Trump voters said they believed what the women were saying. However, most of Trump's supporters said the women were lying, and most of the rest said they weren't sure whether to believe them. Only one in ten said the women's claims were credible.[67]

Scholars use the term "confirmation bias"—our tendency to interpret information in ways that support our preexisting beliefs—to explain such responses.[68] Confirmation bias causes us to respond selectively to information in a way that reinforces what we want to believe. In one study, supporters and opponents of capital punishment were provided two studies, one of which made the case for the death penalty while the other made the case against it. Participants' opinions were then retested. Those initially in favor of the death penalty were now more strongly in favor of it while those initially opposed were now more firmly opposed.[69]

All of us would like to think that we're an exception to confirmation bias, but our minds don't fully allow it.[70] It is the rare sports fan who thinks a close call should have been awarded to the opposing team. Why should politics be any different? In late 2009, for example, Barack

Obama concluded that the situation in Afghanistan was deteriorating and ordered the deployment of an additional thirty thousand U.S. troops. In a subsequent poll, respondents were asked whether the troop level in Afghanistan under Obama had increased, decreased, or stayed the same. Most Democratic respondents claimed Obama had not increased troop levels—a perception in line with their desire to see U.S. troops pulled out of Afghanistan.[71]

On most issues, the misinformed are concentrated in one party or the other. They have greater reason to jigger the facts. As the rumor spread that Hillary Clinton was part of a child sex ring run out of a pizza shop, Republicans were far more likely than Democrats to think it was true.[72] After 9/11, when it was rumored that George W. Bush knew in advance of the terrorist attack and chose to let it happen to further his geopolitical ambitions, Democrats were far more likely than Republicans to believe it.[73]

Americans have a sense that the nation has a reality problem. A recent Pew poll found that four in five partisans think the opposing sides "cannot agree on basic facts."[74] This admission might be a sign that Americans are awakening to the fact that they are losing their grip on reality. Alas, that's not the case. Partisans are convinced their side has command of the facts. The thoughtless ones are those in the other party. "While men are willing to admit that there are two sides to a question," journalist Walter Lippmann wrote, "they do not believe that there are two sides to what they regard as fact."[75]

Some partisans do prize factual accuracy, but there are fewer such citizens today.[76] Faced with alternative realities, Americans are increasingly inclined to choose the one associated with their party, even if a moment's reflection would indicate that it's less plausible. Political scientist Lance Bennett calls it "the democratization of truth."[77] People get to choose their own reality. What could be more democratic than that?

———

Political parties have been around since George Washington's administration, when policy disagreements between Thomas Jefferson and Alexander Hamilton led them to form opposing parties. But if parties are old, why is misinformation suddenly so prevalent? What changes in the parties could account for the recent surge?

Party polarization is one of the factors. Over the past several decades, the parties have been moving apart, such that there is barely an issue today on which Republicans and Democrats see eye-to-eye. Over the past few decades, the gap between Republicans and Democrats on the issue of legalized abortion has increased by a factor of five. On the question of human-caused climate change, the gap is now nine times greater. In terms of a ban on assault weapons, the divide has tripled.[78]

The partisan divide in Congress is even wider. By the 112th Congress (2011–12), the middle had been hollowed out. As measured by roll-call votes, the least conservative Republican in the House or Senate was more conservative than the most conservative Democrat.[79] Four decades earlier, roughly a fourth of House and Senate members were out of step with their party's majority—more conservative in the case of Democrats and more liberal in the case of Republicans.[80]

As party differences have increased, so have the political stakes. And as the stakes go up, so does the skullduggery. In the summer of 2009, Betsy McCaughey, the former lieutenant governor of New York, falsely claimed on a conservative talk show that the health care reform bill under debate in Congress "would make it mandatory—absolutely require— that every five years people in Medicare have a required counseling session that will tell them how to end their life sooner."[81] From there, McCaughey's allegation snaked from one right-wing talk show to the next, buoyed by passionate op-eds she wrote for the *Wall Street Journal* and *New York Post*.[82] Talk show host Glenn Beck called the legislation "euthanasia." "Sometimes for the common good," Beck said, "you just have to say, 'Hey, Grandpa, you've had a good life.' Sucks to be you."[83]

Although supporters of the health care bill pointed out that it didn't contain a death panel provision, Republican leaders stuck to the fictional version. They weren't about to spoil a winning issue. Sarah Palin, who had been the GOP's vice-presidential nominee the year before, called the death panels "downright evil" and upped the ante by invoking her child's Down syndrome, claiming that health care would be withheld based on a person's "level of productivity in society."[84] House Republican leader John Boehner put out a statement saying, "This provision may start us down a treacherous path toward government-encouraged euthanasia if enacted into law." On the floor of the House, Republican representative Virginia Foxx said the health care bill would "put seniors in a position of being put to death by their government." GOP senator Charles Grassley echoed the charge at a town hall meeting in Winterset, Iowa.[85]

As the Republicans' attack escalated, the death panels allegation spilled over to the mainstream media and quickly lodged itself in people's minds. A Pew Research Center poll found that six of every seven adult Americans were aware of the claim. Of those familiar with it, half said it was true or probably true. Two out of every three Republicans accepted the possibility.[86]

A few decades ago, lawmakers had a harder time playing tricks on the American people. The presence in Congress of conservative Democrats and liberal Republicans meant there would be vigorous dissent if cheap ploys were attempted. A false claim loses traction when partisans hear lawmakers of their own party say it's phony.[87] Such lawmakers still exist, but they are now fewer in number and less vocal. Politicians now pay a higher price for speaking out against their party. Nobody likes the skunk that spoils the party line.

The public is at fault, too. They recognize that much of what politicians say is self-serving. But messages don't arrive with a warning sign or seal of approval that would allow people to separate fact from fiction. And studies indicate that most citizens are not very good at distinguishing between the two.[88] It doesn't help that we are in a post-truth age where alternative realities are being peddled at every turn. We have slipped into a time when facts are increasingly what people would like them to be.

The flight from facts began in the 1960s and 1970s with writers on the far left. Rebelling against "the establishment," they argued that reality is a social construction used by elites to manipulate the masses. Although some of this work was thoughtful, much of it was far-fetched. And as the ideas worked their way into the minds of some of those in the counterculture, they became one-dimensional—reality is a fiction and what you think about the facts is as valid as what the next person thinks.[89] Science got folded into the mix with claims that it is riddled with "myth," "dogma," and "bias" and should not be granted "overriding authority."[90]

Two decades later, conservatives turned that idea into a political strategy. After the 1997 Kyoto agreement, conservative leaders became alarmed that climate abatement would cut into corporate profits. Heeding the advice of Republican strategist Frank Luntz, they launched a

coordinated media attack on the science of climate change.[91] It kicked
into overdrive when *An Inconvenient Truth* garnered an Oscar and
Nobel Peace Prize for former vice president Al Gore in 2007. Conservatives labeled Gore a fraud, claiming that global warming was a hoax
concocted by self-serving environmentalists and government-funded
scientists.[92] The campaign worked like a charm. At the time of the Kyoto
agreement, polls indicated that most Republicans accepted the idea that
the climate was changing as a result of human activity; by 2010, only a
third of Republicans believed it.[93] Luntz had predicted as much, saying
that emotion rather than reason drives political opinions. "When you're
talking issues like the environment," Luntz said, "a straight recitation
of facts is going to fall on deaf ears."[94]

Political elites bear much of the blame for the recent sharp rise in
misinformation. Many of them are more than willing to employ false
claims if it gives them an edge. A 2015 study found that misinformation is highest for issues "on which elites prominently and persistently
[make] incorrect claims."[95] If only a few people are misinformed on an
issue, it could be dismissed as the work of oddballs. It takes a gang to
hoodwink a nation.

————

Misinformation on the scale of recent years is unprecedented. And it
couldn't have happened without help from the news media. In the month
or so after Palin weighed in on the death panel myth, the nation's top fifty
newspapers ran over seven hundred articles on the allegation. In more
than 60 percent of the stories, journalists made no effort to debunk the
claim. In three-fourths of the stories where journalists challenged the
claim, they did so without giving a reason. And in a third of the stories
where they said the claim was false, proponents were given space to say
it was true.[96]

Rather than take responsibility for the facts, journalists strive for
"balance"—giving each side a chance to make its case. It's a sensible
approach in many situations and protects the journalist from accusations
of bias.[97] Yet the approach breaks down when one side is making things
up. Balanced reporting then devolves into what the *Atlantic*'s James
Fallows calls "false equivalencies"—the side-by-side presentation of
statements that differ wildly in their factual integrity. When a politician

tells a bold-faced lie, and the press reports it, the press is complicit in the deception; the claim gets publicized and gains credibility from appearing in the news.[98]

To be sure, reality is not always clear-cut. People can reasonably disagree, for instance, on Hillary Clinton's role in the 2012 Benghazi attack that left four Americans dead, but that's different from the claim, made by her opponents and reported in the news, that she "slept soundly in her bed" during the attack. The attack on the American compound in Benghazi occurred in the evening. But when it's nightfall in Libya, it's mid-afternoon in Washington. Clinton was at work when the attack occurred.[99]

Misinformation also gets spread by the publish-it-now pressure of today's hypercompetitive news system. Withholding a story can mean getting scooped or ignoring a story that others are reporting. When Rep. Gabrielle Giffords, a Democrat, was shot at a political gathering in Tucson in 2011, the hurried initial reports hinted that the gunman was a conservative fanatic who had been prodded into action by right-wing talk shows. Sarah Palin's name got folded into the story when reporters discovered that her website featured a midterm election map showing the crosshairs of a rifle scope aimed at several Democratic districts, including Giffords's.[100] A CNN poll taken within days of the shooting found that a large proportion of Democrats believed that Palin was partly to blame for the shooting. Many of them clung to that belief even after it was discovered that the assailant had a personal grudge against Giffords but no history of right-wing activity.[101]

News exposure once served as protection against misinformation.[102] That is still true, but much less so. Harvard's Yochai Benkler, Robert Faris, and Hal Roberts examined four million online messages transmitted or shared during the 2016 election campaign, including those from the websites of traditional news outlets like the *New York Times* and fake news sites like those of Russian operatives. The research team expected the Russian effort to be a leading source of disinformation, and it was. But they discovered that traditional media were a larger contributor. They found that traditional news outlets were a frequent source of hoaxes, false statements, and rumors. Rather than weed out such claims, journalists relied on their "objective" reporting model, which leads them to report what newsmakers say regardless of its factual accuracy.[103]

———

Is it possible to institutionalize misinformation? Are there ways through policy to entrench it? In 1987, the Federal Communication Commission (FCC) unwittingly did so. It revoked the "fairness doctrine."

The fairness doctrine had discouraged the airing of partisan talk shows by requiring stations to offer a balanced lineup of liberal and conservative programs. Prior to strict enforcement of this doctrine, partisan talk shows were aired on some radio stations. The most prominent was the conservative *Manion Forum*, hosted by Clarence Manion, a former dean of law at Notre Dame. It was carried by more than two hundred radio stations, but most of them dropped it when the FCC in 1963 tightened the fairness doctrine's balancing requirement.[104]

When the doctrine was eliminated in 1987, station owners no longer had to worry about carrying programs that ran counter to their political beliefs. Hundreds of radio stations shifted to partisan talk shows, most of which had a conservative slant. Within a few years, the highest-rated program, the *Rush Limbaugh Show,* had millions of weekly listeners. Unlike Manion, Limbaugh had neither a college education nor a record of public service. He got his start as a radio shock jock.[105]

Limbaugh's success led Rupert Murdoch to start Fox News. To run it, he hired Republican political consultant Roger Ailes, who scheduled partisan talk shows in prime time. Other cable outlets followed with prime-time partisan talk shows of their own. The combined radio and television partisan talk show audience now exceeds fifty million weekly listeners.[106]

On some of these programs, listeners are fed a distorted version of truth. To sell it, talk show hosts claim to be wiser than just about anyone. Others lie, they say, but I will give you the truth. Facts are not to be trusted, they say, unless you hear them from me. Limbaugh told his listeners to stop following traditional news outlets. "I'll let you know what they're up to," he said. "And as a bonus, I'll nuke it!"[107] Rachel Maddow prefaces many of her attacks with "This is not personal," implying that it's truth rather than her opinion that the viewer is about to hear. When Trump launched cruise missiles in response to Syria's use of chemical weapons, Maddow's "This is not personal" claim was that Trump was trying to divert attention from the investigation into Russian meddling in the 2016 election. "Even if the tail is wagging the dog," she said, "even if this decision was taken with absolutely no regard for whatever else is going on in the President's life right now unavoidably creates a real perception around the globe that, that may have been a part of the motivation."[108] People who wouldn't consider asking their plumber to diagnose a hacking cough take as gospel what a favorite talk show host tells them about the intricacies of public policy.

Partisan talk show hosts traffic in outrage, seeking to convince their listeners that the other party is hell-bent on destroying America.[109] On that score, there is not much difference between conservative and liberal hosts. Sarah Sobieraj, coauthor of *The Outrage Industry*, notes that "their political ideologies are different, but the way they speak, the types of images they use, their techniques of belittling people, of name calling, of character assassination, are similar."[110]

Consider what Keith Olbermann said of members of the Tea Klux Klan (his label for the Tea Party) when he was an MSNBC talk show host. Ignoring their anger over taxes and government spending, which had been building on the right since the 1970s and was brought to a boil in 2009 by the bank bailout, the $786 billion dollar stimulus bill, and the prospect of health care reform, Olbermann accused them of being driven by one thing and one thing only—the color of Barack Obama's skin. His proof? The color of *their* skin. Olbermann said: "Why are you surrounded by the largest crowd you will ever see again in your life that consists of nothing but people who look exactly like you?"[111] Olbermann was not wrong in identifying race as an element in the Tea Partiers' opposition to Obama.[112] But the anger at government spending and taxes that fueled the movement predated Obama and persisted when he left office.

Partisan talk show hosts rely on a few themes, which is a key to their influence. Familiarity with a claim, simply hearing it again and again, can lead people to think it's true.[113] The tendency stems from our habit, learned early in life, of taking cues from those around us. If we repeatedly hear the same thing from sources we rely on, there must be something to it. As it turns out, it helps if a familiar claim is actually true. In that case, there's a near certainty we will accept it as fact. But even if it's false, we are likely to think it's true.[114]

People who spend hours listening to partisan talk shows have the distinction of being among America's most misinformed citizens.[115] If Exhibit

A is the death panels claim, which sprang from talk radio, the list is long.[116] The talk show audience skews heavily to the right and helps account for the higher level of misinformation among conservatives.[117] Each day millions of them tune in to the likes of Limbaugh or Sean Hannity, where they are treated to the story of how god-fearing conservatives are saving America from godless liberals. It's an immersive propaganda experience closer to what one would expect to find in China or Russia than in the United States. A pundit remarked that, if you marinate your brain in a talk show host's blather long enough, you won't have one.[118]

The internet is an extraordinary advance. It has changed our lives in positive ways, giving us a level of access to information that was unimaginable a few decades ago.[119] Yet mixed in with the internet's reliable content is misinformation, so many shades of it that it would put a lipstick counter to shame.

The internet allows anyone with the time and interest to be a reporter, editor, and publisher, as well as a self-declared expert. Every second of every day, someone is pumping misinformation into the internet, out of carelessness, stupidity, greed, or malice. Outrage is a big draw, getting far more shares and "likes" than does reasoned argument.[120] The result is a flood of misinformation, much of it presented with the self-righteousness of a Sadducee.

Every wacky idea imaginable can be found on the internet. You probably weren't aware that Sen. Mitch McConnell funneled Russian cash to Donald Trump or that Edward Snowden was part of a years-long Russian plot to torpedo Hillary Clinton's presidential ambitions or that Andrew Breitbart was murdered by Vladimir Putin in order to put Steve Bannon in charge of *Breitbart News*. Well, it's all there on the internet, located on sites operated by extreme left-wingers.[121] The alt-right has even a larger presence on the Web. Until the major social media platforms shut it down, Alex Jones's *InforWars* was among the most prominent of the alt-right outlets. Jones claimed that the massacre of twenty-six children and teachers at Connecticut's Sandy Hook Elementary School in 2012 was faked.[122] When seventeen students were murdered in early 2018 in the shooting at Marjory Stoneman Douglas High School in Parkland, Florida, Jones claimed that one of the surviving students, David Hogg, was a "crisis actor"—a term used for individuals who get paid to pretend to be disaster victims. Hogg, like several of the other students, had spoken up forcibly for gun control, which Jones opposes. A video claiming Hogg was a crisis actor reached the top spot on YouTube's trending page.[123]

There are at least a hundred alt-right YouTube channels that draw tens of thousands of viewers. One such operative, who calls himself "Black Pigeon Speaks," espouses a white nationalist ideology wherein Jewish bankers are trapping us in debt slavery, Muslim immigrants are plotting to impose Sharia law, and women are betraying their biological heritage by placing their careers above childrearing. Black Pigeon Speaks said of women, "This half-century long experiment of women's liberation and political enfranchisement has ended in disaster for the West." Black Pigeon Speaks is not the biggest independent in the alt-right network, but his video essays have attracted more than fifteen million viewers.[124]

The reach of the alt-right's solo actors, like Black Pigeon Speaks, pales alongside that of deep-pocketed alt-right internet outlets. *Breitbart News* draws roughly seventy-five million monthly visitors.[125] Even at its peak, the John Birch Society, the top alt-right outlet of its day, had less than one hundred thousand members.[126] One of the wilder ideas perpetrated by the John Birch Society was the claim that a "one-world government" was being promoted by a shadowy group of conspirators, many of them holding powerful positions in Washington. Other than the Birchers, few Americans took the claim seriously. The notion got new life a few years ago when *Breitbart News* began promoting it. Today, a third of Americans think it's true.[127]

Unlike in the broadcast era, when most Americans were exposed to a common rendition of the news, the internet offers customized versions— "cyber-ghettos" in the words of British scholar Peter Dahlgren.[128] People rely on internet sites that cater to their opinions. When directed to other sites, they find more people who think like they do—90 percent of links are to sites that traffic in the same beliefs. And the more they listen to the like-minded, the more entrenched their beliefs become. "We're increasingly able to choose our information sources based on their tendency to back up what we already believe," says *Vox*'s Ezra Klein. "We don't even have to hear the arguments from the other side."[129]

Online exposure to the like-minded reinforces people's beliefs and gives them a false sense of how much they know. There's something about the process of accessing information online that leads people to think that they are suddenly a lot smarter. A Yale University study found that "people who search for information on the Web emerge from the process with an inflated sense of how much they know."[130]

When people are asked to compare their preferred internet sites with traditional news outlets, they claim their sites are more accurate.[131] And how reliable are they? A study of internet sites dedicated to childhood vaccines found that they reject "biomedical and scientific 'facts'" while promoting dubious alternative therapies.[132] As for partisan Facebook pages, nearly a third of the posts have false or misleading information.[133] More toxic yet are political chain messages—those that come with a request to share them with others. A *Politifact* assessment found that four of every five such messages include false claims, most of which contain lies so outrageous that they get *Politifact*'s "pants on fire" rating.[134]

"Buyer beware" signs should also be posted on social media. It's not simply that social media contain a staggering amount of misinformation. We tend to believe much of it because it is forwarded by friends and acquaintances. Just as familiar claims are more likely to be believed, claims that come from people we know are more likely to be seen as true.[135]

In his classic book *Public Opinion,* Lippmann noted that our opinions stem from how we think the world works whereas our behavior plays out in the real world.[136] Misinformation about childhood vaccines has led many parents to forego immunizing their children, resulting in a rise in preventable disease, an increased number of hospitalizations and deaths, and the need to spend millions of dollars on public information campaigns aimed at persuading bull-headed parents to vaccinate their kids.[137] Whooping cough, which had been nearly eradicated, has come roaring back. In the past five years in the United States, there have been more than one hundred thousand reported cases, accompanied by a number of deaths, nearly all of them children under the age of five.[138]

The odds of unintended consequences increase when misinformation is clustered in the minds of loyalists of one political party or the other, which is the normal pattern. If misinformation was randomly distributed across the electorate, it would be a nuisance. But when it's concentrated among one party's loyalists, the odds increase that their side will make a policy decision that makes society worse off, exemplified by Republicans' "voodoo economics" in the 1980s. Instead of providing the promised increase in tax revenue, it delivered an exploding federal deficit and an accelerated path to income inequality.[139]

Asymmetric misinformation—its concentration within one of the parties on any given issue—is also a barrier to policy negotiation. When Republican and Democratic lawmakers agree on the facts, they can negotiate their differences—tough enough, but doable if both sides engage in honest give-and-take. It becomes harder when they can't agree on the facts. As Sen. Daniel Patrick Moynihan complained when negotiation over a legislative bill broke down, "Everyone is entitled to his own opinion but not to his own facts."[140] Facts do not settle arguments, but they're a necessary starting point. If people can't agree on facts, they won't be able to find their way to a settlement. Recent debates on everything from foreign policy to climate change have fractured or sputtered because of factual disagreements.[141]

Aside from the delusional comfort it offers, misinformation doesn't have much to recommend it. But there's arguably something worse: people who know they are being fed false information and embrace it.

It's impossible to know how many of Donald Trump's diehard supporters are of this type, but Trump makes too many false statements for his backers to accept everything he says as gospel. In an assessment of Trump's pronouncements during his first two years as president, the *Washington Post* tallied over seven thousand false or misleading claims—an average of ten a day. The falsehoods started with his claim that his inaugural crowd, which photos showed to be relatively sparse, was record breaking. "The audience was the biggest ever," Trump said. "This crowd was massive." When polls showed his approval rating dropping, Trump tweeted, "Any negative polls are fake news."[142]

When politicians lie, they usually try to disguise it. Trump usually doesn't bother with a pretext, which, according to Princeton University's Harry Frankfurt, makes him more of a "bullshit artist" than a "liar." The bullshitter, Frankfurt writes, "does not reject the authority of the truth, as the liar does, and oppose himself to it. He pays no attention to it at all."[143] However useful that distinction is, it glosses over a deeper question. Why do Trump's fabrications work? The answer speaks to a troubling feature of American politics—the distrust that Americans feel toward politicians. The distrust is so deep that many of them have changed their test of lying. Authenticity, not factual accuracy, is their yardstick. Was Trump ever going to build "a big, beautiful border wall as high as 55 feet" and "have Mexico pay for it"? The chances are remote. A literal reading of Trump's claim misses the point. It was his way of saying he'd be tough on immigration. That's what many Americans were seeking and, in Trump, they thought they had finally found a politician who would stick to his word.

Trump has another tendency, one that is shared by many politicians. It's the tendency to portray policy problems as having simple explanations and easy solutions. During the 2016 presidential campaign, Trump and Bernie Sanders took aim at free trade. Playing to rapt crowds, they attacked trade deals and promised to negate those in force. Trump said he would "kill" NAFTA and called the recently negotiated Trans-Pacific Partnership the "rape of our country." Sanders said, "With the passing of each free trade agreement, we see a decline in good-paying manufacturing jobs as well as the destruction of many communities." Neither candidate was giving voters the full story. Foreign trade has indeed resulted in a loss of factory jobs, but it is not anywhere near the leading job killer. It accounts for only one in eight lost factory jobs. Automation is the real killer. Since the 1950s, manufacturing has shed two-thirds of its jobs, but its productive output has increased sixfold because of automation.[144] And the problem will only get worse as advances in artificial intelligence enable machines to take over more of our jobs.

Americans' flight into fantasy has tilted our politics in favor of politicians who indulge our capacity for wishful thinking. Sanders claimed that a vote for him would fix health care, the costs of college, and a host of other problems, notwithstanding the fact that his proposals had virtually no chance of getting through Congress. Sanders's followers, as political scientists Christopher Achen and Larry Bartels found, didn't seem to notice or care. Their positions on most policy issues were actually closer to those of Hillary Clinton than to those of Sanders.[145] What they saw in Sanders was the prospect of a miraculously transformed America. For his part, Trump is the expert-of-everything. "I have a gut," he said, "and my gut tells me more sometimes than anybody else's brain can ever tell me."[146]

It can be political suicide to tell the truth. When Hillary Clinton inadvisably said during the 2016 campaign that mining jobs "weren't coming back," it cost her dearly in coal states like Pennsylvania, West Virginia, and Ohio. And when she said in the next sentence that miners need retraining and other forms of support, they didn't want to hear it. It wasn't that they didn't know fracking had unearthed abundant low-cost natural gas or that they hadn't seen the gigantic draglines that are powerful enough to strip the top off mountains, doing more work in a day than a miner can do in years. Accepting the implications of changing technology would mean giving up a way of life that has supported tens of thousands of mining families for generations.

The constituency for easy answers is larger than might be thought. As political scientists John Hibbing and Elizabeth Theiss-Morse show in *Stealth Democracy,* a third of Americans now believe that the process of compromise and negotiation on which our constitutional system is based is a waste of time.[147] If, as they think, policy problems are simple and have an easy fix, there is no reason for debate and deliberation. All that's required is for lawmakers to get out of the way and turn the job over to no-nonsense leaders. If you are looking for a reason Trump won the presidency, or why so many artless ideologues have been elected to Congress in recent years, that's one of them. During the 2016 campaign, Trump said, "I will give you everything . . . every dream you've ever dreamed."[148]

America's misinformation crisis thus runs deeper than a bunch of errant thoughts banging around in people's heads. As the *New York Times*'s David Brooks said, there has been "a breakdown in America's ability to face evidence objectively, to pay due respect to reality, to deal with complex and unpleasant truths. . . . Once a country tolerates dishonesty, incuriosity and intellectual laziness, then everything else falls apart." Decades ago, the philosopher Hannah Arendt drew a darker lesson, saying that the rise of demagogues is abetted by "people for whom the distinction between fact and fiction, true and false, no longer exists."[149]

———

Have we been here before? Has America ever been plagued by so much magical thinking? The 1850s—the heyday of the "Know Nothings"—is arguably the closest period.

The immigration of millions of Catholics from Ireland and Germany beginning in the 1830s had put Protestant America on edge, sparking the Know Nothing movement.[150] It was driven by a belief that the newly arrived immigrants were conspiring with Rome to take over America and put the pope in charge. The movement had outspoken leaders but was organized as a secret society. If asked about it, members were told to say "I know nothing." Judging by what was coming from their lips, they were bragging. They had all sorts of cockeyed beliefs, including the notion that the Irish were a racially separate and inferior group.[151]

In the mid-1850s, the Know Nothings had a burst of electoral success, sweeping a statewide election in Massachusetts, winning a number of mayoral races, including those in San Francisco and Philadelphia, and nominating a presidential candidate who finished third in the balloting. But they were out of business before the 1850s ended. Their governing policies were as zany as their theories.[152]

Outrageous ideas abound today but, unlike those of the Know Nothings, they are not likely to disappear in short order. The conditions necessary for misinformation to thrive are firmly in place, held there by three of America's sturdiest anchors—the lust for money, the lure of celebrity, and the drive for power. The chapters that follow explain the long-term developments that have empowered America's partisan firebrands, media marketers, talking heads, and reckless disrupters at the expense of the nation's level-headed citizens.

CHAPTER 2

THE TRIBES

*There is no crime, absolutely none, that cannot be condoned when
"our" side commits it. Even if one does not deny that the crime has
happened, even if one knows that it is exactly the same crime as one
has condemned in some other case, even if one admits in an intellectual
sense that it is unjustified—still one cannot feel that it is wrong.*

George Orwell, "Notes on Nationalism"

Appearing before the Senate Intelligence Committee, former FBI director
James Comey testified that he was fired shortly after spurning President
Donald Trump's plea to drop his investigation of former national security
advisor Michael Flynn. As rumors then circulated that special counsel
Robert Mueller was investigating Trump for obstruction of justice in
the firing of Comey, Newt Gingrich rose to Trump's defense. Calling the
investigation of Russian meddling in the 2016 election a "witch hunt,"
Gingrich claimed that a president cannot be charged with obstruc-
tion of justice. "Technically, the President of the United States cannot
obstruct justice," Gingrich told a gathering at the National Press Club.
"The President of the United States is the chief executive officer of the
United States."[1]

Two decades earlier, as House Speaker, Gingrich led the effort to
impeach President Bill Clinton for obstruction of justice. As articles of
impeachment were making their way through the House of Representatives, Gingrich said, "What you have lived through for two and a half long
years is the most systematic, deliberate obstruction-of-justice cover-up
and effort to avoid the truth we have ever seen in American history."[2]

Gingrich is not alone in letting blind partisanship do his thinking for
him. Two days into Trump's presidency, four of every five Democrats had
already concluded that Trump was doing a lousy job.[3] Republicans had
reacted the same way when Barack Obama took office. It is no surprise,
of course, that Republicans and Democrats would judge a president

differently. That's been true in every Gallup poll since the question was first asked in 1945. But the gap is wider now than at any time in the past. Through the 1970s, those who identified with the president's party were about 30 percentage points more likely to approve of his performance. The gap steadily widened thereafter, climbing to an average of 70 points during Obama's presidency, when 85 percent of Democrats but only 15 percent of Republicans approved of the job he was doing.[4] From the day a president takes office, tens of millions of Americans of the other party have decided that nothing the president can do will be acceptable.

Although partisanship has been part of our politics from the beginning, rarely has it colored so many of our judgments. In 1960, less than one in twenty parents objected to having a child marry across party lines.[5] Today, more than six times that many feel that way, and marriage statistics indicate that they are not joking. Only one in ten new marriages today unites a Republican and a Democrat.[6]

———

When I was a small boy growing up in a Minnesota town of a thousand people, Friday and Saturday nights were moments of joy. Farm families came to town and the three-block-long Main Street was packed with cars from one end to the other. People filled the streets, stores, cafes, and bars. Farmers chatted with townsfolk, Lutherans with Catholics, Republicans with Democrats. A popcorn machine sat on one street corner, a lure for every kid my age, as was the town's small movie theater.

A few years later, the streets had grown quiet. The popcorn machine was stored away, Main Street was not even half filled with cars, and the movie theater was mostly empty and on its way to closing down. It was not that my hometown had suffered an exodus of people or been wiped out by a tornado. Television had come to Westbrook, and people were at home, parked in front of their TV sets.

In *Bowling Alone,* published in 2000, my Harvard colleague Bob Putnam documented the decline in Americans' face-to-face interactions. Americans had become less involved in local clubs and civic organizations, and community volunteering was waning.[7] It was a radical change from what Americans had known. Writing in the 1830s, Alexis de Tocqueville noted that "the principle of association" was nowhere more evident than in America. The United States, he said, was "a nation of joiners."[8] That inclination carried into the twentieth century in the form of organized membership groups, everything from local hospital auxiliaries to national organizations like the Boy Scouts, the Rotary, and the Elks. But in the 1960s these groups began losing members.[9] And as they did, the benefits of civic involvement were eroding. When people work together in their community, they learn teamwork and tolerance. When they lose contact, they grow wary. The number of Americans who believe "most people can be trusted" has fallen by half since 1960. Today, less than a third of Americans believe that most people are trustworthy.[10]

Trust between Democrats and Republicans has fallen sharply, as has the amount of time they spend together. America has undergone what writer Bill Bishop calls the "Big Sort"—a geographical redistribution along party lines. Most states are now more solidly Republican or Democratic than they were three decades ago.[11] The same is true of America's 3,007 counties. Compared with the early 1990s, ten times as many counties today have at least twice as many members of one party as they do members of the other party.[12] Between 1980 and 2012, in the nation's fifty largest metropolitan areas the partisan gap between urban and suburban counties doubled.[13] Neighborhoods are even more out of balance. The odds are high that your next-door neighbor has the same party allegiance as you do.[14]

The Milwaukee metropolitan area illustrates how extensive the sorting has been. A University of Wisconsin study looked at the Milwaukee-area counties at twenty-year intervals beginning in 1952. During each time period, largely as a result of the role of race and income in housing choices, urban Milwaukee County became increasingly Democratic while the three largest suburban counties—Waukesha, Ozaukee, and Washington—became increasingly Republican. Today, in terms of their partisanship, the counties are reverse images. Urban Milwaukee County is more than two-to-one Democratic and the three suburban counties are each more than two-to-one Republican.[15]

Most Americans today don't have many friends in the other party. Democrats are eight times more likely to say that most of their friends are Democrats than to say that most of them are Republicans. For Republicans, the ratio is six to one. Americans without close friends of the opposite party are twice as likely as those with such friends to have a negative opinion of that party.[16]

The physical separation of partisans also affects those who happen to be in the minority. In *The Spiral of Silence*, Elisabeth Noelle-Neumann, who came of age in Germany as Hitler was gaining power and saw that people go silent when confronting a police state, explored the possibility that social situations can silence people. Noelle-Neumann found that people grow quiet in situations where their opinions appear to be in the minority.[17] They also tend to go silent in the company of brash talkers.[18] It doesn't take a police state to silence people. The dominant voices among us have the power to quiet us.

They can also shut down political leaders. Three out of every five Republicans believe that God created people in their current form less than ten thousand years ago, a belief that is at odds with evolutionary science. It has prompted demands by Republican voters that creationism be taught alongside evolution in high school biology classes.[19] Only one of the candidates for the 2016 Republican presidential nomination dared to say that he believed in evolutionary biology. And Jeb Bush was quick to note that it was a personal belief. "It does not need to be in the [public school] curriculum," Bush said.[20]

Religion has shut off more than one debate in conservative circles. Liberals also have a discussion killer—political correctness. As first conceived, it was a much-needed corrective to the casual or deliberate use of words and symbols that malign and demean historically disadvantaged groups, including women, blacks, and Hispanics. Designed to promote respect and understanding, it has acquired additional meanings over time, some of which curb thoughtful discussion. At the height of the #MeToo revelations, actor Matt Damon said in an interview that there's a difference between rape and patting someone on the butt. He went on to say that "both of those behaviors need to be confronted and eradicated without question, but they shouldn't be conflated." Damon was widely attacked for suggesting that there are levels of sexual misconduct, capped by actress Minnie Driver's tweet that "You don't get to be hierarchical about abuse."[21]

Shutting down discussion saves time, but that is the best that can be said for it. The real measure of our opinions is not whether we believe they are sound but whether they hold up to scrutiny. Opinions—those that are honest and not held out of malice, self-defense, or to gain an advantage—are tentative truths about what we think the world is like.

As such, they need to be tested against the alternatives. "He who knows only his side of the case knows little of that," the philosopher John Stuart Mill wrote. "His reasons may be good, and no one may have been able to refute them. But if he is equally unable to refute the reasons of the opposite side, if he does not so much as know what they are, he has no ground for preferring either opinion."[22]

Our interest in listening to the other side is fading, replaced by the small-mindedness that comes from listening only to our side. Many Americans who opposed Donald Trump during the 2016 presidential election could not understand why someone other than a misogynist or racist would back him, which led them to define his supporters in that way. And many of the Americans who opposed Hillary Clinton during the 2016 campaign held similarly one-sided thoughts about her supporters. Without a fuller understanding and appreciation of those with whom we differ politically, it will be difficult to bridge our partisan divide.[23]

———

The partisan divide runs deep, as Emory University's Alan Abramowitz and Steven Webster found when studying voters' likes and dislikes. Although today's voters like their own party about as well as voters did in 1980, they have come to dislike, even despise, the opposing party. Compared with 1980, twice as many partisans today have a strongly negative view of the opposing party. A growing number of Americans dislike the opposing party more than they like their own party.[24]

Their dislike goes beyond words. Party identification was once the best predictor of how people would vote on election day—Democrats lining up behind their party's candidate and Republicans backing their party's nominee. But party identification no longer has that distinction. When Abramowitz and Webster examined elections since 1992, they found that "ratings of the opposing party were by far the strongest predictor" of the vote. "The greatest concern of party supporters," they wrote, "is preventing the opposing party from gaining power."[25]

Negative partisanship is not new. There have been numerous times in American history when one of the major parties was defined largely by what it was against rather than what it was for. What's unusual is the situation where both major parties have defined themselves in that way. The 1850s, when the nation was on the cusp of civil war, was such a period, but there aren't many others.

What is it that Americans don't like about those in the opposite party? Most everything, as it turns out. At the top of Democrats' list, according to a recent Pew survey, is a belief that Republicans are more "closed-minded" than other Americans. "Close-minded" is also at the top of Republicans' list when they think about Democrats. "Dishonest" and "immoral" rank high when Democrats think of Republicans, which are also traits that Republicans associate with Democrats. But each side has a special complaint. Democrats see Republicans as "unintelligent" whereas Republicans see Democrats as "lazy."[26]

And what positive traits do Americans assign to opposing partisans? None, or at least none that more than one in nine partisans is willing to concede. Open-minded? Nope. Honest? Nope. Moral or hardworking? Nope yet again. Large numbers say the other party makes them feel "frustrated," "angry," or "afraid." How do you feel about your neighbors? If they are of the other party, you would probably be happier if they weren't. Two-thirds of Democrats and Republicans, when talking with people of the other party, say they had "less in common" than they had expected. Half say such talks are "stressful and frustrating."[27] If our politics were Shakespearean theater, partisans would be hunched over a fire stirring up a curse—"fire burn and cauldron bubble"—to cast on those of the other party.

Partisan differences are strong enough to outweigh other things we value.[28] In a 2011 poll, only 30 percent of white evangelicals said they would support a candidate who had engaged in immoral behavior. Yet, in the 2017 election for an Alabama Senate seat, 80 percent of white evangelicals voted for Roy Moore, who was credibly accused of sexual molestation when he was in his thirties and his victims were in their teens.[29]

As our party tribalism has intensified, we've taken to insulting each other.[30] A thousand insults are better yet. During the 2016 election, Trump rejected the FBI's conclusion that Clinton's emails did not rise to a criminal offense. "Lock her up" and "Crooked Hillary" were his daily chant, repeated by his crowds and in news reports. On CNN alone, "Crooked Hillary" and "Lock her up" were voiced 2,998 times during the course of the campaign.[31] Did the message sink in? A *Washington Post/*

ABC News poll found that 90 percent of Republicans thought Clinton should be charged with a crime.[32] Guilt by accumulation!

Democrats got their chance to call Trump a crook when early in his presidency the news highlighted allegations that his campaign colluded with the Russians. In the five-week period after the appointment of special counsel Robert Mueller, the Russia story accounted for more than half of Trump's television coverage, receiving twenty times the attention paid to his role in the health care bill that Congress was debating.[33] Although there was as at the time no firm evidence that Trump was guilty of the constitutionally prescribed "high crimes and misdemeanors," polls showed that two-thirds of Democrats thought he should be impeached.[34]

Americans' declining trust in government has been a source of concern. Our lack of trust in each other is equally troublesome. When trust disappears, politics can turn ugly in a hurry. When Republicans chanted "Lock her up" during the 2016 campaign, Americans were witnessing a scene unlike any in the nation's history. A recent survey found that large numbers of Republicans and Democrats believe the other party's policies are so misguided that they "threaten the nation's well-being."[35]

When partisans see the other side as the enemy, the stakes go up dramatically. The loss of an election, rather than being seen as part of the normal ebb and flow of party politics, is seen as a threat—one perilous enough to justify an otherwise unthinkable response, everything from suppressing the vote to denying the legitimacy of the outcome. Orderly government also suffers. Loyalists of the party in power support constitutional overreach by their leaders; loyalists of the party out of power embrace obstructionist tactics that would otherwise be seen as dirty tricks.

―――――

Is it possible to distrust the opposing party and still have an open mind? It's possible, but that's not how things normally work. Yale's Dan Kahan has shown that, as party distrust widens, we stop listening.[36] Republicans say that the fast pace of immigration in recent decades has put a strain on local schools.[37] Democrats would prefer to think that crowded classrooms in some localities are only an issue of inadequate funding. Democrats have climate science on their side in saying that human activity is driving global warming. Most Republicans prefer to think that climate change is a hoax or caused by sunspots.[38]

Scholars use the term "motivated reasoning" to describe the process by which we protect the beliefs we already have. All of us do it to a degree, and we do it most often for strongly held beliefs.[39] In controlled experiments, political scientists Brendan Nyhan and Jason Reifler exposed subjects to information that contradicted what many of them believed. Republican subjects were provided information about the failure of the United States to find weapons of mass destruction in the aftermath of the Iraq invasion; Democratic subjects were provided information on President George W. Bush's policy on stem cell research. Diehard Republicans and Democrats with false beliefs didn't budge after reading the corrective material. They were convinced that the information was wrong and that what they'd believed all along was right.[40]

Research stretching over decades shows that individuals are skilled at protecting what they believe.[41] It can occur through selective retention—the tendency to remember supportive items and forget conflicting ones.[42] It can happen through selective exposure—closer attention to supportive messages than to opposing ones.[43] And it can work through selective perception—seeing what we want to see in a situation.[44] Leon Festinger, the founder of cognitive dissonance theory, was struck by the difficulty of getting people to change their minds. "A man with conviction is a hard man to change," wrote Festinger. "Tell him you disagree and he turns away. Show him facts and figures and he questions your sources. Appeal to logic and he fails to see your point. . . . [When] presented with evidence—unequivocal and undeniable evidence—that his belief is wrong, he will emerge not only unshaken but even more convinced of the truth of his beliefs than ever before."[45]

Selectivity heightens with bias, which is why racists see signs of racial inferiority in behaviors common to us all. Partisan bias is no different. When we're committed to a party, we tend to see the world through its lens. When watching a presidential debate, Republicans and Democrats are looking at the same event but seeing different ones. When their party's candidate is speaking, they tend to see sincerity and strength. When the other party's candidate is talking, they tend to see evasion and weakness.[46] There has never been a presidential debate where party loyalists thought their party's candidate got whipped. Even Donald Trump's performance in the first 2016 presidential debate—widely regarded as one of the most inept ever—did not convince most Republicans that he had lost.[47]

Even scientific theories have bent to our capacity to believe what we want to believe. A recent study exposed subjects to a set of scientific theories. Conservatives tended to discount those that contradicted what they believed. Liberals did the same. Rather than question the validity of their beliefs, they questioned the validity of the science.[48]

Motivated reasoning numbs the mind. Unlike other forms of reasoning, it makes us dumber. People turn off "the critical faculties they usually apply to political speech and forgive . . . any amount of exaggeration, contradiction, or offensiveness."[49] Inconvenient facts are rejected outright or twisted into a form that turns them on their head. Even common sense gets tossed aside. When Trump blamed his popular-vote loss in the 2016 election on millions of votes cast by undocumented immigrants, he made believers out of three of every five Republicans.[50] Researchers have found no evidence for the claim, and a moment's reflection should convince even the most bull-headed Republican that the claim is absurd. Undocumented aliens go to great lengths to avoid detection for fear of deportation. It is hard to imagine a worst place for millions of them to hide out than at the nation's polling stations on election day.

Even our opinions about the democratic process, as *Vox*'s Ezra Klein points out, are subject to motivated reasoning.[51] Democrats were angry when Trump in his first days in office signed one far-reaching executive order after another, forgetting that they had earlier applauded when Barack Obama pushed the limits of executive authority. Republicans spoke out loudly about a rigged system when it appeared Donald Trump would lose the 2016 election. When he won, and evidence mounted that Russia had interfered in the election, they dismissed the meddling. A poll found that three in four Republicans saw the claim of Russian meddling as nothing more than "a distraction."[52]

––––––––

Our flight into blind partisanship began with passage of the Civil Rights Act in 1964. America took inexcusably long to grant legal equality to black citizens, but many white Americans thought that even a century after the Civil War was too soon. Most were southern Democrats, and they were angry with northern Democrats for taking the lead on the civil rights bill. They began moving to the Republican side, urged along by Richard Nixon's "southern strategy."[53]

The late 1960s and early 1970s introduced yet another divisive issue, what Richard Scammon and Ben Wattenberg called the "social issue"—a loose set of controversies including crime, abortion, drugs, school prayer, and changing sexual and family norms.[54] Conservative Christians were the ones most alarmed by the change, solidifying Republican gains in the southern and border states, particularly among white evangelicals.

Ronald Reagan's presidency added the final piece to the GOP's transformation. Like the two earlier developments, Reaganism was a response to unwanted change. President Lyndon Johnson's Great Society programs, which included such programs as Medicare and Medicaid, had expanded the federal government's social welfare role and increased federal spending. Conservatives felt the government was spending way too much and doing far too many things that were better left to the states. Many of them also believed that the money was going to people who hadn't earned it and didn't deserve it. Reagan gave voice to their concerns, vowing to cut welfare, trim the federal budget, and devolve power to the states.

Reagan's presidency marked the ideological transformation of the Republican Party. It had been the federal party, priding itself after the Civil War on being called the Union Party. Now it was a states'-rights party with a power base in the once solidly Democratic South. Some long-time Republicans were uncomfortable with the shift. Business-minded Republicans had little in common with newcomers drawn to the GOP by its stand on issues like abortion, but they stayed put, anchored by the party's promise of lower taxes and less regulation. Socially progressive Republicans, who were concentrated in the Northeast and West Coast, began to bail out.

America's political parties were approaching ideological purity for the first time in history. It happened most quickly in Congress. Before passage of the Civil Rights Act, the congressional parties were diverse. Southern Democrats were more conservative than northern Democrats, and Republicans from coastal and midwestern states were more progressive than Republicans from other states. By 2010, conservative Democrats and progressive Republicans had been all but weeded out. Every House or Senate Democrat was more liberal than even the most liberal Republican in their chamber.[55]

Voters have also split into ideological tribes, though less sharply than have party leaders. Only a small proportion of voters have the

well-defined and consistent belief system that is the mark of a true ideo-
logue.[56] Nevertheless, voters' opinions on most issues tend to align with
prevailing opinion in their party, a tendency that has increased in recent
decades. In 1987 there was a 17 percentage point gap in Republicans' and
Democrats' opinions on whether government should take care of people
who can't take care of themselves. Today the gap is twice as large. On the
question of giving minorities a helping hand, the partisan gap has also
doubled. In response to the statement "I have old fashioned values about
family and marriage," the partisan gap has widened by a factor of four.[57]

Three decades ago, half of all voters had a roughly equal mix of
conservative and liberal opinions. Now only a third of them do. The
result is that there's less overlap in the opinions of Republicans and
Democrats. More than 90 percent of party loyalists hold policy views
closer to those of the typical member of their party than to those of the
typical member of the opposing party.[58]

———

Writing about 1950s politics, Cornell University's Clinton Rossiter
described America's parties as "creatures of compromise."[59] The parties didn't have much choice. Each party was a "big tent." It had large
numbers of voters from nearly every group in society. If it tried to play
one group off against another, it risked alienating part of its base. Even
the racial divide, except in the South, was not easily exploited. Although
black Americans had moved from the GOP to the Democratic Party in
large numbers during the Great Depression, nearly 40 percent of them
in the 1950s were loyal to the Republican Party.[60]

Today's parties are anything but creatures of compromise, and they
are now much less diverse. The Republican Party is a white party. Nearly
nine out of every ten votes that Republicans received in the 2016 election
was cast by a non-Hispanic white voter. Not since Lyndon Johnson's
landslide victory in the 1964 election has the Democratic presidential
nominee won a majority of the white vote.[61] For its part, the Democratic
coalition is nearing the point where most of its votes will come from
minority group members. Black Americans vote roughly nine-to-one
Democratic. Hispanics once divided their votes evenly between the
parties but, as Republican leaders drew an ever harder line on undocumented aliens, they moved to the Democratic side. Hispanics have voted

two-to-one Democratic in recent elections. Asian Americans are the most recent converts. As recently as the 1996 presidential election, most of them voted Republican. They flipped sides in 2000 and since then have voted Democratic; the margin in the 2018 midterm elections was three-to-one Democratic.

The parties are also divided along religious lines, a throwback to the period before the Great Depression. Except in the South where race was the larger issue, religion was for a long period the major dividing line between the parties. Catholics voted heavily Democratic; Protestants voted strongly Republican.[62] An influx of Catholic immigrants had sparked all sorts of religious hatred including the rebirth of the Ku Klux Klan, which resurrected itself in the early 1900s as anti-Catholic, as well as anti-Jewish, anti-Mormon, and anti-black. At the Klan's peak in the 1920s, one in every six Protestant adult males—four million in total—was a Klan member.[63] It took the nation's all-out effort in World War II to convince the Protestant majority that Catholics weren't their enemy. Although religion resurfaced briefly as a wedge issue when John F. Kennedy, a Catholic, ran for president in 1960, it was no longer easy for either party to exploit religion for political gain.

Religion came back into partisan politics in the 1970s on the heels of cultural issues like abortion. But this time the fault line was different. Rather than a Catholic-Protestant divide, the split was between the religiously devout and those with a secular bent.[64] Regular churchgoers vote about 60 percent Republican. Irregular or non-churchgoers vote about 60 percent Democratic. White evangelical or born-again Christians are the largest Republican religious voting bloc, making up a fourth of the electorate and voting Republican by a four-to-one margin. Religious "nones" are their Democratic counterpart. They constitute about a sixth of the electorate and vote two-to-one Democratic.[65]

Tribalism comes more easily when those in the opposing camp differ in lifestyle and appearance.[66] Asked in polls how warm or cold they feel toward various groups, Republicans give "evangelicals" a much warmer rating than do Democrats. "Blacks" and "Hispanics" are viewed less favorably by Republicans than by Democrats, who rate "whites" less highly. "Feminists," "immigrants," "Muslims," and "gays and lesbians" get a chillier response from Republicans than from Democrats. Is there any group that gets a colder response than any of those mentioned? As it happens, there is. Democrats reserve their coldest rating for Republicans, who return the favor.[67]

When geographical, racial, gender, and religious identities dovetail with partisan identities, you have a combustible mix. We reject the other side's facts, question its motives, disparage its values, and sneer at its lifestyles.[68] Those on the left see the right as anchored in bias and bigotry. Those on the right see the left as rooted in political correctness and a perverse form of identity politics.[69] When, at one point, a third of Republicans said they thought that Barack Obama was or might be the anti-Christ, you know that partisanship had spiraled out of control.[70]

Although the United States was never the melting pot of fable, it was a place where people of different faiths and positions in life mixed more freely than they did elsewhere. That mixing didn't break down society's walls, but it lowered and softened them. That is true even today. The simple act of knowing someone of a different background weakens our tribal instinct. A Pew Research Center survey found, for instance, that non-Muslim Americans who know a Muslim are twice as likely as other Americans to think favorably of Muslims, twice as likely to say that the Muslim religion discourages violence, and three times as likely to say that the Muslim religion has a lot in common with their own.[71]

But we are less likely today to be around people who differ from ourselves. That is true not only in our neighborhoods but also when we are on the job. As income level and specialized training have increasingly shaped where we live and with whom we work, we have come to interact less with individuals of a different background or lifestyle.[72] It's true also of age. Younger and older adults mix less often than in the past.[73]

The lines that divide us have also been sharpened by the postwar era's "identity" politics, everything from the 1960s civil rights movement to the more recent gay rights movement. If heightened identity was a natural result of group-based civil rights, it was exacerbated by a tendency of some on the left to demonize whites, particularly those of the working class. The irony is that working-class whites were hearing of "white privilege" at a time when stagnant wages and declining factories were eating away at their economic security.[74]

Political leaders on both sides of the aisle have exploited our differences. Many of them have built their careers on playing to the resentments that Americans feel toward fellow Americans.[75] And in Donald Trump we have for the first time since Richard Nixon a president for whom division is a strategy. The *New York Times* compiled a list of the groups and individuals that Trump has insulted through Twitter; the list numbered in the hundreds.[76]

Although Trump's attacks are so unrelenting that they have come to seem normal, they are not. Even in dark times, presidents have usually avoided demonizing their opponents, and most have sought to dampen our divisions: Jefferson's "We are all republicans, we are all federalists"; Lincoln's "with malice toward none"; Franklin Roosevelt's "We all go up or else all go down as one people." To find relevant comparisons to Trump, we need to look to the democracies of South America and the rhetoric of autocrats like Juan Perón and Hugo Chávez.

Dislike of the "other" side is useful in time of war but is otherwise destructive. It is an invitation to demagoguery and an excuse for selfishness. When you lose your sense of being part of a larger community, why should you care what happens to those on the other side of the divide?

———

Where can we find relief from party tribalism? Where can we find voices that seek to bring us together? Washington is an unlikely place. It is populated by people who delight in tearing things down. One of the first of this breed was Newt Gingrich. When he first ran for Congress, Gingrich said: "You're fighting a war. . . . This party does not need another generation of cautious, prudent [leaders]. . . . What we really need are people who are willing to stand up in a slug-fest."[77] Once in Congress, he circulated a vocabulary for Republicans to use when talking about Democrats. On the list were "radical," "sick," and "traitors."[78] But Americans were not yet ready for Gingrich's unyielding style. When he became Speaker of the House after the GOP swept the 1994 midterms, he was unable to transition from antagonist to governing leader and was forced by his Republican colleagues to resign. "We . . . need to prove that we can be conservative without being mean" was how one Republican lawmaker characterized Gingrich's ouster.[79]

But Gingrich's style was an indicator of things to come. Politicians of his ilk were multiplying. Obstructionism was their aim, and they didn't hide it. After the GOP's sweeping victory in the 2010 midterms, Republican Senate leader Mitch McConnell said, "The single most important thing we want to achieve is for President Obama to be a one-term president." We plan, McConnell said, "to take him down, one issue at a time." Republican House leader John Boehner said of Obama's legislative agenda, "We're going to do everything—and I mean everything we can do—to kill it, stop it, slow it down, whatever we can."[80]

That strategy was on full display when the 2010 health care reform bill was working its way through Congress. It was an imperfect bill in many ways, but one of its strengths was the individual mandate. Requiring people to obtain insurance or pay a tax penalty was the key to bringing enough healthy individuals into the marketplace to offset the high cost of caring for the chronically ill. Republicans fought the provision, even taking it to the Supreme Court for a ruling on its constitutionality. The irony, as many have noted, is that the individual mandate was initially proposed and championed by conservatives. But when Democrats adopted it, Republicans fought it. To be sure, Republicans disliked many aspects of the new health care program, and removing the individual mandate was the easiest way to try to kill it. But Republicans made no effort in 2010 to work with Democrats to craft a bill that would have combined their marketplace concerns with Democrats' health coverage concerns. Not a single House or Senate Republican voted for the bill. In 2017, Democrats reciprocated by withholding their votes when Republicans, now in control of the presidency, Senate, and House, sought to repeal and replace the 2010 legislation in its entirety.

Bull-headed partisanship spilled over to passage of the 2017 Tax Cut and Jobs Act. In an op-ed, McConnell said, "I hope [Democrats] will work with us in a serious way to get this crucial reform accomplished for our country."[81] McConnell then proceeded to shut Democrats out of negotiations on the bill, although it's not clear that Democrats would have embraced the chance to participate.

For years on end, our lawmakers have dedicated themselves to stymieing the other party, with the result that the two sides barely trust each other. "Just say no" signs have been used in campaigns to promote celibacy and end drug abuse. "Just say no" could just as well be stenciled across the dome of the Capitol.

———

Although we need voices that can bring us together, most of those that have our ear are in the business of dividing us. Never before have there been so many places to go for political advice, but they are increasingly bent on accenting our differences. When partisan talk shows emerged in the late 1980s, their hosts discovered through trial and error what listeners wanted to hear. Thoughtful give-and-take between guests turned out to be a ratings bust. What listeners liked best were rants about the opposing party, a discovery that turned outrage into the industry standard. It would be one thing if talk show hosts thoughtfully explained why the other side's policies are a bad idea. Instead, they claim that the other party is trying to destroy America. In 2018, Republican congressman Devin Nunes authored a memo alleging that unsubstantiated information was used to obtain a warrant to conduct surveillance on a Trump campaign advisor. The memo was widely debunked, but that didn't stop talk show host Sean Hannity from claiming, "This makes Watergate look like a Snickers bar."[82]

As Tufts University's Sarah Sobieraj and Jeffrey Berry found in their landmark study, outrage is the trademark of many partisan talk shows. Name-calling, misrepresentation, mockery, character assassination, belittling, and imagined catastrophe are but a few of their tools. The goal is to make the target look stupid, inept, or dangerous. Senator Charles Schumer is "Up-Chuck"; Hillary Clinton is a "feminazi"; Tea Party members are "a bunch of greedy, water-carrying corporative-slave hypocrites"; Obama supporters are "Obamatards"; Trump is "a clown" and "an orange-utan." Lesser figures get generic labels like "idiot," "pompous," "asinine," and "tyrant."[83]

The partisan divide is the main point of attack for these talk show hosts, but the cultural divide is a close second. Issues are played less as policy questions than as questions of tribal identity. Issues, says Yale's Dan Kahan, express "who they are."[84] On conservative talk shows, gun control isn't about trigger locks or background checks but instead about guns as cultural identity. Attempts to control guns are portrayed as a liberal plot to destroy a way of life that has been around since frontier days. Liberals aren't seeking sensible restraints on gun ownership. They're trying to take our guns away.

There is no meaningful dialogue on partisan talk shows. The formula doesn't allow for thoughtful give and take. The conclusion is preordained. It's a closed loop. The argument ends where it begins, giving host and listeners the satisfaction of knowing that they were right all along.

Studies of partisan talk shows have had difficulty finding positive effects. These shows tend to warp people's sense of the other party, prod people into taking more extreme positions, and foster distrust of opposing partisans. They also encourage incivility; after listening to talk show rants, some listeners head to social media to launch copycat attacks.[85] Outrage is easy to mimic. What's hard is taking the time to understand the opinions of those whose views differ from our own.

The internet arrived in the early 1990s full of promise as a digital commons where citizens would thoughtfully exchange views, a marketplace of ideas so vigorous that the likes of John Stuart Mill, John Dewey, and Oliver Wendell Holmes would turn blissfully in their graves. Such rhapsodies overlooked the human element.[86] The internet is mostly a place where people go not to exchange ideas about politics but to find people who think like they do.[87] There are relatively few political blogs or websites that cater to moderates or that are receptive to liberals and conservatives alike.[88] They are gathering places for the like-minded who rail against those who think differently.[89] Those who assert a dissenting view are likely to be driven off or belittled.[90] Even when people are not looking for like-minded individuals, they are likely to encounter them as a result of what writer Eli Pariser labeled "the filter bubble."[91] Internet algorithms are designed to give us content similar to what we usually access, so we're likely when surfing to encounter those who think like we do.[92]

Many political blogs and websites operate in the mode of partisan talk radio. They traffic in outrage, much of it fabricated. The headline of a heavily trafficked story in the blog *Politico.com* read, "Mike Pence: 'Allowing Rape Victims to Have Abortions Will Lead to Women Trying to Get Raped.'" The story went on to put words in Pence's mouth about a nonexistent provision of the abortion bill that he signed when governor of Indiana. He is quoted as saying that the bill didn't have an exception for rape victims because "we'd then have an epidemic of women claiming to have been raped just so they could get an abortion."[93]

The internet has unleashed all sorts of unsavory characters. Traffic is booming at sites that promote absurd notions of racial superiority. There's a geographical pattern to online racism. There is more of it to the east of the Mississippi, and it's not confined to the South, although the heaviest concentration is there. The other dense area starts in West Virginia and is bounded on the east by the rural areas of Pennsylvania and New York and on the west by the rural areas of Illinois and Michigan. These are areas where Obama did less well in 2008 and 2012 than would be expected for a Democratic presidential nominee and where Trump ran stronger in 2016 than would be expected for a Republican presidential nominee.[94]

In a review of studies of the internet, the University of Colorado's Carmen Stavrositu concluded that online use leads people "to hold even stronger views than the ones they started with, and . . . to manifest increasing hatred toward those espousing contrary beliefs." Liberals and conservatives respond similarly, although conservatives are somewhat more likely to seek out supportive sites, whereas liberals are somewhat more likely to block or "defriend" those who express opposing ideas.[95]

———

Surely the mainstream media are the place to find constructive voices. There are such outlets, but fewer than in the past as a result of the rise of a type of journalism that thrives on attack and counter-attack.

When the television networks launched their thirty-minute nightly newscasts in the early 1960s, they soon gained a huge following. In most media markets, news was the only available dinner-hour programming, and habitual viewers stayed tuned. Two-thirds of American adults watched the ABC, CBS, or NBC evening news on a daily basis.[96] Each network gave equal billing to Republican and Democratic leaders, and the discourse was civil. Research found that exposure to television news had a depolarizing effect; differences in Americans' opinions narrowed and respect for the opposing party grew.[97]

In the late 1960s, television news began to change in response to the coarsening political debate surrounding civil rights and the Vietnam War. By the time the tensions quieted, journalists had become accustomed to playing up conflict and had even taken to orchestrating it. When a politician said or did something, they went looking for someone to attack it. "You go shopping," the *Los Angeles Times*'s Jack Nelson said.[98]

Attack journalism got another boost with the onset of party polarization.[99] Journalists no longer had to "go shopping" to find their assassins. The bipartisanship of the postwar era had faded, and a new breed of politician, less given to compromise, was emerging. Their kind had once been dismissed as hotheads, but their blistering attacks made them good copy.[100] A study found that members of Congress from the extreme wings of the parties were being quoted more often in the news than moderate party members.[101] Even today, ideologically extreme politicians get heavier news coverage than their numbers alone would predict.[102]

To be sure, politicians are the ones who are attacking each other. But journalists are the ones who decide what gets aired. A study of candidates' stump speeches found that journalists largely ignore the candidates' policy statements, which account for most of what they say, choosing instead to report the moments when they go on the attack.[103] Political scientists Tim Groeling and Matthew Baum found the same tendency in a study of newsmakers' appearances on *Meet the Press, Face the Nation,* and other Sunday morning interview programs. Although newsmakers on these shows talk mostly about their policy goals and only occasionally attack their opponents, it is the partisan attacks that are most often reported on the Sunday night newscasts and in the Monday morning papers.[104]

Conflict feeds on itself, as the opposing sides respond tit-for-tat, creating what one observer calls "an atmosphere of perpetual mudslinging." It has all the elements of a melodrama, with journalists writing the script and politicians acting it out, all the time trying to tilt the storyline in their direction.[105] When a disruptive character like Trump comes along, he is handed the keys to the newsroom. Reporters twitch with each new tweet, many of them attacks on opponents and vulnerable groups. Journalists have compiled a list of the lies that Trump has told as president.[106] They might find it instructive to compile a list of their Trump-driven stories that have given voice to our divisions.

We don't get many news stories about politicians working together. Even in our polarized age, a third of the bills passed by Congress have bipartisan support.[107] They are not always ignored by the press, but they are nearly always underplayed. When the No Child Left Behind Act (NCLB) was passed in 2001, it had bipartisan support and was accorded fifty-eight articles in the *New York Times.* In the next legislative session, which was marked by partisan conflict over NCLB's implementation, the *Times* devoted six times as many articles to the issue.[108]

At that, the level of conflict in traditional news outlets pales alongside what is found on cable television. News on CNN, Fox, and MSNBC gives politics the look of a war zone. The cable networks differ in who is getting hammered, but not in their tendency to play up conflict.[109] And they are not shy about inciting their viewers, as when Fox claimed that the Black Lives Matter movement had declared war on cops.[110]

Almost no group is spared from attack. A recent study found, for example, that negative stories about Muslims on broadcast television news outnumber positive ones by four to one. And rarely are Muslims given a chance to speak on their own behalf. Fewer than 5 percent of television news stories about Muslims include a Muslim voice. In a recent year-long period, Donald Trump was heard speaking about Muslims seven times more often on television news than were all Muslim voices combined. "Terrorists," "criminals," and "murderers" are just a few of the invectives that Trump has directed at Muslims.[111]

America's news media do not see themselves as being in the business of deepening our tribal divide, but their obsession with conflict has had that effect. Studies indicate that conflict-based journalism increases distrust in politics, politicians, the opposing party, and marginalized groups.[112]

———

Our tribal politics threaten to take us places we haven't been in a long time. To be sure, we have had plenty of tribal episodes in the past, most of them centering on race, and not just the black-white divide that has plagued America since its beginning. When the survivors of the *Titanic* arrived by rescue ship in New York Harbor in 1912, they were taken ashore except for a handful of Chinese crewmen. Chinese were prohibited by law from entering the United States.[113]

Perhaps today's politics are not as tribal as they were in the early 1900s, when America was struggling to absorb millions of immigrants from southern and eastern Europe. But our tribalism easily surpasses anything we have seen since then and is more dangerous. America back then was on the upswing. Its factories were booming, and jobs could be had nearly for the asking. No one doubted that the twentieth century would be the American century. That is not the mood or reality of today's America.

Three of our deepest divides—geographical, racial, and religious—have merged and have found voice in our political parties.[114]

The polarization that defines today's politics goes beyond ideological differences between liberals and conservatives. The fault line also separates Americans by how they look and where they live, which has made partisan conflict as much, if not more than, a question of identity as a question of issues.[115]

It's an explosive mix. When parties differ over issues, there is always the possibility of compromise. When parties are divided by identity, almost nothing is off-limits. We excuse lying when committed by our side and reject cooperation, fearful that it will help the opposing side. Even the traditional notion of accountability—a party's ability to deliver on its policy promises—has been discounted. Undermining the other party is the overriding goal.[116]

We could be approaching the type of politics that James Madison warned against in *Federalist* No. 10. Unrestrained factionalism, Madison wrote, is democracy's soft spot—the one thing that can weaken it from within. It starts democracy on a downward spiral. With each shift in the parties' fortunes, the party newly in power seeks to undo what the previous administration has done. Government becomes unstable, and the parties and their followers, rather than acting as rivals, become enemies. At that point, Madison said, policy is determined "not according to the rules of justice and the rights of the minor party, but by the superior force of an interested and overbearing majority."

My optimistic side says America has too much going for it to be flattened by hyperpartisanship. But fear and loathing feed on themselves. Once unleashed, they are hard to stop. And it's not like Americans' differences are made of smoke and will drift away in the morning breeze. They are a product of deep changes that have unsettled tens of millions, everyone from the West Virginia coal miners who have no hope of getting their jobs back to the newer citizens who fear an undocumented family member will be forcibly deported. We have not divided ourselves into rival tribes simply because we like a good fight.

Our parties are two different cultures, each with its own version of reality and each with its own look. On the right—the Republican side—is two-thirds of white America, aging and longing for a time when economic security was nearly taken for granted and when moral codes were more sharply defined. It was a time of white privilege, one that was, and remains, so deeply embedded in society that most of its beneficiaries fail to see it and thus fail to acknowledge the legitimate grievances of the disadvantaged. That version of America is not coming back. Never in history has time reversed itself in a way that many on the populist right are hoping it will. Trump might not be their last gasp, but there will be a last gasp.[117] But what happens when even their illusion of reversible time is stripped away? What happens when anxiety slips into perpetual disappointment?

On the left—the Democratic side—is emergent America. It is younger, less white, and more urban. Its narrative is that of a fairer and more equal America, but the left has not coupled that goal with a large and coherent program for achieving it.[118] Perhaps we are at "the end of history" in the sense that the social welfare state created through Roosevelt's New Deal and Johnson's Great Society is the left's apotheosis and the best it can do now is stay the course, hoping that the digital revolution, multiculturalism, secularism, and who knows what else will bring us to a better place.[119] That is possible but by no means certain. We are in the early stage of a new industrial revolution, centering on artificial intelligence, where smart machines will take over many of the jobs now done by humans. What happens when those jobs are lost? How will the left manage the fallout, given the difficulty it's had in responding effectively to the economic and social dislocation of recent decades?

To be sure, there are millions of Americans who are not aligned with either tribe.[120] Many of them care so little about politics that they never vote. But many others do care and, in the short term, they're the key to whether our politics will continue to harden or retain enough resilience to overcome the damage of hyperpartisanship.

There is reason for hope. Political moderates say they would like a return to the time when political civility and compromise prevailed. But their numbers have been declining, and we don't have to look hard to understand why. Many Americans are immersed in echo chambers. Some are there by choice, relying on media outlets that reinforce what they already believe. Others find themselves in echo chambers by virtue of where they live or with whom they work. The small rural Minnesota town where I grew up is Trump territory. On my two most recent visits, in the summers of 2017 and 2018, nearly every Trump supporter with whom I talked told me the same story about why they supported him. Their opinions were honest and heartfelt, rooted in a lifestyle they've always known. But the story varied little from one Trump backer to the next. Echo chambers work that way. We hear one version of reality, and we hear it again and again. It's a vortex that's been slowly drawing Americans into one camp or the other.

When operating properly, political parties manage change in ways that reduce disruption.[121] Today's parties have become instruments of division and disorder. When compromise and accommodation are thrown to the wind, bad things happen: instability and resentment rise, civility and unifying values erode, democracy begins to weaken.

CHAPTER 3

THE DISRUPTORS

Sharp knives, of course, are the secret of a successful restaurant.

George Orwell, *Down and Out in Paris and London*

Within a few months of starting the website *Ending the Fed,* Ovidiu Drobota, a twenty-four-year-old Romanian, was king of social media. His top four stories generated three million Facebook engagements during the 2016 presidential campaign—more than did the top four stories of the *Washington Post, New York Times,* or *Wall Street Journal.*[1]

A top-rated Drobota story was headlined "Pope Francis Shocks World, Endorses Donald Trump for President." Another told of how President Obama had cut billions of dollars from veterans' programs in order to allocate billions to help Muslim refugees relocate to the United States. Drobota's stories were fakes. Interviewed after the election, he expressed admiration for Donald Trump, saying that the American media were telling lies about Trump and migrants. Drobota had been working as a hacker but said it was "dangerous" and that he could make more money from the display ads on his Facebook site. "Just to be clear," he said, "I don't have any relation with Russia or WikiLeaks." Asked what might come next, Drobota said that he had never been to America but would like to travel there and "visit some places like NASA and take a picture with Donald J. Trump."

Drobota is one of thousands of foreign disrupters, based mainly in eastern Europe, who produce disinformation and distribute it to Americans. Some do it to advance a cause, make a buck, amuse themselves, or simply mess with Americans' minds. In one small Macedonian town alone, more than three hundred people are involved. The town's mayor proudly said that the work has solved the town's unemployment problem. A local bar owner boasted of booming vodka sales to the newly employed.[2]

Fake news has drawing power. During the last three months of the 2016 presidential campaign, the top twenty fake news stories produced more shares, likes, and other forms of engagement on Facebook than did the mainstream media's top twenty stories.[3] Although most of the stories favored Trump, some aimed to help Hillary Clinton. The most trafficked of the pro-Clinton stories told of how Trump had groped drag queen RuPaul in the 1990s. RuPaul is quoted as saying, "Trump pulled my dress up. . . . He suddenly became very angry. He started yelling and cursing, and he left the party."[4]

Elections are not the only or even the main target of disinformation coming from abroad. The disruptors seek to sow confusion and discord, tarnish the reputation of political leaders, undermine faith in the country's political institutions, and raise doubts about the accuracy of the news media.[5] It is a new and insidious form of warfare. Testifying before Congress in 2017, former director of national intelligence James Clapper said, "If there has ever been a clarion call for vigilance and action against a threat to the very foundation of our democratic political system, this is it."

Nevertheless, for all the mischief they cause, foreign disruptors are late to the game. Very late in fact. Americans didn't need to be taught how to disrupt their political system. They had been practicing it for years. Our political system has been hammered by home-grown disruptors for so long, it's a wonder that it's still running.

————

Democracy rests on political trust. People need to have confidence that their political leaders will govern in their interest even when they are not being watched.[6] Trust gives leaders the time and support they need to tackle tough problems, particularly those that impose short-term costs. And trust helps citizens on the losing end to accept as legitimate the outcome of elections and policy disputes. Trust is what gives democracy its resilience.[7]

Political trust is at its lowest level in polling history. Name a political institution and most Americans are likely to say they don't trust it.

Even government data are suspect. A survey found that more than 40 percent of Americans "somewhat" or "completely" distrust government unemployment, hiring, and consumer spending statistics.[8]

It was not always this way. In the early 1960s, three-fourths of Americans said they trusted the federal government to do the right thing "almost always" or "most of the time." More than twice as many Americans said the government was "run for the benefit of all the people" as said it was "pretty much run by a few big interests looking out for themselves." Today, four times as many Americans think "a few big interests" control the government as think it operates "for the benefit of all."[9]

In the 1960s, President John F. Kennedy spoke of politics as "a noble profession." Many Americans today would scoff at that notion. Relatively few parents say they would like a son or daughter to enter politics.[10] Most Americans find it hard to think of a politician they deeply trust. *Reader's Digest* asked a thousand respondents to name the "most trusted Americans." No political figure was in the top ten. Seven of the top ten were entertainers. Tom Hanks was number one. Not until numbers 23 and 24 did an officeholder appear, and both were retired. One of them was former secretary of state Madeleine Albright. The other was former president Jimmy Carter. A judge came in at number 28, but she didn't sit on the federal or state bench. It was Judge Judy. Only one current elected official slipped into the top 100. Barack Obama, who was president at the time, came in at number 65.[11]

Americans' distrust of politicians runs deep. Ninety percent of Americans believe that "most politicians are more interested in winning elections than doing what is right." More than two-thirds of Americans believe that "our system of government is good, but the people running it are incompetent."[12] Less than a third of Americans think "honest" is a word that describes elected officials, whereas three in four think "selfish" is an apt description. Three-fourths say that most elected officials put their "own interests" ahead of the "country's interest."[13]

Nor do Americans think they can control their elected leaders. Three in every four are convinced that "most elected officials don't care what people like me think."[14] Two of every three have little or no confidence "in the people who run the government to tell the truth to the public."[15] Three of every four believe that most elected officials "lose touch with people quickly."[16]

Most people say that "ordinary Americans" would do a better job than "elected officials" of "solving the country's problems."[17] At that, Americans don't think all that highly of their fellow citizens. Fully half of them say they have little or no confidence "in the wisdom of the American people when it comes to electing their national leaders." Seven in eight say that "most Americans vote without really thinking through the issues."[18]

Americans once had a shared narrative about their country's prominence. Nearly nine in ten said they were "extremely proud" to be an American. Now, according to a recent Gallup poll, only half feel that way. The image of America as a beacon of hope—what Ronald Reagan called "the Shining City on the Hill"—is fading. Only a third of Americans today believe that the United States "stands above all other countries."[19] In a monthly poll that dates back nearly a decade, there has not been a single month in which the number of respondents who thought the country was heading in "the right direction" exceeded in number those who thought it was on "the wrong track."[20]

Some observers think democracy itself might be at risk, which seems unlikely given the nation's many civic associations and its layered system of checks and balances.[21] But democracy in America is frayed. Over the past two decades, the number of Americans saying democracy might not be the best system has increased from 9 to 16 percent.[22] One in five believe the president "should be authorized to act without congressional support."[23] A similar number think a military-led government is a "fairly good" idea.[24] Roughly the same number think courts should have the power to close down news outlets that present inaccurate or biased information.[25]

Americans' distrust has been decades in the making. Stubborn policy problems, leadership failures, and a host of disruptors—some acting deliberately and some unwittingly—have brought trust in government to its knees.

———

For most of its history, the United States was blessed with good fortune. The country's open frontier with its abundant cheap land—called "The Great West" by nineteenth-century historian Frederick Jackson Turner—offered opportunities that ordinary people in the Old World could only dream of having.[26] The relatively late onset of America's Industrial Revolution was also a godsend. The industrial age began in Europe, but the delay here did not affect America's prosperity, because of westward expansion. When the United States finally got serious about industrialization, it was not held back by outmoded factories and quickly leapfrogged Europe in manufacturing output. World War II, which left Japan and much of Europe in ruins, also worked to America's advantage. The country emerged from the war with its industrial base intact. The United States was producing more than half of the world's goods and services, which launched an era of unprecedented shared prosperity—good-paying jobs, rising levels of home ownership, growing numbers of college graduates.[27]

Even young adults had it easy. My high school class in rural Minnesota had forty-five students and, upon graduation, each of us had a job or was headed off to college. If you went to a public university, tuition was next to free—mine was less than $500 a year. I came from a large family, and we had very little money, but college was within reach. Summer jobs for students were plentiful. I spent one summer working for the U.S. Forest Service, another as a laborer on the missile sites being built in the western Dakotas, a third at ROTC summer camp, having decided to do my military service as a U.S. Army officer. I was debt-free upon leaving college.

But good fortune doesn't last forever, and it began running short for America when European and Japanese production recovered from the war. Global demand for American-made goods slowed, reducing the need for factory workers, who were being displaced at an even faster rate by machines. As the higher-paid manufacturing workforce was shrinking, the lower-paid service-sector workforce—food servers, store clerks, hotel staff, artists, lower-level administrators, and the like—was growing.[28] Wage stagnation set in and has continued for decades. The pay of the average worker, adjusted for inflation, is roughly the same today as it was in 1970.[29]

America's middle class, which was once the envy of the world, has been shrinking. In 1970, three in every five Americans lived in a middle-class household, and they enjoyed a proportionate share of the nation's income. Today, only half are in the middle class and their share of income has shrunk to 40 percent. Lower-income Americans have fared even worse. Their average income, adjusted for inflation, has fallen by 20 percent from its 1970s level. The big winners in America's income redistribution have been those at the top. Real income for those in the top fifth has jumped from an average of roughly $100, 000 a year in the 1970s to roughly $170,000 today. The top 1 percent are flourishing—their average real income has gone from roughly $200,000 a year to roughly $1,000,000.[30]

Economic conditions affect political trust.[31] When jobs are plentiful and income is rising, trust increases. Democracies thrive when people think that they can get ahead in life.[32] Personal optimism creates a halo effect that bolsters people's confidence in their political leaders and institutions. On the other hand, trust declines when difficult times persist. Most modest-income Americans describe their current financial situation as precarious; they are only half as likely as higher-income Americans to express trust in government.[33]

As the U.S. economy was starting to weaken in the early 1970s, American politics was rocked by the Vietnam War and the Watergate scandal. They were massive disruptions, precipitating the steepest decline in political trust in polling history. Only 35 percent of Americans expressed confidence in the federal government, less than half the level of a decade earlier.[34]

Since then, whenever political trust has started to creep up, a shock of one kind or another has pushed it back down. America, a once provi-dential nation, has become star-crossed. A first shock was stagflation, a combination of high unemployment and high inflation in the late 1970s. Policymakers had no answer. They had economic models to deal with high unemployment or high inflation, but not when they happened simultaneously. As the problem persisted, trust dropped to the level where only one in four Americans expressed confidence in the federal government.[35] And so it's been. Confidence has edged up, only to be beaten down by an unwanted development—the Iran-Contra scandal, recession in the late 1980s, the Monica Lewinsky scandal, the bursting of the tech bubble in the late 1990s, wars gone badly in Afghanistan and Iraq, the 2008 crash of the housing and financial markets, the bitter fight over health care reform, the disruptive presidency of Donald Trump.

Gridlock in Washington has aggravated the situation. When the writers of the Constitution designed Congress, they took pride in the intricate legislative process by which a bill becomes law. The division of legislative power between two coequal chambers—apportioned differently and with a longer term of office for senators—was intended to encourage compromise. And Congress worked that way until recently. What the framers didn't foresee, and what has happened, is that the structure of Congress makes it an obstructionist's dream. Each party has been strong enough to block the other from acting and rarely strong enough to act decisively on its own. Urgent policy problems have festered for a lack of bipartisanship.

Lawmakers have behaved badly in other ways as well. As more and more of them have looked upon their time in Congress as a full-time career, they've become a political class dedicated to keeping their jobs, which for many has meant putting personal interest ahead of the national interest.[36] A recent study of 1,779 policy decisions by political scientists Martin Gilens and Ben Page found little evidence that the opinions of ordinary citizens affect lawmakers' policy decisions. Their decisions align instead with the policy goals of wealthy citizens and well-funded corporate lobbies.[37] And many lawmakers are shameless in denying responsibility for the gridlock and favoritism that's taken place under their watch. When running for reelection, they attack government for its failures, as if they were somehow not part of the problem.

During the past decade, the number of Americans saying they trust the federal government to do the right thing "most of the time" or "almost always" has averaged a mere 19 percent and has never exceeded 25 percent. Poor performance tops the list when Americans are asked why they distrust the federal government. Older Americans are the most disillusioned. They knew a time when government worked, and now it doesn't.[38] "In recent years," writes the University of Michigan's Ronald Inglehart, the federal government "has become appallingly dysfunctional."[39]

———

One group of lawmakers has made it their mission to tear down government. Concentrated on the right, they call themselves conservatives even though their beliefs don't fit the traditional definition of a political conservative. A commitment to strong institutions was once a core principle of American conservatism.[40] Right-wing Republicans seek to destablize institutions. They're radicals.

Their assault on government is strategically brilliant. If people can be convinced that government doesn't work, they can more easily be convinced to oppose government programs. In *Why Trust Matters,* Marc Hetherington shows that, as trust declines, so does support for government action. People do not necessarily change their minds about the need for action but, as trust diminishes, they doubt that government can deliver.[41]

Newt Gingrich was the first of the radicals to try a hand at shredding the federal government. Upon becoming House Speaker in 1995, Gingrich declared that "1960s-style federalism is dead" and took aim at federal programs, starting with the decades-old policy that granted cash assistance to poor families with children. The 1996 Welfare Reform Act put work and time limits on welfare recipients and, within five years, their ranks had been cut in half.[42] Gingrich also abolished the Office of Technology Assessment, a congressional agency that provided scientific advice on energy, climate, national defense, and other policies under consideration in Congress. There was no need for legislation to be informed by science. Political ideology would supply the answers.

Gingrich's revolution faltered after that, but the anti-government rhetoric continued and got a boost when the Tea Party emerged in 2010 in reaction to the bank bailout, stimulus spending, and health care reform. "We've come to take our government back," Republican senator Rand Paul said. "This movement, this Tea Party movement, is a message to Washington that we're unhappy and that we want things done differently."[43]

The Republican Party's most conservative voters have a deep distrust of government. They're the Americans most likely to say they're "angry" with the federal government, to say it needs "sweeping reform," to say it's "almost always wasteful and inefficient," and to rate its performance as "poor."[44] Tom Keane, a *Boston Globe* contributing columnist, notes that right-wing Republicans "are a surly bunch, filled with naysaying: no to Obamacare, no to gay marriage, no to new immigrants, no to taxes, and no to government in general."[45]

When historians look back on this period in our history, however it ends, they'll puzzle over how a great American political party could have been hamstrung by radicals who share almost none of its founding principles. They will have an easier time telling the story of the consequences—dysfunctional government, unrestrained partisanship, and the unleashing of tribal instincts.

———

The Democratic Party has a stake in creating trust in government, but many of its efforts have backfired, making the task harder. Democrats have found themselves in the position of having to convince voters that a program is needed while also trying to convince them that government can do the job.

The Democratic Party's transition from its greatest legacy—the creation of an economic safety net—has been anything but easy. For decades, party conflict in America divided along class lines, with Republicans arguing for unfettered free markets and Democrats fighting for the interests of workers. The 1930s New Deal and the 1960s Great Society capped that struggle. Democrats were able to enact economic security programs that included Social Security, the minimum wage, collective bargaining, Medicare, and Medicaid. But Democrats were then thrust into the position of having to protect their programs. They'd been the party of a better future for ordinary people. They became the party of big government. Given America's tradition of individualism and small government, it has been a tough sell. To be on the side of the little guy in America is to be on the side of the angels. To be on the side of big government is damnation. "My symbol of hell," wrote novelist C. S. Lewis, "is something like the bureaucracy."[46]

Democrats have struggled to tell their story, as scholars Robert Entman and Julie Wronski found in their study of more than ninety thousand statements made by party elites on Sunday morning talk shows between 2009 and 2015. They focused on what scholars call "framing"— the way in which party elites define their party's positions and ideology.[47] They found that Republican leaders tell a coherent story that seeks to feed distrust in government and build support for market-based policies. The Republican message can be boiled down to a few words: "Big government is the problem, cutting taxes and regulation the solution; a rising tide will then lift all boats and those who work hard will live the American Dream." Supporting the message are short, pithy phrases: "big government," "tax-and-spend liberals," "government is the problem, not the solution," "tax relief."[48]

For their part, Democratic leaders don't tell a large story about why Americans are struggling to get ahead and how government can help. They talk about policy issues but not in the context of a larger message about government's role in society. Democrats even lack a favorite word for their party. Republican elites use the label "conservative" to describe their party eleven times more often than Democratic elites use the terms "liberal" or "progressive" to describe their party. In fact, Republicans use the label "liberal" four times more often than do Democrats, using it to criticize what Democrats represent. Democrats lack a crisp rejoinder to the Republican claim that they're the "tax-and-spend" party.[49]

Democrats have also been hampered by persistent divisions within America's working class. In *Strangers in Their Own Land,* Arlie Russell Hochschild describes how working-class whites see themselves as having waited patiently in line for a piece of the American Dream only to see minorities and immigrants cut the line, ushered there by affirmative action and other policies promoted by the Democratic Party. Although working-class whites are better off economically than minorities, they see themselves as being held back so that minorities can get ahead.[50] A recent poll found that two-thirds of working-class whites believe that reverse discrimination—discrimination against whites—is as prevalent as discrimination against minorities.[51]

The perception that Democrats have abandoned the little guy also owes to Democratic leaders' embrace of economic globalization and wealthy campaign donors. Republicans had started doing these things earlier, and in a larger way, but voters expected that of America's pro-business party. It was jarring when the party of labor did so. Whose side were the Democrats on?

Trust in government has fallen among all demographic groups, but none more so than working-class whites. They are today twice as likely as blacks and Hispanics to be distrustful of government.[52] They are today the demographic group most distrustful of the two parties—seeing both of them as favoring the rich.[53] They are today the Americans most likely to say that they "feel like a stranger" in their own country.[54]

Trump leveraged white working-class Americans' sense of deprivation by promising to "make America great again." And by portraying immigrants as their enemy, he gave voice to their belief that less-deserving individuals were getting ahead at their expense.[55] There was nothing new about Trump's playbook. It dates to the earliest days of politics. When people feel unjustly deprived, they're open to leaders who demonize "the other."[56]

———

"The press is your enemy," the president said. "Enemies. Understand that? . . . Because they're trying to stick the knife right in our groin."[57] These words were spoken, not by Donald Trump but by Richard Nixon, whose vice president famously said that the television networks were "nattering nabobs of negativism." Ever since Nixon, Republicans have feuded with the press, accusing it of having a liberal bias. Nixon worked largely behind the scenes, threatening to take away broadcasters' licenses if they didn't shape up. Ronald Reagan created what amounted to a White House news service, feeding print stories directly to local news outlets in an effort to bypass the national press. A bumper sticker in George H. W. Bush's 1992 reelection campaign read, "Annoy the Media, Re-Elect Bush." George W. Bush took to sending video feeds to local TV stations to bypass the White House press corps. What's different about Trump is that he has confronted the press head on and without restraint: "fake news," "enemy of the American people," "fake media," "the opposition party," "disgusting media," "corrupt media," "lying media." He has ordered journalists removed from his rallies and threatened to change the libel laws to make journalists easier to sue.

Scholars have not found what Republicans say to be true—that America's mainstream media have a decidedly liberal bias. Dozens of studies have investigated the issue and, although there is evidence of liberal bias, it's not anywhere near the level that Republicans say.[58] And partisan slant varies from one news outlet to the next. Those with more liberal audiences tend to provide more liberal content whereas those with more conservative audiences tilt conservative in their coverage, suggesting that marketing, rather than politics, drives some of the slant.[59]

Nor is it true that Republicans routinely get the short end of the news coverage. Over the full course of the 2016 presidential campaign, the candidate with the most negative coverage was Hillary Clinton, not Donald Trump. Not until Trump had secured the Republican nomination did the press cut loose on his candidacy. Until then, he had come as close to getting a free pass as today's journalists are willing to give. His coverage before the primaries and during the contested primaries was more than three-to-two positive over negative. As for Clinton, she was pounded in the press from the day she announced her candidacy to the day she conceded the election. Her coverage was two-to-one negative during the pre-primary and primary periods, and also two-to-one negative during the general election.[60]

Trump's edge went beyond the tone of the election coverage. According to a study by Harvard's Berkman Klein Center, Clinton's coverage included three times as many references to scandals as did Trump's, whereas his coverage included nearly three times as many references to policy as did her coverage. Reporting on Trump was based more heavily on his policies; reporting on Clinton was rooted largely in alleged scandals, which received roughly four times as much attention from journalists as did her policy positions.[61]

Nevertheless, the Republicans' decades-long attack on the press as politically biased has undermined trust in the press.[62] After Watergate, when the press played a key role in exposing the scandal, it was America's most trusted institution. Now it's nearly the least trusted. When asked in Gallup polls how much they trust the press to present the news "fully, accurately, and fairly," the number of Americans who say they trust it "a great deal" or "a fair amount" has declined from more than 70 percent in the mid-1970s to roughly 30 percent today. Republicans are the least trusting. Only about 15 percent of Republicans say they trust the press.[63] Three of every four Republicans are convinced that the news media invent fake stories designed to make Trump look bad.[64] Half of all Republicans accept Donald Trump's claim that the press is "the enemy of the people."[65]

Republicans' distrust runs so deep that few things are more likely to whip Republicans into a frenzy than a blistering attack on the media.[66] In a 2016 Republican presidential primary debate, Senator Ted Cruz went after CNBC's moderators. "This is not a cage match," Cruz said. "You look at the questions—Donald Trump, are you a comic book villain? Ben Carson, can you do math? John Kasich, will you insult two people over here? Marco Rubio, why don't you resign? Jeb Bush, why have your numbers fallen? How about talking about the substantive issues?" Cruz scolded the moderators: "The questions that have been asked so far in this debate illustrate why the American people don't trust the media." The debate audience erupted with wild applause. Republican pollster Frank Luntz's focus group, which was scoring the candidates' debate statements, gave Cruz's attack 98 points out of a possible 100—the highest score that Luntz had ever recorded.[67]

Although the news media have been a punching bag, they have landed more than a few blows of their own. They've been pounding away at politicians for decades. It began after Watergate when journalists decided that politicians needed to be policed.[68] That conviction quickly turned into a litany of what's wrong with our political leaders and institutions.

For decades, news coverage has been relentlessly negative in tone. A study found that, when a president's use of military force is the subject of a TV news story, critics of the policy get four times the air time as those who back it.[69] Another study found that the press largely ignores the minority party in Congress except when the opposing party controls the presidency. Then, as a prime source of attacks on the president, the minority party gets as much coverage as the majority party.[70] Newly elected presidents no longer get the "honeymoon" that traditionally followed their inauguration. Except for Barack Obama's first one hundred days in office, no president since George H. W. Bush has caught a break from the press early in his term. And Obama's soft entry in 2009 quickly ended. During his second hundred days in office, his coverage turned negative and stayed low for his remaining years in office.[71] As political scientist Michael Robinson put it, journalists seem to have taken some motherly advice and turned it upside down: "If you don't have anything bad to say about someone, don't say anything at all."[72]

Critical reporting can alert the public and discourage wrongdoing by officials, but, when it's relentless and directed at all things large and small, the only sure effect is political distrust.[73] As one analyst said of reporters, "You know, the ones who bring us daily, even hourly, tales of hypocrisy, corruption, jealousy, infidelity, gaffes, ambition, lies, double-crosses, distortions, unsubstantiated rumors."[74] By choosing to present politicians as scoundrels unworthy of the public's trust, the press has helped create that very belief.[75]

Ironically, the so-called liberal media's negative slant serves the interests of the right wing by reinforcing its anti-government message. Having been told by the media for years on end that political leaders are devious and that the government is badly run, many Americans have come to believe it.[76]

Negative coverage has also undermined the media's authority.[77] If journalists had picked their fights, saving their attacks for instances of gross misconduct, they might have retained a measure of the public trust gained during their Watergate coverage. By defining themselves as nitpickers, they have wasted much of that trust.[78] A poll found that three times as many Americans believe that the news media "[get] in the way of society solving its problems" as believe that the news media "help society solve its problems."[79]

———

Elimination of the fairness doctrine in 1987 launched partisan talk radio, which sparked partisan talk shows on television, which have been joined by partisan internet sites. These outlets are less visible than the mainstream media, largely because their main platforms are radio and the internet. But it would be a mistake to underestimate their contribution to Americans' political distrust or the size of their audience—more than fifty million Americans tune in each week. Conservative outlets attract roughly 90 percent of the audience.[80]

Right-wing media are hooked into a large network that includes conservative think tanks, some of which are little more than propaganda outlets. They have, for example, funded scores of climate-change denial books, picking authors who dispute the scientific consensus.[81] Wealthy donors are also part of the conservative media network. *Breitbart News* is backed by Robert Mercer, cofounder of a successful hedge fund, and *The Daily Caller* is backed by the billionaire Koch brothers.[82] The brothers are following in the footsteps of their father, Fred Koch, whose money helped underwrite the John Birch Society.[83]

Whatever the level of partisan bias in the traditional media, it pales alongside the bias in right-wing media. Traditional notions of objectivity count for little in what they convey.[84] They operate from an ideological model that conveys a version of truth in which virtually all the answers are found on one side of the political divide. Their intolerance extends to those who stray even a few steps from the party line. In her study, journalist Jackie Calmes found that many Republican lawmakers live in fear of conservative talk show hosts. Calmes cites the example of House majority leader Eric Cantor, who lost his seat to a little-known right-wing challenger after angering the talk show folks by suggesting that he was open to a bipartisan compromise on immigration. "If you stray the slightest from the far right," former Republican senate majority leader Trent Lott told Calmes, "you get hit by the conservative media."[85]

Government is a prime target of partisan media. From outlets on the right, we hear that government serves the undeserving at the expense of hardworking taxpayers. From those on the left, we hear that government serves the rich and well-connected at the expense of hardworking taxpayers.

The "establishment" is also a target. Before being forced out at *Breitbart News* for critical comments about Donald Trump Jr., Steve Bannon had made removing "establishment Republicans" a higher priority than ridding Congress of Democrats. "We are declaring war on the Republican establishment," Bannon said. "Nobody is safe. We're coming after all of them."[86]

Research on partisan media has focused on right-wing outlets, which got an earlier start and have the larger audience.[87] These outlets, as one study found, replaced the traditional media's "talking heads" with "screaming heads."[88] Listening to them has all sorts of adverse effects, including a dislike of government, the traditional media, and the Democratic Party and its loyalists.[89] The effect is heightened by listeners' behavior. The more people are exposed to uncivil voices, the more cynical they become. And the more cynical they become, the more they prefer uncivil voices.[90]

Studies of left-wing outlets have focused on comedy shows like those hosted by Bill Maher and Steven Colbert. Such shows are said by some to reflect a long-standing tradition in American humor—poking fun at politicians. Mark Twain quipped: "Suppose you were an idiot. And suppose you were a member of Congress. But I repeat myself." But today's political humor is nothing like that of yesteryear. It's like comparing sex scenes in films of the 1950s with those seen today on HBO. Today's humor is pitiless. Politicians are dupes and institutions are beyond hope.[91] Unlike partisan news outlets, which try to disguise their exaggerated claims, comedy shows carry them to the point of absurdity. The attacks hit home anyway.[92] A leading study concluded that political comedy shows "foster distrusting attitudes—whether it concerns individual politicians, the media, or the political system overall."[93]

———

Americans don't need help when it comes to tearing down their politics, but they're getting it anyway. Foreign agents have joined in. The scale of foreign disruption is striking. There are thousands of foreigners pumping false or divisive information into America's media stream. During the 2016 presidential campaign, Russia alone is believed to have paid more than a thousand individuals to spread false information about Hillary Clinton.[94] Facebook estimated that 150 million Americans, more than half of the adult population, received Russia-sponsored content during the election. Twitter uncovered more than thirty-six thousand Russia-linked disinformation accounts. Russia was able to exploit our tendency to sort ourselves on the internet into like-minded communities.[95] The Russians targeted users from particular locations and then zeroed in on individuals by identifying their user profile, such as "Jew hater" or "homophobe."[96] A capacity for hatred is part of the human condition, and the Russians are skilled at exploiting it.

Russia assigns each of its trolls a quota. Russian Twitter trolls are required to open at least ten accounts and tweet fifty times a day on each one.[97] Some Russians operate from a "troll farm" in St. Petersburg, which is organized around multiple online accounts, coordinated to give the impression that the messages reflect a groundswell of opinion. And then there's Fancy Bear, a Russian cyber-espionage group that specializes in hacks. It was Fancy Bear that penetrated the files of the Democratic National Committee in 2016 and stole emails that were handed over to WikiLeaks in order to damage Hillary Clinton's campaign.[98] When the emails were released, the mainstream American media did exactly what Fancy Bear anticipated. Journalists didn't stop to dig deeply into the source of the emails or the motive behind their release. They headlined the most damaging ones, thereby legitimizing the information without delegitimizing the source.[99]

As the story of Russia's attempt to disrupt the 2016 election was unfolding, a news agency interviewed a Russian who had worked in the

St. Petersburg troll factory. He told of how workers were required to read a strategy document and watch *House of Cards* in order to understand the issues that divide Americans. "Tax problems, the problem of gays, sexual minorities," he said. He was instructed to participate in social media chats—"fire it up, try to rock the boat." One of the best ways, he said, was "to write that sodomy is a sin. This would always get you a couple of dozen likes."[100]

Russia also enlisted the help of unsuspecting Americans. Pretending to be Republicans, the Russians posted ads offering jobs to Trump supporters. One assignment was to organize pro-Trump rallies. One such rally was held in Twin Falls, Idaho, which has a resettlement program for Muslim refugees. The rally's publicity falsely claimed that the town's Muslim refugees were infecting the locals with tuberculosis.[101]

Russian trolls haven't stopped with Trump's election, jumping on nearly every subsequent event that has the prospect of dividing Americans. When a gunman in 2018 killed seventeen students at Marjory Stoneman Douglas High School in Parkland, Florida, Russia's automated Twitter bots swung into action. One tweet falsely claimed that the shooter had searched the web for Arabic phrases, suggesting that he was a home-grown Islamic terrorist.[102]

———

Disrupters have gained our attention, and they've made it their business to fill our heads with all sorts of nonsense. They tell us government is not working even when it is, an argument that has added force when people distrust government.[103] When Congress in 2008 enacted the Troubled Assets Relief Program (TARP) to help ailing financial institutions, it was widely portrayed as a boondoggle aimed at helping rich bankers while government ignored the ordinary Americans who had defaulted on their home mortgages. A Pew Research Center poll asked respondents whether TARP had "helped prevent a more serious [economic] crisis" or "did not help." "Did not help" came out on top, even though economists credit TARP with helping prevent an implosion of the financial sector that could have taken down the global economy and, with it, many of Americans' remaining financial assets.[104]

Conspiracy theories flourish when distrust is high. They acquire credibility when people think that politicians will do anything to get and hold power. That thinking spawned the Seth Rich murder conspiracy theory. Rich, a DNC staffer, was murdered soon after the WikiLeaks release of hacked DNC emails embarrassing to the Clinton campaign. Did Rich have a role in the hack? Did he have additional emails so explosive that they would have torpedoed Clinton's campaign? By the logic of conspiracy buffs, even though Washington police said that Rich was killed in a botched robbery attempt, there was only one explanation: Clinton had arranged for Rich to be assassinated.[105]

There was a time when conspiracy buffs were isolated oddballs. They are now in the mainstream, and one of them sits in the Oval Office. Trump's conspiracy theories have ranged far and wide: pharmaceutical companies are burying research that shows vaccines cause autism, Barack Obama forged his birth certificate, Ted Cruz's father was involved in the Kennedy assassination, Justice Anthony Scalia might have been smothered to death while he slept, global warming is a hoax invented by China. To support his theories, Trump often cites himself ("I'm a very instinctual person, but my instinct turns out to be right") or the public response to rumors that he starts. David Muir, anchor of ABC's *World News Tonight*, asked Trump, "Do you think that talking about millions of illegal votes is dangerous to this country without presenting the evidence?" Trump replied, "No. "Not at all! Not at all—because many people feel the same way that I do."[106]

Social psychologist Ilan Shrira notes that conspiracy theories have many of the same origins as scapegoating. They tell us that bad things don't just happen on their own, that someone is responsible and that they need to be stopped or punished. "It's not our fault," Shrira writes. "It's them."[107] The most psychologically satisfying conspiracy theories are those that impugn individuals or groups we dislike.

No conspiracy theory is more closely tied to political distrust than the notion that the United States is run by a "deep state." Popularized by *Breitbart News* and other right-wing outlets, it holds that high-ranking people in government and corporations are, in the words of one proponent, "effectively able to govern the United States without reference to the consent of the governed as expressed through the formal political process."[108] Trump shared a tweet of talk show host Sean Hannity in which Hannity pledged to expose the deep state. Hannity has yet to do so, and investigative journalists have uncovered nothing of the kind.

No matter. A 2017 *ABC News/Washington Post* poll found that half of Americans believe the deep state is real. Only a third of the poll respondents said the idea of a deep state amounts to nothing more than "a conspiracy theory."[109]

Conspiracy theorists thrive on the absence of information. Trying to reason with someone who believes George W. Bush conspired in the 9/11 attacks invariably leads to a demand for evidence to the contrary. In the normal world, a claim is judged to be valid because it's backed by confirming evidence. In the conspiracy world, a claim is judged to be valid because some people say that it's true.[110]

For over two centuries the United States operated on informal norms governing debate, deliberation, and standards of proof.[111] The norms didn't prevent repulsive behavior. Every era has had its sleazy characters. But the norms shuttled them to the fringes and kept our thinking within the limits of what is reasonable and plausible. Sensible governing is at risk when false narratives are accepted as fact by large numbers of Americans.

Distrust does more than create misinformed and jaded citizens. Distrust gives license to irresponsibility.[112] Americans who are most distrustful of government are the most opposed to taxes and are the biggest tax cheats.[113]

Distrust leads people to seek someone to blame for their problems. The "establishment" is always on the list of scapegoats. So, too, are the more vulnerable members of society. If they weren't around, or so it's claimed, we'd be better off. Xenophobia has characterized every difficult period in the nation's history, and today is no exception. A Pew Research Center poll asked Americans whether they were "angry" or just "frustrated" with the federal government. Those who said they were "angry" were more than twice as likely as other respondents to say that the increased number of people of different races, ethnicities, and nationalities has made America "a worse place to live."[114]

When trust falls, some people lose interest in politics. Citizens have always found it easy to come up with excuses not to vote. They're too busy, registration is too hard, their single vote won't make any difference.[115] When they believe that officials can't be trusted, it becomes even easier to bail out. The *Washington Post*'s David Broder put his finger on the problem when he said, "If the assumption is that nothing is on the level, nothing is what it seems, then citizenship becomes a game for fools, and there is no point in trying to stay informed."[116]

If the voter decides to get involved anyway, why not back the firebrands who are railing against the system? They are saying what the voter is thinking—that the system is broken and that it's time to throw the rascals out. Yet firebrands are rarely good at governing. By temperament or belief, they're not interested in the negotiation and compromise that are the bedrock of the democratic process.

———

As distrust of government increased steadily after the 1980s, analysts said that a major disruption to the political system could be in the offing. Many of them thought a competitive third-party candidate was the likely possibility. None predicted what actually happened—the election to the presidency of a real estate mogul/TV reality show host.

It's impossible to explain Donald Trump's rise to the presidency apart from the disruptions that have roiled American politics in recent years. He rode the wave of distrust all the way to the Oval Office. Although it is popular in some circles to say that Trump's victory owed to racism, studies indicate that race, though it played a significant role, ranked behind economic dislocation and Americans' distrust of government as a factor in voters' decisions. Somewhere between seven and nine million Americans voted for Barack Obama in 2012 and switched to Trump in 2016. Their main reason? Convinced that government wasn't working, they were persuaded by Trump's promise to "drain the swamp."[117]

Trump flooded the swamp that he vowed to drain. He took dysfunction to new heights, all the while undermining the nation's institutions. During the 2016 presidential campaign, he refused to say whether he would accept the result of the election, "except if I win." He won but still refused, claiming that millions of illegal votes had deprived him of a popular vote victory. In office he became the destructor-in-chief, belittling members of Congress, cabinet members, federal judges, the news media, the nation's allies, and nearly everyone and everything else imaginable. As the FBI pursued its investigation of Russian meddling in the election, and the possibility of collusion with his campaign, Trump attacked the FBI, fired its director, forced out its deputy director, and enlisted like-minded congressional Republicans to discredit the Bureau.

Trump has been praised in some quarters for being transparent. He's been compared in that respect to Franklin D. Roosevelt, who used a new platform, radio, to speak directly to the American people through his fireside chats. Trump too has employed a new platform, Twitter. But the comparison ends there. As Roosevelt spoke to Americans during the Great Depression and World War II, he sought to calm their fears and bring them together. Trump has used his tweets to inflame Americans' fears and pit them against each other.[118]

There is power to be gained through division, and that's been Trump's playbook. Soon after becoming president, he had gained the steadfast loyalty of most Republican voters, which enabled him to silence critics within his own party. With a few notable exceptions, including Arizona senators John McCain and Jeff Flake, few congressional Republicans spoke out against his attacks on the nation's institutions, including the one of which they were a part. Congress's check on presidential power, which is a core principle of the U.S. Constitution, was effectively put on hold.

Nevertheless, it would be inaccurate to say that Trump is the cause of America's disorder. Trump is a product of the disorder, a presidential nominee who was a plausible choice only for an electorate distrustful enough of government to believe that the problem could be fixed only by someone who would blow up the system.[119]

CHAPTER 4

THE PERFORMERS

It was not the man's brain that was speaking; it was his larynx.

George Orwell, *Nineteen Eighty-Four*

On April 18, 2017, instruments at the Mauna Loa Observatory in Hawaii, the world's premier atmospheric research facility, recorded the highest carbon dioxide reading in the facility's sixty-year history. The level was reached sooner than scientific models had predicted, suggesting that the pace of climate change was accelerating. Judging from core samples of ancient air trapped in the ice sheets of Antarctica, the carbon dioxide concentration was now at its highest level in more than a million years.[1]

The landmark reading caused barely a ripple in Washington circles. The Beltway crowd was buzzing about yet another presidential trip to Mar-a-Lago.[2] Donald Trump had spent a third of his time away from Washington, most of it at his Florida estate. Each trip was costing taxpayers nearly a million dollars, and local officials in Florida were complaining that overtime pay for police security was draining their budgets. Republican senator Joni Ernst was quoted as saying, "I do wish that he would spend more time in Washington, D.C. That's what we have the White House for." Republican congressman Ted Yoho sought to shift reporters' attention to Obama: "He went to Hawaii a lot," Yoho said. "He went to Africa quite a bit. He went around the world."[3]

Trump's golf outings were part of the buzz. During the presidential campaign, Trump had blasted Obama for spending time on the golf course. "I'm going to be working for you," Trump said. "I'm not going to have time to go play golf." Yet, by the end of his first hundred days in office, Trump had racked up nineteen rounds of golf, compared with one round for Obama during his first hundred days.[4]

The Washington crowd lives in a bubble of its own. It's hardly surprising that nine out of ten Americans believe that "political events these days seem more like theater or entertainment than something to be taken seriously."[5]

———

When the legendary showman P. T. Barnum decided in 1870 to get into the circus business, he called his spectacle "The Greatest Show on Earth." In January 2017, that show opened in Washington under the name of Donald J. Trump. Replete with fiery news conferences, early-morning tweets, overnight policy shifts, insults to foreign leaders, slams of congressional leaders, the firing of political aides, fits of temper, and one false claim after another, it was mesmerizing. And unsettling. "We're in unchartered waters in all of this," a Republican leader said. "This is all new territory."[6]

Although Trump's confrontational style was new, the territory that he inhabited was old. It had been decades in the making. In the early 1960s, television news changed and so did our politics. The networks lengthened their evening newscasts to thirty minutes and hired the reporting crews needed to produce video news. The networks quickly discovered that they had to come up with something different than the newspaper model of reporting. Viewers didn't have to be told what they could see with their own eyes. A livelier and more stylized form of reporting was needed.[7] NBC's Reuven Frank instructed his correspondents: "Every news story should, without any sacrifice of probity or responsibility, display the attributes of fiction, of drama. It should have structure and conflict, problem and denouement, rising action and falling action, a beginning, a middle and an end."[8]

Politicians adjusted to the change.[9] They held their events in eye-catching settings and scheduled them to fit the deadline for the evening news.[10] Following consultants' advice, they wore bright ties and honed their presentation skills—"It's not what you say, it's how you say it." Historian Daniel Boorstin ridiculed the practice by telling the story of a woman and a baby. A bystander remarks, "My, that's a beautiful baby you have there!" She replies, "Oh, that's nothing—you should see his photograph."[11]

Journalists became uneasy with the theatrical turn. They had created the model but worried that it was getting out of hand. Nothing but "phony events," one reporter said.[12] When George McGovern appeared unannounced at New York's Columbus Day parade during the 1972 campaign, CBS's news story was filled with footage of bands playing and revelers strutting down Fifth Avenue. But tucked into the story were sly put-downs ("Marchers grumbled that politicians ought to go find their own fun and leave other people's parades alone") and disdainful asides ("A Republican dignitary huffed and puffed about the political impropriety of turning up at parades without an invitation").[13]

As the theatrical form of politics was taking hold, the Vietnam War was imploding. The Johnson and Nixon administrations had insisted the war was being won. When purloined secret documents, the "Pentagon Papers," revealed otherwise, journalists felt duped. "The air was thick with lies, and the president was the lead liar," *Washington Post* editor Ben Bradlee declared.[14]

Journalists' traditional reporting model had abetted the lying. "It's my job to report the [newsmaker's] words, whether I agree with them or not," is how one journalist described it.[15] That approach had to be abandoned if politicians were going to lie.[16] But what was the alternative? Investigative journalism was the ideal solution, but it was too slow and painstaking for daily reporting. An expedient alternative was needed, and reporters found it in the voice of others. When a politician did something newsworthy, they turned to his adversaries to tear it apart. The manufacturing of conflict was an old technique, but it became a daily practice. It turned the suspicion that some politicians were lying into the assumption that virtually all of them lie.[17] It was, as one observer said, "a declaration of permanent war between journalists and the political classes."[18]

The tone of the news coverage turned sour. In the 1960s most of what was reported about political leaders was favorable in tone. By the end of the 1970s most of it was unfavorable. As the news turned negative, so did Americans' opinion of their political leaders. It would remain low, anchored by relentlessly negative news coverage.[19]

The change made some old-line journalists uneasy. *Washington Post* editor Russ Wiggins said, "Journalists belong in the audience, not on the stage."[20] But the stage appealed to many journalists, and they gradually worked their way into the lead roles. In the late 1960s the average "sound bite"—a block of uninterrupted speech by a newsmaker on television evening news—had been more than 40 seconds; by 1980 the average had shrunk to 12 seconds (and would eventually drop to less than 10 seconds).[21] Shortening meant simplifying. Whatever nuance or explanation there might have been in a newsmaker's statement was left out. Much of the time that newsmakers were visible on the screen with their lips moving, their words could not be heard. Journalists were doing the talking.[22]

It was more than a change of voice. Elected officials talk mainly about policy problems and issues. Journalists do not. Their norms prohibit them from taking sides on issues, so they focus instead on political strategy and infighting. As journalists became the larger voice in the news, news of the political game came to the forefront. A study of four decades of congressional coverage found that reporting on policy issues and the policy process gradually gave way to reporting on which side was winning and which was losing.[23] Studies of presidential coverage and election reporting revealed the same trend.[24]

Elected officials were caught by surprise by the change in journalism. "I feel like bait rather than a senior member of Congress," Texas congressman Jack Brooks said.[25] But it was the new reality, and politicians had to figure out how to make the best of it.

There is no exact date when politicians realized that attack journalism provided an opportunity to tear down their opponents, but the 1988 Bush presidential campaign was one of the first to turn it into a full-blown strategy. When *Time* magazine's cover story, "The Year of the Handlers," highlighted campaign consultants who manipulate symbols and bring "hot button" issues into play, the Bush campaign was the prototype.[26] Its symbol became a felon, Willie Horton, who not by chance was also an African American male. (He was "William," not "Willie," Horton before the spin doctors latched onto him.) "Americans for Bush," a conservative action group, ran a TV ad saying Horton had brutally raped a white woman while on weekend furlough from a Massachusetts prison. The ad sent the press into a frenzy, and the Bush campaign hurriedly produced an ad to keep it going. "As governor, Michael Dukakis . . . gave weekend furloughs for first degree murderers not eligible for parole. While out, many committed other crimes like kidnapping and rape. And many are still at large."

The Bush campaign hit Dukakis with every charge imaginable, catching him off guard. After the election, Dukakis acknowledged his "failure to understand" the new brand of politics. He had stuck stubbornly to the issues, even as his campaign collapsed around him. "I said in my acceptance speech in Atlanta that the 1988 campaign was . . . about [governing]. I was wrong. It was about phraseology. It was about 10-second sound bites. And made-for-TV backdrops. And going negative."[27]

In an exhaustive study, the University of Pennsylvania's Kathleen Hall Jamieson and Paul Waldman examined the impact of attack journalism. They found that citizens don't learn much about policy problems or issues from exposure to it. Such coverage, they concluded, suppresses "the factual information citizens need to make sense of the political world."[28] They did find one large effect. The coverage generated distrust of politics and politicians.[29] A 2017 study by political scientist Mary Layton Atkinson expanded that research by examining the impact of attack journalism on people's policy opinions. As citizens are exposed to media coverage that highlights the fighting surrounding legislation, they increasingly think the legislation itself is flawed. That's true, Atkinson writes, even for "policies that seem to give Americans what they want—more education funding, more affordable health care, lower taxes, and so on."[30]

———

The political game lacked hecklers until partisan talk radio came along in the late 1980s. The radio hosts quickly discovered that the way to attract listeners was to fire away at the opposing side. "Blood on the floor" was how journalist John Carroll described the formula.[31] Talk radio hosts also figured out that their listeners expected to be entertained. When Glenn Beck in an unguarded moment called himself "a rodeo clown," he put his finger on the other part of a successful talk show.[32]

Few of the radio talk show hosts had a talent for humor, so they resorted to tall tales, of which the Clintons were leading villains. One tale insinuated that the Clintons had a hand in several deaths, including that of Vince Foster, who committed suicide while serving as White House counsel. "How many other politicians have you heard of who have had so many mysterious deaths associated with them?" asked Rush Limbaugh. "It's a lot of people they know who have died, who have been murdered. . . . There's a Clinton body count."[33] When Fox and later MSNBC introduced partisan talk shows to the cable audience, they adjusted the format to fit the television medium. A host sitting alone in a studio talking into a microphone worked on radio but fell flat on television. Roger Ailes tried it with Limbaugh, but the show wasn't a ratings hit and was cancelled.[34] Cable TV settled on a format that coupled hosts with "guests" and "regulars."

Cable TV's partisan talk shows solidified developments that had begun in the 1960s. Airing from Washington, they focused on the Beltway. Endless spats about which side had the better day became their specialty. Time-honored rules of political discourse—fair treatment of each side, verification of sources, and transparency of methods—were ignored. "There are no rules," said Donna Brazile, a longtime talk show guest.[35]

Aside from the format, many of television's partisan hosts differ not at all from their radio counterparts. They're in the assault business. When Wisconsin governor Scott Walker set about eviscerating the state's public employee unions, MSNBC's Rachel Maddow set about eviscerating Walker, an effort that contained false allegations, including the claim that "the Wisconsin middle class is shrinking at a faster rate than any other state in the country."[36]

Truth is a routine casualty on partisan talk shows. Early in Trump's presidency, Fox's Tucker Carlson hosted a self-described Swedish documentary filmmaker who brought along video clips, including one that showed a dark-skinned man hitting a policeman. The filmmaker claimed that Sweden was suffering from a crime wave perpetrated by Muslim immigrants. At a political rally the next day in Florida, President Trump highlighted the Swedish crime wave, saying it proved his claim that Muslim immigrants had to be blocked from entry. Fox's Bill O'Reilly followed up by interviewing a self-described Swedish security expert, Nils Bildt, who confirmed that a Muslim-inspired crime wave was sweeping Sweden.[37]

It was pure fiction. When Swedish authorities learned of the claim, they said there was no crime wave of any kind in their country, Muslim-driven or otherwise. As for Nils Bildt, the self-styled Swedish security expert, it turned out that he wasn't an expert and wasn't even Nils Bildt. The name was an alias, presumably to hide the fact that he had recently spent a year in a Virginia prison.[38] Now, there's no evidence to indicate that Carlson and O'Reilly knew they were being hoodwinked, but they didn't bother to check their guests' credentials before putting their lies on the air.

In the pre-cable era of television, talk shows were models of public discourse. The networks' Sunday morning interview shows and programs like William Buckley's *Firing Line* were a time for serious hosts and guests to talk seriously about serious issues. Today's partisan talk shows have lowered the level of public discourse. It would be inaccurate even to describe their content as discourse, given the disorderly and irrational nature of much of it.

————

The Washington circus would not be complete without its magicians. They had been there all along, but they suddenly began the wholesale transformation of words. What's a patriot? One dictionary says it's "a person who vigorously supports their country." Not according to the 2001 USA Patriot Act. A patriot is a government that's been granted broad new authority, including the power to snoop into your medical records. And what lawmaker of sane mind could vote against a "Patriot" bill? Only one senator dared to do so, although several worried later that they had handed the president a blank check to wage war.

Word manipulation is as old as politics itself. George Orwell wrote that "political language is intended to make lies sound truthful."[39] But rarely have political wordsmiths been as creative as they've been in the past few decades. Until the late 1990s, the estate tax was not on Americans' minds, and for good reason. Most heirs paid no taxes because the estate was too small (less than $650,000 for a surviving spouse). But heirs to an estate worth $3 million or more had to pay a hefty tax. Such estates accounted for less than 1 percent of the total, which meant such heirs would need help from the other 99 percent if they were to get the law changed. Believing that ordinary Americans could be enlisted if the estate tax was relabeled, Republican politicians and conservative groups began calling it a "death tax." Family farms lost, small businesses shuttered, every imaginable "death tax" story was told but one—the fact that wealthy heirs would gain the most if the tax rate was changed. As the death-tax campaign escalated, polls showed that Americans were increasingly worried about the taxes they would owe upon the death of a loved one. Congress responded with legislation that raised the exemption threshold by a factor of four while also cutting the tax rate on the wealthiest estates. Nearly all of the tax gains went to those with large inheritances.[40] In 2017 the Republican-controlled Congress topped that by raising the exemption to $11.2 million for an individual and $22.4 million for a couple—a change that benefits less than two in one thousand Americans.[41]

Many of today's word games are the handiwork of Republican consultant Frank Luntz, who is hailed in the press as "the messaging guru." Democrats have a celebrated magician of their own, the University of California's George Lakoff—"the linguistic guru."[42] The partisan war on words confirms a proposition set forth seven decades earlier by Edward L. Bernays, the founder of modern public relations. "The cure for propaganda," Bernays wrote, "is more propaganda."[43]

Trump has compounded the word game, using words to give life to things that never were. In late 2018 he recast a flow of migrants heading toward America's southern border as a "caravan." Falsely claiming that more than a hundred "unknown Middle Easterners" had infiltrated the group, Trump said that they were "terrorists" bent on "storming the border." He claimed that young adult males made up most of the group, that many of them were "cold stone criminals," and that they were using the accompanying women and children as props to hide their intent. "It's a lot of young people, lot of young men," he said. "They are pushing the women up to the front—not good—and the kids right up to the front." When the migrants were still hundreds of miles away from the United States, Trump dispatched U.S. troops to guard the border. Authorizing them to use lethal force, Trump said, "I have no choice. You're dealing with a minimum of 500 serious criminals."[44]

When language becomes a manipulative game, it is increasingly difficult to hold onto anything resembling facts or truth. As the historian John Miller noted, "The temptation to exaggerate, mischaracterize, fuzz up the truth, and deliberately lie ramps up greatly."[45]

———

At an earlier time, governing and campaigning were kept largely separate, with governing taking up most of Washington's time and attention. Campaigning and governing are now inseparable.[46] In the mindset of the nation's lawmakers, what's good for one party is bad for the other. Although the dynamic isn't all that new to politics, it has accelerated as the tools of communication have expanded. It's been estimated that half of a president's time is now consumed by communication planning and delivery and that about half of congressional staff time is devoted to that purpose.[47]

The point of all this communication might appear to be lawmaking, but most of it is salesmanship. In *Beyond Ideology,* political scientist Frances Lee cites example after example of congressional leaders introducing sham bills on hot-button issues solely to create the kind of conflict that will capture the media's attention and motivate the party's base. Their messages are aimed, not at other lawmakers, but at voters and talking heads. As Lee describes it, it's "messaging" rather than "governing." Politicians aren't trying to legislate. They're trying to win votes. Reflecting on the practice, Republican senator Susan Collins had a straightforward explanation: "If I could compress all that has gone wrong in one phrase, it would be 'perpetual campaign.'"[48]

The problem goes beyond the question of immediate partisan advantage. The perpetual campaign deepens mistrust between opposing lawmakers such that, even when they're not all that far apart on a policy issue, mistrust can block agreement. The more they suspect the other side's motives, the harder it is for them to engage in compromise.[49] When you spend your time worrying that you'll get knifed in the back, there is not much reason to spend time trying to find out whether there is a position that both sides could support.

———

While lawmakers have been playing at their game, journalists have been busy playing up the competitive game—reporting on who's up and who's down. Rare is the development that doesn't generate speculation about its impact on the fortunes of this or that party or politician.

Politics can trump substance even in situations where it's decidedly secondary. When a U.S. special operations team in 2011 conducted a secret raid into Pakistan that killed Osama bin Laden, the killing dominated the news. During the week following his death, the major storyline was the planning and execution of the military raid. But what was the second-biggest storyline? The press could have focused on the reaction of the Arab world to the killing, or the operation's effect on U.S. relations with Pakistan, or the effect of bin Laden's death on terrorists' operational capacity. Instead, second billing went to the impact of Bin Laden's death on the political game. Would it help Barack Obama win a second term? "President Obama," an ABC reporter said, "is getting a significant bump up in the polls."[50]

There are times, of course, when strategic considerations deserve top billing. But a focus on the political game—whether coming from the press, talk show hosts, or politicians—now so thoroughly dominates the agenda that it can numb the mind to the purpose of politics. And then there is the never-ending stream of opinion polls. There are so many polls now that barely a day passes when a new one is not cited as proof that the game is now tilting in favor of one side or the other.[51]

The oversupply of political messages reflects what the *Washington Post*'s Dan Balz calls "the gap" between the interests of the Beltway crowd and those of "ordinary folks."[52] To be sure, citizens take an interest in political goings-on. During a presidential campaign, people naturally want to know how their side is doing. But they also want to know how they'll be affected by what happens, a topic of lesser interest to reporters. A study found that journalists are seven times more likely to say how campaign developments might affect the candidates than to say how they might affect the voters.[53] That tendency is true even of the top news outlets. During the closing weeks of the 2016 presidential election campaign, only five of 150 front-page *New York Times* articles compared Trump and Clinton's policy stands, and fewer than a dozen discussed their policy positions in detail.[54]

What do "ordinary folks" get from the media's game coverage? A better question is what don't they get. Policy issues are presented in a way that can make it hard for even attentive citizens to know what's at stake, other than the fate of individual politicians. It's no surprise that studies have found that citizens don't learn all that much about policy issues from news exposure or that some of what they learn is wrong. There's not much substance to begin with, and the war of words between the opposing sides is often a war over alternative realities, giving listeners a chance to pick the one they like.

To be sure, the news would not be the news if political wrangling was ignored by reporters. There's truth in *Dallas Morning News* reporter

Jacquielynn Floyd's claim that the news would be "a mighty dry and colorless affair" without it.[55] But the balance is off, and by more than a little.[56] Game-centered coverage is just about the laziest form of reporting imaginable. Such stories can be constructed merely by observing what public figures are saying and doing—talking heads without a drop of journalism training do it in real time all the time. In his best-selling *The Making of the President* books, Theodore H. White had taken Americans behind the scenes, giving them an inside look at politics for the first time. As his approach crept into daily reporting and then came to define it, White had misgivings. "I invented [this] method of reporting," White said. "I sincerely regret it."[57]

———

History is a distillation that obscures small things. In thinking about the driving forces of elections past, we think of depressions, wars, and other large issues, forgetting that the 1884 presidential election was decided on an anti-Catholic slur.[58] But, until recently, such instances were rare.

Three of the past five presidential elections have been upended by media frenzies. When in our history did anything as small as an email server get far more media attention than all major policy issues combined and tip the balance in a presidential campaign?[59] Or consider the 2004 presidential election, when a concocted story that a five-time decorated combat veteran was lying about his military service occupied the press's attention for nearly a month and influenced the outcome of a historically close election.[60] Or consider the 2000 election, which was nearly decided on a drunken-driving arrest many years earlier. During a three-day period near the end of the 2000 campaign, George W. Bush's DUI arrest in 1976 got more media attention than did everything he and his opponent Al Gore said about foreign policy during the entire general election campaign.[61]

If elections were the only things warped by the interests of the Washington crowd, the damage could be contained. But nearly every aspect of politics gets distorted. As seen through the media's lens, one institution towers above all others. The White House is the main story, allowing it to control much of the narrative. When Congress makes news, its members are usually responding to what the nation's newsmaker-in-chief has said or done.[62] As he was leaving Congress, House Speaker Tip O'Neill was asked whether he had any unfinished business. He said that he would like to teach the media that Congress "is a co-equal branch of the federal government."[63]

The executive branch bureaucracy gets even less attention than Congress. Over the past century, as policy has become more complex and as government has become more deeply involved in the day-to-day workings of the country, power has devolved from the elected institutions to administrative agencies. Yet bureaucratic activity is not easily fitted into the game narrative. Except when agencies mess up, they might as well be located in Canada for all the attention they get. During his first months in office, Trump failed to get his legislative agenda through Congress but was busy signing executive orders. His attempts to ban immigration from several Muslim nations, blocked as they were by federal judges, got intense news coverage. But they were only a fraction of his executive orders, which covered everything from financial regulation to climate-change policy. Such orders accounted for less than 1 percent of Trump's news coverage, and rarely did a reporter investigate how an order was being implemented.[64]

Lobbying groups? Also in Canada. It's widely known that the United States has election campaigns awash in money. What's less known is that lobbying spending far exceeds that of election spending.[65] Lobbying groups are lightly reported. When the auto industry flooded Capitol Hill with lobbyists in a successful effort to kill a provision of the Dodd-Frank bill that would subject car loans to closer scrutiny, it got barely a headline.[66]

There are plenty of actors on the national stage—journalists, talk show hosts, press secretaries, talking heads, political consultants, pundits. Given that, the narrow range of discourse is remarkable. But it's easy to understand why that's the case. The talkers know a lot more about the political game than they do about policy and government. "Talking mainly to each other" is how scholar Lance Bennett puts it.[67]

In 2017, after nearly 150 years in the business, the Ringling Brothers and Barnum & Bailey Circus folded its tent. The Big Top was no longer drawing a crowd. Not so for the circus in Washington. The Greatest Show on Earth that was the Trump presidency was packing them in.

The audience ratings of CNN, Fox, and MSNBC news shows were up sharply.[68] And there was no mistaking who was in the center ring with Trump. With their nonstop news and talk, the cable networks were a perfect match for Trump's impulsive style. Some years earlier, noting how quickly the media jumped from one big story to the next, the *Atlantic*'s James Fallows said that politics had become "an endless stream of emergencies," the effect of which "is to make the week the fundamental unit of political measurement."[69] Trump's presidency made Fallows's thesis obsolete. The unit of measurement was now the daily tweet. Each new one prompted the cable networks to drop what they were doing and talk nonstop about what Trump had just said.

Heat, speed, trivialization, and deceit virtually guarantee that citizens will be misinformed and more than a bit confused. Under such conditions, the facts get jumbled. In a slower age, the 1960s, cyberneticist Karl Deutsch worried that "noise" in the information system was undermining citizens' ability to make sense of public affairs.[70] Today's information system is awash in noise, much of it intended to confuse or mislead.

Trump has added to the noise, but his political genius was in recognizing how to exploit it. If our information system is an unholy mix of the real and the fake, then it's easy to label the real as fake and replace it with an alternative version. And when Trump got called out for his lies, he doubled down and his aides provided cover. When asked on a talk show about Trump's false statements, White House advisor Kellyanne Conway offered a line that could have come straight out of George Orwell's *Nineteen Eighty-Four*. It would be good to remember, she said, "the many things that he says that are true."[71]

Writing in the 1960s, when the political game was in its infancy, President Kennedy's press secretary, Pierre Salinger, foresaw the destructive possibilities inherent in what was developing. "Perhaps in the long run," Salinger surmised, "we will find that the communications revolution has run away from us and that we have neither the ability nor the desire to adjust life and our practices to meet the challenges with which it has presented us." If this happens, Salinger said, the public "will ride from crisis to crisis, from crest to crest of 'happenings,' many of which are completely fabricated."[72]

CHAPTER 5

THE MARKETERS

I offer you a good time.

George Orwell, review of Hitler's *Mein Kampf*

Donald Trump's presidential campaign began with a theatrical ride down the escalator in Trump Tower. Hired actors were at the bottom, cheering wildly as he descended. Before long, news outlets were doing the cheering. He was a ratings hit.[1] During every month of his presidential campaign, Trump was by far the most heavily covered candidate, allowing him to define his opponents—"Lying Ted," "Little Marco," "Crooked Hillary." During the general election, Trump's cries of "Make America great again" and "Lock her up" were voiced more than twice as often in the news as were Hillary Clinton's calls of "Stronger together" and "He's unqualified."[2] Trump predicted as much. "If you get good ratings," he said, "you'll be on all the time. . . . It's a very simple business. Very simple."[3]

News outlets justified their one-sided coverage by saying Trump made himself readily "available" to reporters.[4] If that were the standard, cash-poor and third-party candidates would be lined up outside the newsroom door. Trump filled the airways during the campaign because he was good for business. Even as they thought his candidacy would collapse, reporters lavished him with publicity. In a rare bit of candor, one network executive said of Trump's candidacy: "It may not be good for America, but it's damn good for CBS. . . . The money's rolling in and this is fun." One estimate put the advertising windfall at more than a billion dollars for the cable networks alone.[5] Did Trump's media advantage help him win the presidency? News executives flatly deny it.[6] They might be the only insiders on the planet to believe it.

When it comes to the marketing of news, America is in a league of its own. CNN shamelessly prefaces its commercial breaks with the promise of "breaking news" and then resumes its newscast with the same old story. America's marketing mania extends to politics. The "marketing style of politics" was invented in America, and other democracies have never come close to catching up.[7] Annual spending on political marketing of one kind or another in the United States dwarfs the amount spent elsewhere.[8]

"More is better" is the guiding principle of American marketing. The Supreme Court applied that principle in *Citizens United,* opening the door to unlimited campaign spending by corporations, unions, and independent organizations. "There is no such thing as too much speech," the Court's majority said.[9] That's a lofty ideal, but it rests on the assumption that what's being said will enable citizens to make informed decisions. Unfortunately, the marketing of news and politics in America is a better deal for the marketers than it is for the public.

Although the news media are called the "fourth branch of government," their loyalty is divided. They are obligated by their constitutionally protected position to serve the public but driven by their business interests to serve themselves. In the early years of the republic, publishers relied on government printing contracts for revenue, which tethered them to the political parties.[10] The partisan press was brought to its knees, not by a fit of conscience but by a better business deal. The invention of the high-speed rotary press enabled publishers to print their papers more cheaply, driving up circulations and attracting advertisers that paid far more money than the parties ever could—so much money that newspapers killed stories that would upset them.[11] "One set of masters," political scientist V. O. Key Jr. wrote, "had been replaced by another."[12]

Newspapers freed themselves from advertisers' grip by buying up other newspapers until they were the only paper in town.[13] Advertisers had no choice but to come to them. Television networks also had market leverage. The huge national TV audience was split between three networks, ABC, CBS, and NBC. By the 1960s, media companies were among America's most profitable firms.[14]

Media monopoly turned out to be a good deal for America. News outlets were so profitable and had so little competition that many of them didn't mind investing in serious news. William Paley, CBS's chief executive, told his correspondents not to worry about expenses. Paley said, "I have Jack Benny to make money."[15]

As cable spread into American homes in the 1980s and 1990s, the media monopoly began to unravel. The news audience was shrinking. Americans now had choices other than news at the dinner hour, and many of them switched to cable entertainment programs.[16] As the financial losses mounted, some of the first things to go were the foreign news bureaus. They were expensive to maintain, and ratings showed that most Americans weren't all that interested in what was happening elsewhere in the world.[17]

Soon thereafter a theatrical style of news emerged that was designed to compete with cable entertainment. It was aimed at the marginal news consumer—those with a weak interest in news who might be persuaded to stay tuned if the news was made more entertaining. Celebrity gossip, hard-luck stories, good-luck tales, sensational crimes, scandals in high places, and other human interest stories became a larger part of the news mix.[18] Such stories were labeled soft news to distinguish them from traditional hard news stories (breaking events involving public figures, major issues, or significant disruptions to daily routines). "Pretty close to tabloid" was how former FCC chairman Newton Minow described the change.[19]

Although marketing has always been part of the news, it was checked for a long period by the notion that journalists have a civic mission. But news has increasingly been treated as a commodity, something to be developed, tested, and sold.[20] The shift has been dramatic. A study of two decades of news coverage in nearly three dozen print and television outlets found that, in every outlet, soft news stories had increased, often by a large amount.[21] Another study—this one of 154 local TV stations in fifty media markets over a five-year period—found that crimes and accidents were getting twice the coverage devoted to public affairs.[22] A few news outlets, including the *New York Times, Wall Street Journal,* and *Washington Post,* have stuck to the old way of doing things,[23] but most outlets have lightened their news. In other ways, too, the news product has been tailored to audience tastes. A service called CrowdTangle, used by scores of local newsrooms, alerts journalists to topics that are trending on social media, a signal to begin producing stories on that topic until the traffic dies down.[24]

Many of the newer digital publishers have embraced the entertainment strategy, doing little in the way of serious original reporting while letting readers' tastes drive what they display, all the while trying to spot content that will trend on social media.[25] In posting its stories, *Upworthy* puts out a large sampling using a dozen or more alternative headlines. The headline that attracts the most attention—usually a variation of "You Won't Believe What Just Happened"—is then attached to the rest of the feed.[26]

Then there's branded advertising—the placement of paid-for stories in the mix with journalist-generated stories. Such stories assure advertisers that their pitch will be more widely read. "Hook and hold" tactics such as factoid lists are used. The "6 Great Things You Didn't Know about Starbucks Coffee" can be nestled in a mix with the "6 Bad Things You Need to Know about the New Tax Law."[27]

Media marketers exploit our instincts. Danah Boyd, a principal researcher at Microsoft, notes that "we're biologically programmed to be attentive to things that stimulate." That includes content that is "gross, violent, or sexual" and gossip that is "humiliating, embarrassing, or offensive."[28] We're drawn to such material even though we sense that we should avoid it. In surveys, Americans regularly say that they wish the news was more substantial and less sensational.[29]

Media marketers don't have anything against politics. Without it, the news would not be news and would not be marketable at all. The marketing question is a financial one: what mix of content will attract the largest possible news audience? And thus it was that, when the greatest reality show in the nation's history kicked off in June 2015 in the guise of Trump's presidential candidacy, politics was moved to the front burner. And it stayed there into his presidency. During his first hundred days in office, Trump was the subject of two of every five stories on the network evening news—twice the amount normally afforded a newly elected president.[30]

The marketing of news is defended on grounds that it produces the money needed to staff the newsroom.[31] That's true, but the newsroom is more than a revenue appendage. The purpose of journalism is to get people thinking and talking about public affairs. That can't happen when the public has visions of sugar plums dancing in their heads. A study conducted during the Obama presidency found that a B-list actress,

Lindsay Lohan, received more media exposure and was more widely known than any member of the cabinet except for Hillary Clinton.[32]

In *Amusing Ourselves to Death,* NYU's Neil Postman spoke of the peril of treating news as a form of entertainment. "I am saying something far more serious than that we are being deprived of authentic information," wrote Postman. "I am saying we are losing our sense of what it means to be well informed. Ignorance is always correctable. But what shall we do if we take ignorance to be knowledge?"[33]

———

With its twenty-four-hour format, cable television feasts on long-running stories that capture the audience's interest. Such stories are a marketer's dream. Their outcome is unknown, which creates a natural dramatic sequence. Today's developments can to be tied to what happened yesterday and what might happen next.[34] Viewers can be lured into sticking with the story for days on end.

Thus it was that CNN highlighted the story of Malaysia Airlines Flight 370 every day for months. The flight disappeared on March 8, 2014, while carrying 227 passengers and a crew of twelve on a scheduled route from Kuala Lumpur to Beijing. On the way, it turned westward and disappeared from radar, never to be found. CNN began its coverage reporting on a fatal accident before turning it into a global mystery story. Night after night, panels of "experts" offered competing theories on the location of Flight 370. One night, a caller asked whether the jetliner might have been sucked into a small black hole. The host suggested that the possibility deserved consideration before a guest informed him that "a small black hole would suck in our entire universe." CNN's coverage became the butt of jokes on late-night comedy shows, but CNN had the last laugh. Its ratings jumped dramatically. CNN didn't cut the power on Flight 370 until its ratings plunged.[35]

Cable is now on its umpteenth trial of the decade—the Menendez brothers, O. J. Simpson (three times, two criminal and one civil), Scott Peterson, Phil Spector, Clark Rockefeller, Jodi Arias, Casey Anthony, etc. When Anthony went on trial for her daughter's murder, CNN and its sister station HLN gave it more than five hundred stories. CNN even constructed a temporary two-story air-conditioned structure across

from the Florida courthouse where the Anthony trial was being held
so that its crews could work in comfort.[36]

Important topics get addressed on cable, but the accompanying hype
can leave viewers checking their pulse. In 2014 an Ebola epidemic broke
out in West Africa. When the first Ebola patient in the United States was
diagnosed, there was wild speculation that it could lead to a pandemic,
and a deadly one at that—half of those infected by Ebola die. Some reports
went so far as to speculate what would happen if Ebola, which is transmitted by direct contact with bodily fluids, went airborne and could be caught
in the same way as is the flu or a cold. "Ebola in the Air? A Nightmare That
Could Happen" is how CNN headlined one of its stories.[37] However, there
is no recorded case of a fluid-transmitted disease like Ebola transform-
ing itself into an airborne-transmitted disease. It might be theoretically
possible, but the World Health Organization says it hasn't happened.[38]
The sensationalized news coverage scared the bejesus out of millions of
Americans, including those hundreds of miles from the nearest Ebola
patient. Two in every five Americans in a Pew Research Center poll said
they worried that they or a family member would catch the disease.[39]

When it comes to politics, controversy is cable's beat. Unless an issue
sparks controversy, cable can't be bothered to stick with it. The format
of many cable news programs—guests with sharply opposing views—is
intended to provoke controversy. If the guests were of one mind, the show
would have to be cancelled. Political scandals are the juiciest source of
controversy. Rooted as they are in money, sex, power, and wrongdoing,
scandals are a blend of soft and hard news. They are mystery stories that
provoke endless speculation about motives and evidence. A study found
that three-fourths of scandal allegations were attributed to anonymous
or unnamed sources.[40]

Few stories better illustrate cable's love of controversy than does the
"birther" story. In 2011, Donald Trump, while toying with a presidential
bid, questioned whether President Obama was a native-born American.
Trump's statement was seized upon by cable outlets and stayed on their
shows for days on end. Fox trotted out guests who said the claim could
well be true. MSNBC's guests ridiculed the claim and those making
it. On CNN, a veteran correspondent interviewed Trump, justifying
the interview by saying: "There comes a point where you can't ignore
something, not because it's entertaining. . . . The question was, 'Is he

driving the conversation?' And he was." Actually, it was cable news that was driving the conversation, which quieted only after Obama released the long-form version of his birth certificate, as if his release of the short-form version in 2008 was immaterial.[41]

Political scientist Lance Bennett notes that the thinly sourced claims circulating on cable put broadcast news and newspapers on the spot.[42] If they report an allegation, they amplify and legitimize it. If they ignore it, they risk being scooped or being attacked for withholding information that the public has a right to know. In today's intensely competitive media environment, the pressure to publish often wins out. "We are hostages to the non-stop, never-ending file-it-now, get-on-the-Web, get-on-the-radio, get-on-TV media environment," says the New York Times's Peter Baker.[43]

Not surprisingly, as the birther controversy grew on cable, the traditional media jumped in. A Trump interview on ABC's Good Morning America prompted a slew of newspaper coverage. "Trump: I'll Release My Tax Returns If Obama Releases Birth Certificate" was how USA Today headlined its entry.[44] A Gallup poll taken shortly thereafter found that more than 40 percent of Republicans believed Obama was "definitely" or "probably" born in another country. If all such episodes were equally trumped up, one might confuse the news with a parody dreamed up by the clever folks at Saturday Night Live. "There are insane narratives that are popular because of their insanity," says Pulitzer Prize–winning journalist John McQuaid.[45]

Insane narratives are one thing, deceptive narratives are another. Two of the cable news outlets, Fox and MSNBC, are in the advocacy business. They would like to think of themselves as being in the tradition of Europe's partisan newspapers, which have historically aligned themselves with a political party. But Fox and MSNBS operate by a different standard than do their European counterparts. The leading partisan newspapers in Europe pride themselves on the factual accuracy of their reporting.[46] Their slant comes in their selections—the stories they chose to headline, the frames they apply, the arguments they support or oppose. News about Britain's royal family, for example, frequently appears on the front page of the right-leaning London Times while being relegated to a back page of the left-leaning Guardian.

Fox and MSNBC employ those techniques but at the same time sometimes play fast and loose with the facts. During the height of the partisan conflict over climate-change policy, the dominant narrative for four years in a row on *Fox News* was that scientists are conspiring to commit fraud—Fox newscasts claimed they were cooking the data to make it appear as if the climate is changing in order to get attention and obtain grant money.[47] Small wonder that Fox viewers during this period came to see the global warming theory as a hoax.[48]

Americans have never had access to as much news as is available today. Yet never before has so much of the news been so thinly sourced, speculative, twisted, or pointless. Postman was only half right in saying we risk "amusing ourselves to death."[49] We also risk deluding ourselves to no good end.

———

Journalists express dismay at today's ratings-driven news. A survey of U.S. journalists found that 60 percent of them think journalism is headed in "the wrong direction." Only one in eight endorse marketing strategies aimed at attracting as "wide an audience as possible."[50]

Journalists properly distinguish their profession from those of advertising, marketing, and public relations. Journalists operate by professional norms based on fairness, accuracy, and verification—fact rather than opinion. Yet journalism has always had a marketing element. The news is a version of reality that's designed to attract and hold the audience's attention.[51] The legendary publisher William Randolph Hearst said that an "editor has no objection to facts if they are also novel. But he would prefer a novelty that is not a fact to a fact that is not a novelty."[52] Although no self-respecting journalist today would make that claim, "novelty" is built into the definition of news.

The demand for novelty contributes to what *Newsweek*'s Meg Greenfield called journalists' "chronic collective amnesia"—their eagerness to dump the old story in favor of the new.[53] Front-page stories in early 2006, for example, told of church bombings in the rural South and of Arab unrest over a Danish newspaper's publication of cartoons depicting the prophet Mohammed in terrorist garb. Suddenly, those issues disappeared from the front pages, not because they had been resolved or because citizens had figured them out. They disappeared because they had been displaced by news out of Texas. Vice President Dick Cheney had just shot a hunting companion in the face.

During his first hundred days in office, when Trump was sending out tweets by the score, pundits wondered whether they were timed to divert the press's attention from Russia's meddling in the 2016 election. Given that his tweets usually got him in hot water, Trump's impulsive personality would seem the better explanation. Whichever, Trump's tweets got journalists to drop what they were doing and chase the latest one. Trump's tweets attracted a large audience, but it was not because people were glued to his Twitter feed. By one estimate as much as 99 percent of Americans' exposure to Trump tweets was from their coverage by the news media.[54]

Novelty, speed, and brevity are good for business. Quick hits are what news audiences increasingly want. It's why TV news now packs five times as many images into the average news story as it once did, and why it presents facts in rapid succession.[55] Yet novelty, speed, and brevity impede learning. As messages arrive in smaller pieces at an ever faster pace, our ability to remember them diminishes and the likelihood increases that we'll conflate unrelated items.[56]

———

America's partisan media have their own brand of marketing. They're in the business of selling outrage. And sell it does. Their audience is growing, while that of mainstream news outlets is shrinking.[57]

Partisan talk shows and blogs pump out staggering amounts of outrage. Tufts University's Sarah Sobieraj and Jeffrey Berry found that outrage is expressed on average once every minute and a half on television talk shows and more frequently on radio. Two talk show hosts, Michael Savage and Mark Levin, are veritable Gatling guns, cranking out more than one outrage a minute on average. Outrage is the selling card of conservative and liberal outlets alike, but they differ in how much outrage they spew, with conservatives outpacing liberals by roughly three to two per show. "Liberal content is quite nasty in character," write Sobieraj and Berry. "Conservatives, however, are even nastier."[58]

Before cable and the internet came along, the market for outrage was limited. In their desire to attract the largest possible audience, newspapers and television outlets tried not to offend anyone. The *Smothers Brothers Comedy Hour* tested that boundary in the late 1960s and got in hot water over an irreverent skit about Moses and the Burning Bush. When the singer Joan Baez appeared on the show and said that her husband David Harris was in prison for refusing military induction because of his opposition to the Vietnam War, CBS kept in the words about her husband's imprisonment but cropped out the reason he was there. When the show's hosts tried to do a reprise of its religious skit, CBS cancelled the program.[59]

Today's partisan outlets have a different business model. They operate in a fragmented media system, and incendiary language is their calling card. They attract loyal followers by skewering opponents. It's a moneymaker. Network news anchors were once the highest paid TV personalities. Topping the list today is a talk show host, Sean Hannity, whose annual salary is $29 million.[60]

Ultimately, the outrage industry's success owes to the nastiness of today's politics, which has expanded the market for partisan insult.[61] Voices within the mainstream media have joined the outrage business. Sobieraj and Berry examined the level of outrage employed by the most widely syndicated conservative and liberal newspaper columnists. Outrage was not hard to find; the average was six instances per column. Columnists didn't always construct their arguments in this way. When Sobieraj and Berry examined newspaper columnists from 1955 and 1975, expressions of outrage were almost nowhere to be found.[62]

Is there anything to recommend the marketing of outrage? There's evidence that consumers of outrage are more politically engaged and do in fact learn a bit about politics from what they hear.[63] But these benefits are more than offset by the adverse effects—heightened intolerance of other groups, greater distrust of government, more extreme political opinions, increased levels of misinformation, and a pronounced tendency to see politics as a struggle between good and evil.[64]

―――――

The internet was heralded as a Garden of Eden, a place where citizens would frolic amid unlimited amounts of information. It had somewhat of that look until the marketers swooped in, turning it into a medium where traffic is god.

As the internet unfolded, a trend emerged that hadn't been predicted. A handful of sites were gobbling up most of the news traffic. Before long, the internet news audience was more heavily concentrated than either the television news audience or the newspaper audience.[65] The concentration increased when search engines and social media companies consolidated their market positions. Two-thirds of online users rely on Google as their core search engine, and four-fifths of online users have a Facebook account.[66]

In the period before cable and the internet, the mainstream news media acted as a gatekeeper, deciding on the information the public would see.[67] As business entities with an interest in attracting customers, they let some fluff through the gate. But most of their stories, and nearly all of those at the top of the news, dealt with what Pulitzer Prize–winning journalist Alex S. Jones calls "the iron core" of news—major stories about public affairs.[68]

Internet news aggregators operate by a different standard. Their computer algorithms are designed to maximize engagement, which means delivering to consumers their preferred content. The higher the level of user engagement, the larger the user base, which means more clicks, which means more advertising revenue.[69] The algorithm for Google News, for example, evaluates a topic by the volume relating to it and the pages linking to it, giving priority to the highest-ranked items. Quality is irrelevant; heavily trafficked misinformation has equal standing with other heavily trafficked material on the same topic. Traffic is also what's behind bots, which amplify a message by relaying it repeatedly, giving the impression that it's "trending" on social media, which increases the likelihood it will pop up on social media pages.

Such internet algorithms turn us into gatekeepers. The choices we make and the content we share help determine the information that will pop up in other people's search. Each time we click or share an item, we vote to push it toward the top of the list. That makes good sense when we're trying to buy electronic equipment or find an amusing cat video, but not when it comes to politics and public affairs. It would be one thing if we had a strong preference for reliable information. But that's not who we are. We're drawn to sensational tales, susceptible to misinformation, and eager to share content that belittles those we dislike.[70]

Digital companies are the other gatekeepers. Facebook recently changed its algorithms to downgrade feeds from traditional news outlets in favor of feeds from family and friends. It led to declines in traffic to news sites.[71] Social media users were not consuming less content, but the mix was different.

We're also at the whim of those clever enough to game the algorithms. When a crazed gunman killed fifty-nine people and wounded hundreds more at a Las Vegas concert in 2017, far-right trolls operating from a number of sites created a fake story that the killer was "a Democrat who liked Rachel Maddow, MoveOn.org, and was associated with the anti-Trump army." This story was picked up by other websites, which moved it up on the list when people searched Google for information about the gunman. As they then shared it, it moved further up, and before long it was at the top of the search list. Google was alerted at this point and removed it. Facebook also got scammed. Its algorithms highlighted the false information before the company discovered the hoax and physically removed the posts.[72]

The only thing unusual about the Las Vegas case is that the fake information was deleted. There's a mountain of it out there, and the more we traffic in it, the more others will see it. Many of us will pass it along, usually without checking the content. Research has found that most users never go beyond the headline before clicking "share" or "like."[73] And there's something about fake stories that draws users' interest. An MIT study of more than one hundred thousand stories on Twitter found that fake news stories spread six times faster than actual news stories did.[74]

———

Media outlets don't have a monopoly on brazen forms of marketing. Politicians are masters of it. "Politicians are the same all over," Soviet leader Nikita Khrushchev remarked a half century ago. "They promise to build a bridge where there is no river."[75]

In recent decades, our politicians have sold and resold the same bridge time and again, and it's opened a path to power that wasn't as easily traveled in earlier times. The traditional path to high office has been election to lower office, where one builds a power base and learns about politics and policy. That's still a path to office for many. It's the path that Hillary Clinton took.

Donald Trump took a different road. He had no political experience and no political organization when he launched his presidential bid. What he had was a knack for talking about hot-button issues in a way that drew attention. He packed four such issues—immigration, Islamic terrorism, free trade, and Obamacare—into his announcement speech.[76] His campaign was off and running.

Trump's insight was that attention equals power. In an information system that tests our ability to pay attention, there are few things more powerful than the ability, as Trump says, "to keep people interested." "And that gives you power," he said. "It's not the polls. It's the ratings."[77]

Hot-button issues—those that create strong emotions and are inherently divisive—have been part of every era's politics, but never before have so many been available at the same time. Party polarization, combined with the rise of single-issue groups, has created an abundance of wedge issues: gun control, abortion rights, immigration, welfare, climate change, race, and health care reform, to name a few.

Hot-button issues are the opposite of what political scientists call valence issues, which are issues where nearly everyone agrees on the goal. Peace is a valence issue. Prosperity is another. People are not divided on whether prosperity is a good thing, which makes it a difficult issue to market. A candidate or party must make a persuasive case for why its prosperity plan is better than the opponent's. It takes a lot of words and a lot of effort, along with voters who are willing to listen and learn, to sell that kind of pitch. The only time prosperity is an easy sell is when the other party fails to deliver it. The party that's out of power invariably picks up votes following a steep drop in the economy.[78]

In contrast, hot-button issues are a political marketer's dream.[79] Each such issue has a committed set of voters who can be mobilized at the mere mention of it.[80] Hot-button issues can also be bundled, as Trump did, with each one adding to the candidate's following. From a marketer's perspective, that's one of the beauties of today's hot-button issues. There are lots of them.

Hot-button issues are easy to sell but are hard to resolve. They are not like budgetary issues, where the opposing sides can make concessions on the way to reaching a compromise that both can accept. Hot-button issues are all-or-nothing. Conceding to the other side means losing out completely, with the result that each side will do whatever it can to prevent the other side from winning. Few hot-button issues illustrate the point more clearly than does the abortion issue. Ever since the Supreme Court ruled in 1973 that women have the right to choose abortion in the first trimester of pregnancy, the pro-life and pro-choice sides have been battling it out without resolution.[81]

Stalemate might frustrate voters, but it's a godsend for political marketers. Stalemate means that a hot-button issue will be around for use again in the next election.[82] It also keeps the issue alive for the talk show circuit, which never tires of railing about such issues.

Hot-button issues have warped the nation's policy agenda. Abortion and guns, for example, have rarely registered above the 1 percent level when Americans are asked in polls what they see as the nation's most important problem. Topping the list in nearly every such poll are issues of peace and prosperity—the very issues that political marketers have the most trouble selling.

Nowhere is political marketing more on display than in candidates' televised political ads. And like so much of American politics, ads have gone to the dark side. In the 1960 presidential election, positive ads outnumbered negative ones and by a substantial margin—less than 10 percent of the ads were negative in tone.[83] Over the past six presidential elections, negative ads have easily outpaced positive ones.[84] The 2012 Obama-Romney race is the extreme case—negative ads outnumbered positive ones by nearly five to one. And candidate advertising is rosy by comparison with ads sponsored by super PACs and other outside groups. Since the Supreme Court's *Citizens United* ruling in 2010, these groups have steadily increased their spending, such that in 2016 they sponsored a fourth of all presidential campaign ads. Candidates' ads in 2016 ran three-to-two negative over positive, whereas those sponsored by outside groups ran more than ten-to-one negative.[85]

Negative ads get heavy play because they're thought to be more persuasive than positive ads. Although the evidence for that assumption is mixed, negative ads are more readily recalled by viewers.[86] Scholars attribute it to "negativity bias"—our heightened response to threat. Negativity bias may have evolutionary roots—the need in earlier times to be alert to the dangers posed by hostile tribes and wild animals.[87]

Negative ads have another advantage. They get the news media's attention.[88] Four of every five news stories about political ads are based on negative ads.[89] For political consultants, that's a reason to use them.

Attack ads get what British prime minister Margaret Thatcher called "the oxygen of publicity."

Few attack ads have received more oxygen than did the Swift Boats Veterans for Truth ads during the 2004 presidential election. They were aired on local television in only three states, and their message might have died there had reporters not picked it up. The ads claimed that Democratic presidential nominee John Kerry had falsified his service in Vietnam and was undeserving of his heroism medals. Although proof was lacking,[90] the smear sparked a media feeding frenzy. By the time it died out, the allegation had received enough news coverage to make it one of the most heavily reported issues of the election.[91] The Swift Boat controversy got 40 percent more mentions in the news than did the Iraq War. It generated 153 stories in the *New York Times* and 191 stories in the *Washington Post.*[92]

Negativity is only part of the story of political ads. Scholars Travis Ridout and Michael Franz examined candidate ads for the emotions they're intended to evoke—anger, fear, enthusiasm, pride, or compassion. And here the picture is darker yet. Appeals to fear and anger account for the largest share of ads. And the closer one gets to election day, the greater the use of ads that seek to evoke fear or anger. "Anger and fear," a top strategist said, "is what gets people to the polls."[93]

Deception is commonplace in today's political ads. Commercial advertisers are governed by truth-in-advertising regulations, which do not apply to political ads. Candidates can say whatever they like in their ads, the judiciary having ruled that "the voters should decide" what's acceptable.[94] Voters are apparently a tolerant bunch. Many candidate ads contain misleading, inaccurate, and exaggerated claims. Those sponsored by outside groups are even less trustworthy; in fact, the large majority of such ads contain false or deceptive claims.[95]

Studies indicate that political ads can give voters a clearer understanding of the issues. Ads have features—simple direct messages reinforced through repetition—that contribute to voter learning.[96] Yet many political ads present a warped version of the issues. A *PolitiFact* assessment of the most heavily aired ads during the 2016 presidential campaign found that a substantial proportion contained false claims or quoted the opposing candidate out of context.[97] Studies have found that negative ads are particularly troublesome. They sully the image of both the attacking and attacked candidate, reduce trust in government, undermine confidence in elections, darken the public's mood, and foster misunderstanding.[98] As the authors of a meta-study of negative advertising concluded, the implications for our democratic system are "alarming."[99]

"The citizen performs the perilous business of government under the worst possible conditions."[100] Journalist Walter Lippmann wrote these words in 1922, a time when deafening factories, oversized families, and the grind of household chores sapped people's time and attention. A quiet moment with the evening paper was about as close as most people came to a civic education. "For the newspaper in all literalness is the bible of democracy, the book out of which a people determines its conduct," Lippmann wrote. "It is the only serious book that most people read. It is the only book they read every day."[101]

Conditions today are no less perilous for citizens, but for different reasons. Although technology has relieved us of household drudgeries, it has created a world where hundreds of messages—political, commercial, and otherwise—compete each day for our attention.[102] Media abundance overwhelms the recipient. "What information consumes is rather obvious," Nobel laureate Herbert Simon wrote. "It consumes the attention of its recipients. Hence a wealth of information creates a poverty of attention."[103] A 2015 Microsoft study used surveys and electroencephalograms (EEGs) to study the length of people's attention spans and found that individuals lose their concentration after eight seconds on average. When the study was conducted in 2000, the average was twelve seconds, leading the research team to conclude that today's fast-paced media environment is hindering our ability to learn. And just how short is an eight-second attention span? Before the 2015 study was conducted, the baseline average was set by the goldfish, which has an average attention span of nine seconds.[104]

Citizens could take it upon themselves to slow things down. They could do what citizens did in Lippmann's age—find a quiet time each day to read the paper. Research has shown that newspaper reading, more than any other type of media exposure, contributes to an understanding of public affairs.[105] I delivered the daily newspaper when growing up and, to relieve the boredom of walking from house to house, I read the paper from front to back. I might have been the only kid in my small town who could talk about communist China's Chou En Lai in one sentence and the New York Yankees's Mickey Mantle in the next. If they had asked, I could even have provided adults with advice on how to handle their personal lives. I delivered both the morning and evening papers. One carried Ann Landers's advice column, and Abigail Van Buren's column graced the other.

Americans today don't have much interest in the newspaper. Circulation has fallen sharply in recent decades and continues to decline. And those who read the paper now give less time to it. In the past five years alone, the average time spent reading a printed newspaper has dropped from twenty-two to sixteen minutes. When people read a paper online, they give it even less time—less than half as much time, in fact.[106]

In truth, we don't have an interest in slowing ourselves down. We could choose a more reflective life, and doing so would allow us to reap the benefits—heightened insight, creativity, and concentration.[107] But the temptation of speed is irresistible. Marshall McLuhan predicted as much when he said, "We shape our tools and then our tools shape us."[108]

Digital tools condition us to go ever faster. Cognitive psychologist David Meyer calls digital media a modern day "Skinner's box," a reference to psychologist B. F. Skinner's famed stimulus-response studies of the 1930s.[109] Cell phones, TV remotes, and other devices offer instant gratification, conditioning us to seek more of it. "We get an adrenalin jolt every time we receive a new stimulus—a reward for paying attention to the new," says Harvard Medical School professor Michael Rich.[110] The typical American sends more than thirty texts a day, up sharply from just a few years ago and rising by the year.[111] We're so conditioned to the digital rush that we feel lost without it. A study found that more than half of smartphone users suffer anxiety when they forget their phone at home or can't get a signal. The condition has been given a name—nomophobia.[112]

We might be able to manage the marketing onslaught if the information coming our way was trustworthy and focused on questions of governing. The steady beat of such messages would eventually inform our judgment. But that's not what we're getting. Today's messages are marketed to the hilt. They have no core and often no integrity. They're an ungodly blend of the silly and the serious, the reliable and the deceptive, the extraneous and the noteworthy. Perhaps we could still make sense of that mishmash if we were completely logical beings. But our minds prefer easy explanations and those that confirm our beliefs. Toss all of that stuff into the same basket and you have a recipe for confusion and error. The Tower of Babel comes to mind, but closer to our era is a barroom scene from Kurt Vonnegut's *Cat's Cradle:*

> She was remembering a lesson that had impressed her. She was repeating it, gropingly, dutifully. "He said, the trouble with the world was . . ."
>
> "He said science was going to discover the basic secret of life some day," the bartender put in. He scratched his head and frowned. "Didn't I read in the paper the other day where they'd finally found out what it was?"
>
> "I missed that," I murmured.
>
> "I saw that," said Sandra. "About two days ago."
>
> "That's right," said the bartender.
>
> "What is the secret of life?" I asked.
>
> "I forget," said Sandra.
>
> "Protein," the bartender declared. "They found out something about protein."
>
> "Yeah," said Sandra, "that's it."[113]

CHAPTER 6

THE LEVEL-HEADED

To see what is in front of one's nose needs a constant struggle.

George Orwell, "In Front of Your Nose"

In 2019, as a condition for keeping the government open, President Donald Trump insisted that Congress provide $5.7 billion to fund a wall stretching the length of America's border with Mexico. The Democratic-controlled House of Representatives resisted, saying that the government shutdown was entirely Trump's doing. Trump blamed it on the Democrats, despite saying earlier that he would be "proud to shut down the government for border security." As the impasse continued, Trump threatened to declare "a national emergency" and use funds set aside for the military to build the wall. Meanwhile, because of the government shutdown, eight-hundred thousand federal workers went without pay for days on end, even though those that were classified as "essential" had to report to work.

American politics is plagued by disorder. Our political institutions are struggling. When not mired in gridlock and brinkmanship, they're beset by petty feuding and renegade behavior. Our media, which once protected us from fantasy, are indulging in it. Citizens are losing respect for reason and for each other. Stupidity and deception of one form or another are raging, as are anger and anxiety. Intolerance is on the rise. One bad thing feeds off the next.

Americans are understandably worried. Two of every three citizens believe the country has reached "a dangerous low point" that is the "new normal." Four of five Americans say Congress is dysfunctional. Two of every three Americans say the same of the presidency. Half or more lay the blame on wealthy donors, members of Congress, the president, ideologues, the news media, or social media. A large majority in each party point to the other party as a culprit.[1]

French philosopher Albert Camus said that "one should never indulge in useless lamentations over an inescapable state of affairs."[2] Perhaps our political system is so broken that it's in that category and that we have no choice but to wait it out. But if that's our fate, things can be done to hasten a recovery.

Political reform by itself will not be enough. How, as a nation, do we deal with the anxiety resulting from declining rural communities or stagnant wages? Americans are understandably worried about their future. In 1970 only 10 percent of thirty-year-olds were worse off economically than their parents at the same age. Today, half of them are.[3] The problem is particularly acute for working-class whites, whose prospects for upward mobility, as measured against the economic position of their parents, are less than that of blacks and Hispanics.[4] Reforms will not revitalize our politics if there's no measurable change in Americans' everyday lives. The two are more intimately connected than might be thought. Wage stagnation, for example, affects not only how people feel about their economic security but how they feel about other Americans. When people are optimistic about their financial prospects, as economist Alex Tabarrok notes, they become "much less concerned about black vs. white, foreign vs. domestic, immigrants vs. nonimmigrants."[5]

Nevertheless, unless we can restore order to our politics, the likelihood of making progress on our social and economic problems is slim. We need to wrest control of our politics from the ideologues and misfits and entrust it to level-headed citizens and leaders.

———

Until the past few decades, our politics was distinguished by its moderate tendencies. Even during the height of ideological fervor in Europe in the first half of the twentieth century, Americans shied from ideology, preferring to judge their political choices by whether they seemed workable rather than whether they fit an ideological belief.[6] Even in periods when Americans were enthralled by snake oil salesmen, they kept their wits about them when it came to politics. That outlook kept the reins of power out of the hands of demagogues and gave leaders the flexibility to address tough problems, even during hard times.

Today's America has fewer such individuals. In their stead are the party ideologues who find their answers in rigid beliefs. There are untold numbers of conservative Republicans who hold the simpleminded notion that the answer to every policy problem is a cut in government. That response is the feasible and prudent answer in some cases. But not in every case. No matter. They find their answers in dogma rather than in reality. The political left also has its ideologues, although they are fewer in number than those on the right. When they see a problem, they look first to government for the solution.

Moderation is also threatened when people don't know what they're talking about. Rather than deal with inconvenient facts, they indulge in self-serving fantasies. Americans were once distinguished by their pragmatism, a trait that historian Daniel Boorstin labeled "the genius of American politics."[7] The pragmatic mind is anchored in reality and focused on what's practical and sensible. The pragmatist is a problem solver, which is a daunting task if your view of the world is wildly at odds with the reality of it. Sensible interaction with the world around you requires that you have reliable knowledge of how it works.

America's level-headed citizens and leaders have been marginalized, at great cost to our politics. By "level-headed," I refer not only to those with moderate opinions but also to those, on the left and right, who are open to what the other side has to say. These Americans know that their side doesn't have all the answers, recognize the things that we have in common, understand the importance of negotiation and compromise, and realize that prejudice and unyielding partisanship are destructive. They're committed to what works, not just in their personal interest in the short term but in the collective interest over the long run. They constitute what gives democracy its flexibility, and they're ultimately what make it work.

There are tens of millions of Americans who have the traits I've described. I'm confident that they outnumber those who hold unyielding or fantastical beliefs.[8] But America's saner heads have been overshadowed. Ideologues and wild thinkers are driving our politics. They dominate the debates in Washington, hog the media spotlight, and draw our attention when we go online. They're dominating the rest of us, and they're driving us apart. We can't revitalize our politics unless we find ways to give level-headed citizens and leaders a larger say.

———

The change we need could happen as a result of a shift in power between the Republican and Democratic parties. In the long cycle of American politics, the two parties have gone through periods where they've been closely competitive, and periods where one party has been much stronger than the other. Our parties have behaved very differently in those two situations.[9]

When the parties have been closely matched, as they were in the late 1800s and as they are today, each party has sought to deny the other party any claim to success. Legislative debate is rancorous, and the party out of power tries to block the policy initiatives of the party in power. The minority party sees itself as an election away from getting back in power. As a result, it has an incentive to block the stronger party even on small issues. In turn, the stronger party does everything possible to marginalize the weaker party in order to destroy its brand. Each party casts the other in stark terms—too extreme and too beholden to special interests to govern in the interests of ordinary Americans. The hostility flows into the next election, which carries over into the newly elected government, continuing the polarizing cycle. It's a brand of politics that empowers those with extreme and uncompromising positions.

The situation changes when one party is much stronger than the other. Sooner or later, the weaker party recognizes that it will have more influence by moderating its positions and working with the stronger party. That scenario played out when Democrats gained sweeping election victories in the 1930s, giving them control of the White House and huge majorities in the House and Senate. Republicans fought President Franklin Roosevelt's New Deal programs but, by the time Republicans came back into power in the early 1950s, Roosevelt's programs had acquired widespread public support. When the GOP's conservatives then proposed to renew the fight to overturn them, Republican president Dwight Eisenhower shut them down. "Should any political party attempt to abolish social security, unemployment insurance, and eliminate labor laws and farm programs," Eisenhower said, "you would not hear of that party again in our political history."[10]

When one party is dominant, the weaker party foregoes disruptive tactics and moderates its stance by moving closer to the dominant party's position. It no longer has anything to gain from petty fights. The stronger party also moderates its positions. It now includes such a large segment of the electorate that pursuit of a narrow agenda would alienate many of its followers.[11]

Democrats were conceivably in a position after the 2008 election to become the nation's dominant party. They held the presidency, three-fifths of Senate seats, and three-fifths of House seats. The Democrats' landslide victory in the 2008 election, much like their victory in the 1932 election, was propelled by a sharp drop in the economy. But that's where the parallel ends.

When President Roosevelt took office in 1933, he dedicated himself to a single goal—putting Americans back to work. He initiated one jobs program after the next, seeking to gain the public's trust and support. In the ensuing 1936 election, Democrats won an even larger victory than they had in 1932, consolidating their position as America's dominant party.[12] They remained so for the next thirty years.

After their landslide victory in 2008, Democrats pursued a different course. Although polls showed that unemployment was the top issue, President Obama, after quickly getting a jobs bill through Congress, jumped headlong into health care reform, ignoring the fact that the issue had backfired politically on two previous Democratic presidents.[13] A number of leading Democrats, including Vice President Joe Biden, tried to talk the normally prudent Obama out of it. Obama was undeterred, saying, "I'm feeling lucky."[14] It took a year to get the health care bill through Congress. As a policy initiative, it was a substantial achievement. In political terms, it was an unmitigated disaster. It alienated large numbers of Americans and reenergized a demoralized Republican Party, giving rise to the Tea Party movement.[15] In the 2010 midterm elections, the GOP won a landslide victory, gaining control of the House and cutting deeply into Democrats' Senate majority. The parties have been closely matched ever since.

Looking forward, can either party expect to gain a clear-cut majority? A case can be made for each party. If Republicans can develop a credible form of what George W. Bush called "compassionate conservatism," it could expand its base. The Republican message of lower taxes and smaller government has broad appeal, but it's been blunted by a belief that Republicans' real purpose in lowering taxes and reducing federal spending is to help the rich. That belief has limited the GOP's appeal, as has the hostility that some of its leaders have displayed toward Hispanics and other historically disadvantaged groups.

The Democratic Party's best hope for long-term domination is demographic change.[16] By a roughly two-to-one margin, Democrats have had the support of three groups—young adults, Hispanics, and Asian Americans—which are becoming an ever larger part of the electorate. If the trend continues, Democrats will eventually have an ironclad majority. The trend's continuation could depend on whether Republicans change their ways. The GOP's politics of division have alienated these groups, and others as well. As writer and former conservative talk show host Charles Sykes has noted, the Republican Party has created for itself "a demographic bomb" which, if left unaddressed, will eventually make it a second-rate party.[17]

———

History is an imperfect guide. Although I'm inclined to think that a functioning government in the hands of a dominant party would help to restore trust in government and moderate our politics, I worry that we're in uncharted territory.

Our political disputes are deep and cross-cutting. The New Deal addressed the nation's economic divide, answering it by creating a social safety net while preserving market capitalism. We have an economic divide today that needs to be addressed, but it intersects with a cultural divide. Rural America and inner-city America have common economic needs, but they're miles apart in other ways.[18] So it is with one division after the next. Our differences are large and raw, and easily inflamed.

Most of our agitators are on the political right, but their numbers on the left have been increasing.[19] If, as some analysts think, we're in the midst of a culture war mixed with elements of economic and racial populism, the emergence of a dominant party, rather than quieting our divisions, could compound them. Control of government by one party in that case could foster the type of government that most worried the writers of the Constitution—an oppressive majority. The party in power could pursue its interests without regard for the legitimate rights and interests of the minority. Even if it were to act with an element of restraint, powerful voices within the minority party could say it was acting tyrannically and concoct alternative realities to that effect. Either situation would deepen our already deep divide. It would be a dark day in America, one that would test our national unity.

Given America's strengths and traditions, that scenario seems unlikely to me, but the cohering power of our core ideals is weakening.[20] We're caught in an arms race between civility and incivility, fact and fake, unity and division, and it's not clear that America's better angels are winning. Mature democracies don't collapse with a bang. They do it slowly, as expediency, anxiety, and miscalculation erode them a piece at a time.[21] If we continue to separate ourselves into two different tribal cultures, each embracing its own version of reality and seeing the other side as the enemy while blindly marching behind self-referential leaders who have no shame, we could be headed for real trouble.[22]

That's more than a theoretical possibility. White Americans with strong racial and religious opinions are already fighting tooth and nail against social change. How will they react when minorities become a voting majority? And how will minorities react if they become a voting majority and find that they are still on the bottom rung? How much longer will they tolerate second-class status?

Status uncertainty is unnerving. When social dominance is up for grabs, all sides feel threatened. As Amy Chua notes in *Political Tribes,* "Every group feels attacked, pitted against other groups not just for jobs and spoils but for the right to define the nation's identity."[23]

Both political parties bear some responsibility for our descent into rabid tribalism. When Democrats took up the cause of greater equality for minorities, many of them chose to portray it as a zero-sum game—for minorities to get ahead, whites had to lose. That portrayal was also used by some Republicans, who saw it as a chance to make inroads with white voters. We would face a difficult task if the partisan divide was all that we had to overcome. It's a monumental task now that our partisan divide coincides with our racial, ethnic, religious, and geographical divides.[24]

Key to America's future are the millions of Americans who have retained a sense of moderation. If they hold out until our politics take a better turn, they'll cushion the transition. If they get sucked into the vortex of division, it's not clear what will happen. And they are slowly gravitating toward one camp or the other. Deep partisan divisions work that way. They encourage us to take sides. For proof of that we don't have to look further than the Trump presidency. Newt Gingrich, who knows a thing or two about incitement, said of Trump's governing style, "He intuits how he can polarize."[25] Poll after poll during Trump's presidency has shown a widening and hardening of our political divisions.[26]

It's a mistake to assume that our Constitution is sufficient protection against a dark future. As Harvard's Steven Levitsky and Daniel Ziblatt note in *How Democracies Die,* democracies depend on unwritten norms to keep politics in check. One such norm is mutual tolerance, an acceptance of the opposition as legitimate—a rival rather than an enemy. A second norm is forbearance. It rests on the understanding that power should be used with restraint rather than weaponized and taken to its lawful limits. A political party can be expected, of course, to pursue its agenda, sometimes vigorously. But tolerance and forbearance mean that it won't demonize or run roughshod over the minority party. When that happens, retaliation ensues when the weaker party comes back into power. It's a vicious cycle that's hard to reverse.[27]

———

Without change at the top of the political system, there's little hope of change at the bottom. Disruption and disorder at the top filter down, affecting how citizens respond to politics. Change could start with Congress. For better or worse, the presidency is defined in large part by its occupant, which is why it is both the most inspirational and the most dangerous of our institutions. But presidents come and go, whereas Congress is a relatively ongoing institution, defined less by the actions of any one member than by its members collectively. And those members have been behaving in destructive ways.[28] Democracy works best when institutions operate in an orderly and restrained way, under the direction of responsible leadership.[29] That's not the way Congress has been operating.

Senator John McCain rebelled against the change when he cast the decisive vote in a Republican effort to overturn Obamacare. Although an opponent of Obamacare, McCain was angered by how Republican leaders were trying to kill it—negotiating a bill in secret, springing it on members at the last minute, telling them it was better than nothing, refusing to send it to committee for hearings, arm-twisting those who had reservations, stonewalling the other party. When it came his turn to vote, McCain walked slowly to the well of the Senate, stopped a few feet short of Senate majority leader Mitch McConnell, stretched out his arm, and pointed down. His no vote sent the bill to defeat by the narrowest of margins, 51–49. McCain's vote was a repudiation of what the Senate had become—an institution where traditional procedures are ignored and where winning is all that counts. McCain said, "I don't think that is going to work."[30]

Unyielding partisanship, rather than compromise and cooperation, has been the driving force in Congress. Few things illustrate the point more clearly than does House Republicans' Hastert rule, also known as "the majority of the majority" rule. Instituted in the late 1990s, it holds that, when Republicans are in the majority, the Speaker should bring a bill to the floor only if it's supported by a majority of House Republicans. The opinion of Democratic lawmakers is irrelevant. All that matters is what the Republican majority thinks. A Republican Speaker is not literally bound by the rule—it's an informal directive—but Republican speakers have honored it, knowing that they could lose their position if they don't. "Maybe you can [ignore the rule] once, maybe you can do it twice," a former House member said, "but when you start making deals, when you have to get Democrats to pass the legislation, you are not in power anymore."[31]

The Hastert rule, as one observer noted, is "a structural barrier to compromise."[32] It's what enabled right-wing Republicans to shut down the government in 2013. Although a House majority would have voted to keep the government open, a bill to that effect didn't make it to the House floor because it was opposed by a majority of Republican members. When asked why he had let his fellow Republicans shut down the government, House Speaker John Boehner said, "When I looked up, I saw my colleagues going [for it]. You learn that a leader without followers is simply a man taking a walk."[33] The shutdown finally ended when Boehner ignored the Hastert rule and brought a clean bill to the floor. Although the House's most conservative Republicans voted against it, it passed by the lopsided margin of 285–144. When Boehner went against the Republican majority again a year later on another major bill, he was operating on borrowed time. Shortly thereafter, under pressure from the House's most conservative Republicans, he resigned as Speaker.

The Senate filibuster has also been a casualty of unbridled partisanship. For more than 150 years it was used sparingly, and for the most part judiciously. In the first half of the twentieth century, it was employed roughly twenty-five times, about once in every two-year session. Since 1990 it has been employed roughly one thousand times, about sixty times each session on average.[34] It was being used so freely that in 2013, responding to spiteful Republican filibusters of presidential nominees, Democrats eliminated it for all presidential nominees except those for the Supreme Court. In 2017 the Republican-controlled Senate abolished it for those appointments as well. An instrument that was designed to encourage compromise on key issues has become a tool of narrow partisanship and is now diminished in form as well as in practice.

The elimination of the filibuster in the appointment of Supreme Court justices is particularly telling. It weakens a legislative check on the judiciary. In recent decades, the Court has become an extension of our hyperpartisan politics, with Republican- and Democratic-appointed justices on opposite sides on key rulings. Recent presidential nominees to the Court have been picked because they interpret the law through a partisan lens, and there should be no surprise that, once on the Court, they behave that way. When the judiciary bends to partisanship, it strays from what the writers of the Constitution sought to create—"a government of laws, not of men," as John Adams expressed it.[35]

Congress's constitutional responsibility to check the executive branch has also fallen victim to hyperpartisanship. When the president has been of the same party as the House and Senate majorities, Congress has shown little interest in exercising its oversight function. The House Intelligence Committee's investigation of Russian meddling in the 2016 presidential election was a sham, aimed at protecting President Trump rather than at protecting our democratic institutions. The committee's Republican majority refused to call key witnesses or subpoena those who refused to answer questions, then issued a report claiming that Russian meddling was inconsequential—a claim at odds with what the nation's intelligence agencies had concluded. "What's been lost in recent times," a four-term U.S. senator recently said, "is a commitment to Congress as an institution."[36]

It would be comforting to think that Congress is a deliberative body—a place where members of the two parties exchange views on legislation and then weigh what they have heard in deciding how they will vote.

That hasn't happened in the House or Senate in years. Members still stand in the front of the chamber to make their arguments, but they may as well be trying to convince their dog to stop peeing on the carpet.

In his farewell address, George Washington foresaw the predicament and argued that extreme partisanship leads lawmakers to turn a deaf ear to reason. Each year on Washington's birthday, a senator reads Washington's address on the Senate floor. The House also did this but then gave it up, perhaps in recognition that no one in the chamber was listening.[37] A longtime veteran of the House said recently that the House floor is no longer a place where debate occurs. It's become, he said, "a campaign stage."[38]

Congressional Republicans and Democrats don't even talk to each other regularly. In times past, members of Congress often had close friends on the other side of the aisle. The friendship between senators Edward Kennedy and Orrin Hatch was almost legendary. Although Kennedy and Hatch had contrasting personalities and beliefs, they cosponsored a number of important bills that were enacted into law.[39] Members of Congress from the opposing parties now seldom spend time together.[40] Once rare, insults of the other party's lawmakers are common. A recent study found that a fourth of congressional press releases "taunt" the opposing side.[41]

Congressional dysfunction was on full display during the 2018 Senate hearings on Brett Kavanaugh's appointment to the Supreme Court. It was a raw, ugly, no-holds-barred fight that degenerated further when Kavanaugh became the first Supreme Court nominee in memory to level personal attacks at senators who were questioning him.

Perhaps we shouldn't be surprised that partisan hostility is now openly displayed. It's happened before. In the uncompromising period before the Civil War, Southern and Northern lawmakers resorted to fisticuffs; there were more than one hundred separate instances of violence in the House and Senate. One brawl found fifty House members fighting it out on the floor of the chamber.[42] Today's members haven't resorted to slugfests, but Congress is no longer a dignified rules-driven institution. When the other side becomes the enemy, there's not much room for compromise and little interest in comity.

Dysfunction in one institution has a way of spreading to other institutions. Presidents have been pushing the limits of executive power, often as a response to Congress's failure to act.[43] When Congress blocked one after another of his initiatives, Barack Obama shifted to executive orders. "We can't wait for an increasingly dysfunctional Congress to do its job," Obama said. "Whenever they won't act, I will."[44] Many of the recent executive orders have tested the constitutional boundaries of presidential authority; some have been struck down by the courts, some have narrowly survived judicial review. Executive orders are a poor substitute for well-designed legislation and can be negated by the next president, disrupting the orderly administration of policy and programs.

Institutional responsibilities, rules, and norms have a purpose. When they're cast aside without thought as to why they were established, or what purpose they serve, the result is uncompromising partisanship and institutional disorder.[45] If Congress is to serve as a model for how our politics should be conducted, it will have to find ways to restore what's been lost.

───────

Change could start with the election of a larger number of moderates to Congress. They've declined in number, and it's crippling the institution. In dividing power between the branches, the framers of the Constitution sought a lawmaking process that would force officials to engage in compromise and negotiation. As James Madison expressed it, the division of power was designed to prevent the takeover of government by "an interest adverse to that of the whole society."[46] For most of our history, the system worked largely as intended. Each party had its hotheads, but they were greatly outnumbered by a cluster of lawmakers in the political center. They were the dealmakers. They had the power to force other members to come to the middle—the place where the institutional structure created by the framers is designed to work. Not every major policy was decided there, but centrist lawmakers were normally in charge.

Moderates excelled at brokering compromises. They did their job so well that Americans didn't consider how Congress would work if they weren't around.[47] Nor were Americans at an earlier time looking for a different kind of lawmaker. The voters were pragmatic in their thinking and supported politicians of the same temperament.[48] But as the political parties began to move apart in the 1980s, the congressional middle began to weaken. As the polarization continued, it weakened further and is now all but gone. Based on roll call votes, the least liberal Democrat in the House or Senate is more liberal than is the most liberal Republican.[49] There are no longer enough congressional moderates to force other members to come to the center to bargain over policy.

It can be uncomfortable to be a moderate in today's Congress. Often ignored by their party when it comes to the top committee and legislative assignments, they face intense pressure to vote the party line on key votes. Some do it out of a sense of self-preservation, but it's not gratifying.[50] In *Opting Out of Congress*, Danielle Thomsen talks of how the pressure and frustration of serving in Congress have led a number of its moderates to quit the institution. One of the latest is Pennsylvania congressman Charles Dent. In announcing his decision not to seek reelection to the House in 2018, Dent said that his ability to make a difference on legislation had been blunted by "influences that profit from increased polarization and ideological rigidity that leads to dysfunction, disorder, and chaos."[51]

Hyperpartisanship has made it risky for lawmakers even to suggest the possibility of compromise. In 2017, Arizona Republican senator Jeff Flake said Republicans and Democrats should work together to fix health care and immigration. For all the fury it unleashed, you'd have thought he'd been caught selling child porn. "Don't get me started on Jeff Flake," said Kelli Ward, the right-winger who unsuccessfully challenged John McCain in Arizona's 2016 Republican Senate primary. Ward then proceeded to blast away at Flake, accusing him of turning his back on conservative principles, lying to the voters, and being lower than a snake in the grass.[52] Soon thereafter, Flake announced he would not seek reelection.

Viewed from afar, members of Congress would appear to have plenty of maneuvering room. Congress is not like a European parliament. There, the members' first loyalty is to their party. The party organizations pick their nominees and run the political campaign. Once in office, a party's members are expected to back its platform and can be denied renomination if they don't. Members of Congress, on the other hand, are not formally beholden to their party. They organize their own campaigns, run for nomination in primaries, and win election through the support of voters in their home state or district.

Once in office, however, they're able to stay there only if they continue to get the voters' support. And there's the rub. Since the 1990s, most states and districts have become increasingly Democratic or Republican, which has shifted the key contest from the general election to the stronger party's primary election, when extreme partisans make up a large share of the voters. As they have come to dominate primary elections, members of Congress have had to respond to their demands, which has pulled them toward the political extremes.[53] It's become risky to work in the political center, where compromises are forged. It's also risky in terms of retaining the support of the ideological groups and donors that pour money into congressional campaigns.

The problem is more acute on the Republican side. The GOP's most engaged voters are more ideological, and more of one mind, than their Democratic counterparts. A Pew Research Center poll found that staunch conservatives are four times more likely than staunch liberals to say that their representatives should "stick to their positions" rather than engage in "compromise."[54] In 2012, Indiana senator Richard Lugar, the Senate's most senior Republican and its top foreign policy expert, became a target of his party's hardliners. Lugar was defeated in the Republican primary by a right-wing challenger who accused him of having "lost his conservative edge." More surprising yet was the defeat of Eric Cantor, the House majority leader, who was next in line to become Speaker. He lost in a 2014 primary to a Tea Party–backed political unknown who surged on the claim that Cantor was "not conservative enough."[55]

––––––

The influence of party diehards doesn't end on election day. Faced with the reality of primary voters who hold extreme beliefs, lawmakers have protected themselves by moving toward the extreme wing of their party, hoping that it will stave off a primary challenger. And if they end up with a challenger, even a weak one, they shift even closer to their party's far edge.[56]

Running Scared, a 1997 book by political scientist Anthony King, told of how House incumbents, because of high campaign costs and their two-year term of office, constantly worry about reelection. If such a book were written today, it might be titled *Governing Scared.* Many of today's lawmakers today live in fear of their party's ideologues.[57]

Few bills illustrate that point more clearly than does the attempt in 2018 to put together a bipartisan agreement that would protect

"Dreamers"—undocumented immigrants brought to the United States as young children. The legislative package balanced Republican and Democratic demands—protection for Dreamers and their immediate families as a concession to Democrats and heightened border security as a concession to Republicans. Off the record, there was strong support in Congress for the bill. Yet it never came close to passing. It failed to get enough Senate votes to override a filibuster and never even reached the floor of the House. Not enough members were willing to risk the wrath of hardliners opposed to one or another of the bill's provisions.

Lawmakers' fears extend to talk show hosts, who act as an alarm bell for party diehards. It was a right-wing talk show host, Laura Ingraham, who started the campaign that brought down Eric Cantor in 2014. Cantor had said that Republicans should give legal status to Dreamers. For Ingraham, a strident opponent of immigration reform, Cantor's statement was treasonous, and she used her show to tear him down. She bragged that she gave Cantor's opponent "a platform and a bigger microphone."[58]

Lawmakers are also in the crosshairs of wealthy campaign donors. Wealthy contributors have always had outsized influence, but their power increased after the Supreme Court's decision in *Citizens United,* which gave them license to spend freely in campaigns.[59] Many of them, like the Koch brothers and Robert Mercer, are ideologues. If a lawmaker responds to their demands, there's financial backing in the next election. If not, the money may go to a primary election challenger whose views align with the donor's.[60] Unless *Citizens United* is reversed, which is unlikely given the the Supreme Court's present makeup, the power of money will continue to warp our politics.

Lawmakers can't do their job if outsiders are pulling the strings. Congress works well when lawmakers have the freedom to engage in negotiation and compromise. Congress sputters when lawmakers are hamstrung by the demands of ideological voters and wealthy donors.[61] Critics say that lawmakers should stand up to their party's ideologues. That's easy to say when it's not your job that's on the line. Few lawmakers will support legislation that is all but certain to end their political career.

Politics, like the marketplace, cannot function without ambition. The challenge, as political scientist James Sundquist once noted, is "to discover some way to create a degree of harmony between behavior that satisfies personal behavior and behavior that promotes the public good."[62] Party polarization has shifted ambition toward the self-serving end of the scale.

Congress cannot be expected to operate effectively unless the ideologues' grip on it is loosened. It's conceivable that it's too late for that to occur. If political leaders of moderate temperament had done more to stop the rise of the ideologues, rather than teaming up with them at the start for narrow partisan gain, much of what has transpired since the 1990s might have been blunted. It will be much harder today to cut the ideologues down to size.

———

Reform could start with changes that would result in the election to Congress of a larger number of moderates. Their numbers have fallen in part because of a decline in the number of competitive states and districts. Competitive elections have many advantages, everything from a more vigorous campaign to better candidates.[63] They also produce more moderate officeholders. Compared with one-sided elections, competitive ones give moderate candidates a better chance of winning and discourage candidates from pandering to voters with extreme views.[64]

Our elections would be more competitive if there were restrictions on partisan gerrymandering. In most states, the power to redraw congressional district boundaries after each decennial census rests with the party in control of the state legislature. Districts are created that include enough of the majority party's voters to ensure victory for its candidates, and other districts are packed with as many voters of the other party as possible so that that party in effect "wastes" votes, reducing its competitiveness elsewhere in the state. The effect is a large number of uncompetitive districts where the larger party's primary is the decisive election.

The Supreme Court has not ruled on whether extreme forms of partisan gerrymandering are permissible under the Constitution, holding that judges are not equipped to draw the boundaries of congressional districts. In the absence of a Court ruling that would severely constrain partisan gerrymandering, states should be encouraged to entrust redistricting to a bipartisan or nonpartisan commission. A few states, including Iowa and Arizona, already have such commissions, and they tend to draw district boundaries in ways that increase the number of competitive districts.[65]

Nevertheless, a constraint on partisan gerrymandering would not by itself produce wholesale change. In most states, one-sided districts are less a product of gerrymandering than of geographical sorting. Over the past few decades, most states have become more strongly Republican or Democratic. And within nearly every state, cities have become more heavily Democratic while suburban and rural areas have become more heavily Republican.[66] It's difficult in many states to draw compact congressional districts in ways that would make House elections more competitive. My home state of Massachusetts, which has nine House seats, is so heavily Democratic that it's nearly impossible to carve out more than one or two districts that Republicans could conceivably win.

Studies indicate that geographical sorting accounts for twice as many one-sided districts as does gerrymandering.[67] And the geographical problem is hard to fix. It would require overturning a 1967 law that requires states to use single-member House districts. Before 1967, states had the option of using multi-member districts. Such districts, if coupled with a proportional system of allocating the seats between the parties, would increase electoral competition. But the 1967 law is an absolute barrier to such a change. Lawmakers in the party disadvantaged by a change in the law would oppose the change, as would incumbents worried about its effect on their reelection chances.[68]

––––––

Given the reality of uncompetitive states and districts, which have the effect of making the stronger party's primary election the decisive contest, the surest way to increase the number of congressional moderates is to increase the primary election turnout rate of moderate voters.

Primaries have relatively low turnout, and the people who do vote are disproportionally the party's most committed voters. For a long period that didn't make much difference because their policy views were not all that different from those of the party's other voters. But when the parties pulled apart, primaries were increasingly dominated by voters with hardline views.[69] There are still plenty of moderate voters, but they participate in relatively small numbers in primaries.[70]

Open primaries are a way to increase the number of moderate voters.[71] Open primaries allow independents and those willing to switch their party registration to participate. At present, about half of the states have open primaries, although some are open only to unaffiliated voters, as opposed to those who are already registered with the other party. The other states use closed primaries, where participation is limited to the party's registered voters.[72] Closed-primary states have resisted calls to open their primaries on grounds that nominations are a party issue and should be decided solely by the party's voters. A Republican state party chairman said recently that open primaries are a source of "mischief," claiming that voters outside the party participate with the goal of picking a weak nominee so that the other party "will have a better shot at winning in the general election."[73] There's no substantial evidence to back up that claim. It has happened, but the odds of it are only somewhat less than getting hit by a bolt of lightning.

At the same time, there's no substantial evidence to show that open primaries regularly yield more moderate nominees than do closed primaries.[74] Although they're more likely to do so, the difference is small. Low turnout is a reason. Open primaries don't ordinarily attract large numbers of independent or crossover voters. It's rare when their turnout rate is high enough to change the outcome.[75]

Noting the turnout problem, the Brookings Institution's Elaine Kamarck recommends that states hold their primaries on the same date. Unlike the general election, which is held in all states in early November, primary dates are staggered. Some states hold their primaries as early as March, others as late as September. As a result, primaries don't get the huge media buildup that precedes a general election. It's nearly impossible for a citizen to miss the fact that a presidential election is taking place but, as Kamarck notes, "the existence of elections that are spread out over months means that these particular elections are very likely to be missed by even those citizens who consider themselves conscientious voters."[76]

If a common date for primaries was established, some state parties would refuse to participate, concluding that timing or other considerations outweigh the prospect of higher turnout. But some state parties might see a national primary day as an opportunity to increase their voter base and reduce the odds that their primary would be won by an unelectable candidate.[77] In 2010, Christine O'Donnell, who was backed by Tea Party advocates, won Delaware's Republican Senate primary even though she received only thirty thousand votes. O'Donnell knew next to nothing about government and fumbled her way through the general election. During a televised debate, she challenged the ban on teaching creationism in public schools, saying, "Where in the Constitution is separation of church and state?" When told it was in the First Amendment, she challenged the claim. She lost the general election by a landslide—this in a state that Republicans had been expected to win.[78]

Republicans may also have lost three other Senate seats in 2010 because of flawed nominees, and the Republican Party has since tried to prevent such candidates from getting the party's nomination. They haven't always succeeded. Roy Moore, a right-wing religious zealot who was removed as Alabama's chief judge after refusing to uphold federal law, won Alabama's 2017 GOP Senate primary despite opposition from leading national Republicans. He was defeated in the general election, the first time in a generation that the Republican nominee lost a Senate race in Alabama.

A national primary day is not the only reform that could increase the moderate vote. Compulsory voting would do it, as would a European-style system where the government takes responsibility for identifying and registering all eligible voters, but no state has adopted either method. A more realistic option is mail-in balloting. Colorado, Oregon, and Washington use it for their primaries and have higher than average turnout.[79] Oregon, for example, mails out a ballot to all registered voters in the state two weeks before the primary. Early voting and no-excuse absentee balloting can also boost turnout. Nearly three-fourths of the states offer early voting, by which voters can cast their ballot before election day. There is, however, wide variation among the states on when early voting can start. The earliest is forty-five days before the election and the latest is four days, with the average length being nineteen days. Finally, about half the states allow no-excuse absentee balloting, by which a voter can apply for an absentee ballot and mail it in, provided it is postmarked by election day.

These are sensible ballot provisions, but a fourth of the state governments offer none of these options to their voters. An additional eighth of the states require a documented excuse to cast an absentee ballot and substantially restrict early voting by, for example, limiting the number of days and polling places.

Higher turnout is not a goal of every politician. Although politicians are quick to urge people "to get out and vote," some of them are hypocrites. They've manipulated registration and voting rules in order to depress turnout. Ten states, including Texas and South Carolina, shut down registration thirty days before the election, which is the longest period allowed by federal law. States that shut down registration at an early date have a lower average turnout rate than do other states. Other devices for restricting turnout include voter ID requirements, early poll closings, selectively purging of the voter registration rolls, failing to publicize registration deadlines, and limiting the hours and places where citizens can register.[80] If there's anything good to say about how some officials treat the right to vote, it's that the law no longer permits them to use literacy tests and poll taxes as ways to keep poorer and less-educated citizens from going to the polls.

Republicans are behind nearly every effort to limit turnout. They've used nearly every available means to create an electorate that will increase their chances of victory. Of the thirty-odd states that have adopted a stricter voter ID law, for example, all but two were enacted into law when the legislature was controlled by GOP lawmakers.[81]

Republicans are correct in assuming that Democratic voters are more likely than Republican voters to be deterred by barriers to voting.[82] What Republican leaders fail to consider is that moderate voters are also deterred. Ideologues will make the effort to register. Many moderates will not. Republican Party leaders can't have it both ways. They may prefer more moderate nominees, but their strategy of restricting registration cedes power to their party's hardline voters.

The Republican strategy is shortsighted in another way as well. Barriers to registration and voting are felt most keenly among America's minority groups. Blacks, Hispanics, and other disadvantaged groups are less likely, for example, to have a government-issued ID, such as a driver's license or passport, which several states require as a condition for registering to vote.[83] These groups are keenly aware that the Republicans' restrictive policies are aimed at keeping them from the polls. Whatever the immediate gain, Republicans could pay a long-term price for targeting minority group voters. White voters of modest or higher income were about two-thirds of the electorate in 1980. They now constitute about half.[84] That's a dwindling population on which to sustain a political party.

If fixing politics at the top is a necessary step in restoring sanity to our politics, a second step is also required—fixing our reality problem. How do we get government to work properly when millions of citizens are living in fantasy worlds of their own making? Tough policy problems are always difficult to address, and they become unmanageable when citizens deny them or attribute them to imagined causes. We increasingly engage in escapism, preferring self-serving fantasies to hard realities.[85]

Wild thinking has been with us for as long as people have been around. But with party polarization, and an information system where we now can find "proof" for even the wackiest of ideas, we've taken it to new heights.[86] We now have a public that includes millions of citizens for whom facts do not matter or who find it easy to accept as fact that which is fake. It is a situation incompatible with our democracy's long-term health. We need to find our way back to a reality-based politics, not simply to get our feet back on the ground but to fight the intolerance and demagoguery that are being fueled by false realities.

At an earlier time, when the local newspaper and broadcast networks had a monopoly on our attention, the media system served as a moderating force. Americans were exposed equally to Republican and Democratic leaders, and debates were conducted civilly. We had our differences, but they were moderated by what we were hearing from political leaders and through the media.[87] Today's information system exaggerates and inflames our differences while filling our minds with nonsense and disinformation. Unless that system changes, and we change along with it, common sense will continue to be in short supply.

We won't find a solution by looking to partisan talk shows. They're a big part of the problem, and it's inconceivable that they could be part of a solution. Rush Limbaugh's "four concerns of deceit" are "government, academia, science, and the media."[88] Hearing that claim a few decades ago would have led us to think that our crazed uncle was at it again. Today, more than ten million Limbaugh listeners a week nod their heads in approval.

Whether partisan talk shows are the main contributor to the rise in Americans' intolerance and misinformation is anyone's guess, but they're a leading contributor. "A sociopathic alternative reality" is one analyst's description of their content.[89] The likelihood that the FCC's fairness doctrine will be reinstated, which would drive many of them off the air, is near zero, so they'll be around for years. The only cause for optimism on the talk show front is that its average listener is over fifty and getting older by the year.[90]

The internet is also awash in disinformation. Deliberate efforts to sow false claims and our willingness to believe them are a hellish brew, made more deadly by the recent entry of foreign disruptors who seek to turn Americans against each other. A widely circulated fake story during the 2016 election, for instance, told of how Muslim men in Michigan had multiple wives and were collecting a welfare check on each one.[91]

Disinformation on the internet cannot be slowed without concerted action by digital companies such as Facebook, Twitter, and Google.[92] They've been preoccupied with making money. They now need to ask what they can do to protect our democracy. They've dodged responsibility by claiming to be nothing more than platforms—mere aggregators of information created by others. In reality, they are media companies whose decisions affect the content that we see.[93] Given the role of the internet in our lives, we can't make real headway on our information disorder without their help in cleaning it up.[94]

After the 2016 presidential election, as the extent of Russian involvement became clear, major internet providers, including Google, Facebook, and Twitter, began to take steps to clamp down on the flow of disinformation. Nevertheless, even if digital companies commit themselves to screening out disinformation, it is a first-order technical and legal challenge. It bumps up against free speech claims and a corporate culture dedicated to profit. Money will be lost in applying algorithms that promote content based on what people should see as opposed to what they prefer to see. Moreover, such algorithms are technically difficult—algorithms based on quantity, although complex enough, are far simpler than those based on quality.[95] And it's not as though digital companies would be policing a small space. There are more than a billion online sites.[96]

Internet firms can't handle the disinformation problem by themselves, nor are they the only ones working on it. *PolitiFact* and *FactCheck* are among the many organizations seeking to slow the spread of false claims by exposing them as they arise. It's important work that makes a difference.[97] But the effect so far is small and appears likely to remain so. Many of those who go to fact-checking sites aren't there to determine whether they have their facts straight. They're checking to confirm a suspicion that opponents are lying.[98] There's evidence, too, that fact checking, by highlighting false claims, can contribute to their spread. People remember the claim, forgetting that it was debunked.[99]

In 2017 the Pew Research Center asked a thousand technologists, scholars, and practitioners whether they thought online information would improve in quality over the next decade. None suggested disinformation could be eliminated, but half thought the online environment could be improved, citing technical advances that will detect disinformation and give priority to reliable sources. The other half thought that sources of misinformation will always have the initiative and will figure out how to overcome new barriers. One of the pessimists said, "It is too easy to create fake facts, too labor-intensive to check and too easy to fool checking algorithms." Another said, "We will develop technologies to help identify false and distorted information, but they won't be good enough."[100]

————

If we're going to fix our information disorder, the traditional news media will have to shoulder much of the burden. In an earlier time, Americans were closely attentive to what journalists had to say.[101] Their words created an "information commons"—a shared set of facts and ideas about the country and the challenges it faced. Not everyone derived the same meaning from the news they were receiving, and the reporting had its blind spots.[102] But it was a politically balanced rendition of public affairs that helped build a sense of national community. It didn't prevent division, but it had a depolarizing effect.[103] Our news outlets did their job well enough that we took for granted why a shared understanding of politics is important.

The information commons cannot be resurrected in its old form, built as it was on media monopolies. The three broadcast television networks and the local newspaper dominated Americans' attention, so much so that the sum of what they reported was nearly the whole of the news that people consumed. And consume they did. News was the only television programming available at the dinner hour in nearly every media market.

Today's media system is fragmented and includes partisan outlets that offer one-sided versions of reality that appeal to many Americans. These outlets are gathering places for the like-minded. Rather than provide a shared understanding, they offer a picture of the world that's rosy on one side of the partisan divide, dark on the other. The effect is polarizing.

Today's media system also includes nearly every imaginable form of entertainment, everything from electronic gaming to streaming video. If the old media system made it hard for the citizen to avoid news, the new system is an invitation to indulge in fantasy. Although Americans are spending more time on media than ever before, they're spending less time on news.[104]

Nevertheless, the traditional news media are still the backbone of America's news system. Their cumulative audience easily exceeds that of partisan outlets, and most of those who follow partisan outlets also get much of their news through traditional outlets, which also supply most of the news links found on the internet.[105] The audience for traditional news has declined but is still huge, which is an extraordinary asset in today's "attention economy."[106] What other institution has a daily following in the tens of millions? No church or political party gets anywhere near that kind of ongoing attention.[107]

The traditional media also have another strength—a commitment to accuracy. *BuzzFeed News* analyzed the factual accuracy of the internet political news pages of three mainstream outlets (*ABC News Politics*, *CNN Politics*, and *Politico*), as well as the Facebook pages of three major right-wing outlets (*Eagle Rising*, *Freedom Daily*, and *Right Wing News*) and the corresponding pages of three left-wing outlets (*Addicting Info*, *Occupy Democrats*, and *The Other 98%*). Only the mainstream outlets demonstrated fidelity to accuracy. A mere 1 percent of their original claims were shown to be factually wrong, compared with 20 percent for the left-wing outlets and 38 percent for the right-wing outlets.[108]

The problem is that the traditional media have allowed themselves to become a megaphone for the falsehoods of others. A recent Columbia journalism school study concluded that "news organizations play a major role in propagating hoaxes, false claims, questionable rumors, and dubious viral content."[109] News outlets honor their commitment to accuracy by quoting their sources accurately, but that is a flimsy standard when sources are lying or peddling half-truths and rumors.

If traditional media are to deserve their claim to be "custodians of the facts,"[110] they need to recognize that the larger media system is filled with propaganda and that transmitting it in the name of "objective reporting" makes them part of the problem.[111]

The traditional media need to do better. They need to supply what a democracy most needs from the press—a steady supply of trustworthy and relevant information.[112] "The point of having journalists around," says NYU's Jay Rosen, "is not to produce attention, but to make our attention more productive."[113]

We also can't restore sanity to the public sphere if our mainstream news outlets continue to be infected by what a Carnegie Corporation study called "the entertainment virus."[114] Some news outlets, including the *New York Times, Washington Post,* and *Wall Street Journal,* have avoided the temptation to soften their news, but many have not. An informed public cannot be built on infotainment and sensationalism. The media are fostering a public that is losing its sense of what it means to be informed and, with that, its ability to fend off false, baseless, and useless ideas.[115] The best protection against being duped by ideologues and liars is having the facts. Information actually does trump deception and disinformation, but only if you have it.

When news outlets are criticized for lacing the news with entertainment, they tend to blame the audience, saying that they're merely responding to public taste. But the public doesn't necessarily know what it wants until it sees it, a point emphasized by Rueven Frank, who headed *NBC News* during the heyday of broadcast television. "This business of giving people what they want is a dope pusher's argument," Frank said. "News is something people don't know they're interested in until they hear about it. The job of a journalist is to take what's important and make it interesting."[116] Unless journalists find ways to take issues of national policy and make them appealing, they'll continue to underserve the public. Citizens, as Princeton's Martin Gilens has shown, make better choices when they understand policy problems than when they don't.[117] Common sense doesn't exist in a void. It requires that we know what's at stake.

Journalists' obsession with the political game—who's up and who's down—is also a disservice. It's the dominant theme of political coverage and fosters political distrust. By portraying politicians as single-minded in their pursuit of power, the press, as one scholar noted, reduces them "to their worst stereotypes, people possessing no motive but political advantage."[118] What conclusion can one draw from game-centered reporting other than the impression that politicians spend all their time one-upping each other? It would be one thing if the stories explained in detail what's at stake in the competition, but that part is often left out. A University of Pennsylvania study found that competing policy proposals are often reported by their sponsors' names without reference to what the proposals contain or how they differ.[119]

Game-centered stories displace coverage that could help voters better understand the nation's policy problems. Such stories make it into the news, but not regularly. Former U.S. senator Alan Simpson put his finger on the problem when he wrote: "You come out of a legislative conference and there's 10 reporters standing around with their ears twitching. They don't want to know whether anything was resolved for the betterment of the United States. They want to know who got hammered, who tricked whom." Theodore H. White, who pioneered inside-politics reporting, said that so many journalists do it now that there's "no room left on the inside."[120]

Equally destructive is attack journalism. It's not the same as watchdog journalism, which is rooted in careful factual investigation and is aimed at holding officials accountable. In contrast, attack journalism starts with the assumption that politicians can't be trusted and seizes upon any hint or suggestion that a politician acted improperly.[121] Attack journalism fosters cynicism and political distrust. It also makes the press an easy target for politicians. When journalists attack them at every turn, they open themselves to charges of bias.[122]

And when journalism's "bad news is good news" formula is applied to demographic groups, it's destructive. Over the past decade, when immigrants have been the main subject of a national news story, roughly four of every five stories have been negative in tone. That's true also of news coverage of Muslims.[123] And for decades black Americans have been underrepresented in the news except when it comes to crime, where they're not only overrepresented but portrayed in ways that whites accused of crime less often are—handcuffed and in police custody.[124] Journalists can shrug their shoulders and say they're not responsible for how people respond to their stories.[125] That's another dope pusher's argument. Negative coverage of immigrants, Muslims, blacks, and other marginalized groups fosters negative stereotypes that activate prejudice and allow ideologues to justify everything from lengthy prison sentences to border walls.

Positive stories don't come naturally to journalists. They lack the tension that journalists seek and can lead to accusations that the reporter is a shill. But without such stories the news media are failing to show us an entire side of the American story—the positive side. Success is one of the most underreported aspects of politics. After the sharp economic downturn in 2008, the media stayed on the story while the news was bad and then dropped it as soon as the economy began to improve. No wonder most Americans believed that government policies—TARP, the job stimulus, and the like—did little to fix the problem and were a waste of taxpayers' money.[126] Nancy Gibbs, former editor of *Time* magazine, notes, "If we don't show how democracy can work, does work, if we don't model what civil discourse looks and sounds like and the progress it can yield, then we can hardly be surprised if people don't think [such things] matter."[127]

Without news that is balanced, relevant, and trustworthy there's not much hope that the public will anchor its opinions in reality. Such news is not beyond reach. NPR produces it regularly. The type of reporting I'm proposing would require journalists to have a fuller understanding of their subjects, spend more time away from the centers of power, say more about the substance of our politics and less about the horserace aspects, be as attentive to what's going right as to what's going wrong, and recognize that their stories affect the judgments citizens make.

———

Citizens also have to do better. We're part of the reason that our politics have been going downhill. One could say, as did the philosopher Javier Goma Lanzon, "that we are looking for the ideal of a virtuous republic composed of citizens relieved of the burden of citizenship."[128] We're not committed enough to show up regularly at the polls, if we show up at all. The presidential election is still a draw for many. About three in five of us get up and out for that contest. But turnout in many primary and local elections has fallen below 15 percent.[129] The 2018 midterm elections drew the largest midterm turnout in more than half a century. Yet the number of eligible voters who stayed home exceeded the number who showed up at the polls. Small wonder those with extreme views have disproportionate power. They're the ones who take the time to vote.

Nor are we committed enough to inform ourselves. We're intent on amusing ourselves, and we do it well. Compared with the pre-cable era, news consumption has declined in every age group, especially among young adults.[130] Americans are not walled off from news because of its high cost or inaccessibility. They suffer from insufficient interest.

Perhaps, as some have argued, we're victims of an education system that doesn't place much value on the teaching of history, the humanities, civics, or media literacy. It's difficult to know how much weight to attribute to this tendency, but the kind of education that people receive does affect their response to politics.[131]

The past decade or two have exposed faces of America that appeared to have been receding. Perhaps the racism and other forms of bigotry that have been so apparent recently were always there but were merely less visible. If that's correct, the downward turn in our politics and media have simply served to surface them. I'm inclined to think otherwise, believing that recent political and media developments have intensified and enlarged our worst instincts. It's a dangerous development. In the long run, the health of our democracy rests more on the character of our citizens than it does on the strength of our institutions. We need to restore, and deepen, Americans' commitment to democratic values. That effort must go beyond fostering the duty to vote. It also includes fostering tolerance, forbearance, and a recognition that what's good for the individual is inseparable from what's good for society.

Citizens are more dependent on the tone of our politics than might be thought. We have, as a result of scientific polling, nearly a century of reliable public opinion data. What jumps out when looking at the history of the polls is the variation in public opinion. The political distrust expressed by today's public is not how the public has always felt. There was a lengthy period where confidence in government was high. The hostility that many of today's Americans feel toward members of the opposing party is not how Americans have always felt. There was a lengthy period when Democrats and Republicans, though they had their differences, viewed each other with respect. The wacky ideas and conspiracy theories that we now so readily embrace did not always fill our heads. Polls stretching back to the 1930s show that Americans have never been highly informed, but it's only recently that our thinking has gone haywire.

The difference in these periods can be traced to the behavior of our leaders. They can speak honestly and appeal to facts and reason, or they can dissemble, deceive, and appeal to our worst impulses. When they've acted responsibly, the public has responded sensibly. When they've behaved badly, so has the public. "The voice of the people is but an echo," wrote Harvard political scientist V. O. Key Jr. "The people's verdict can be no more than a selective reflection from the alternatives and outlooks presented to them."[132]

Key wrote those words in the 1960s, but they capture what has happened since. Party polarization started at the top, among political elites, rather than at the bottom.[133] Disinformation and demagoguery are not naturally occurring phenomena. They are the result of deliberate choices made by political and media operatives. When they engage in name-calling, exploit our divisions, and put expediency ahead of principle, it's a green light for us to do the same. Trump's subtle and not-so-subtle appeals to white Christian America have unleashed forms of bias that were there all along but kept largely in check. Since Trump came on the political scene, there's been a sharp rise in hate crimes directed at Hispanic, black, and Muslim Americans.[134] But Trump's presidency is a product of our dysfunctional politics rather than the source of it. The seeds of division were being sown long before he announced his presidential bid. How did Democratic and Republican voters learn to see each other as enemies rather than rivals? We didn't learn that from our neighbors. We learned it from our warring party leaders and the messengers allied to their cause.

From the nation's earliest days, most of America's leaders understood that their privileged position carried with it a public trust. They differed in their beliefs, but they stopped short of destructive words and actions. When Thomas Jefferson won the election of 1800 and declared it a "revolution" of the common people, he refrained from demonizing his opponents, knowing that to do so would unleash the populist resentments that had been building against the wealthy.[135]

Level-headed leadership has been in short supply in recent decades, and it's turned us against each other. Citizens can be faulted for their lack of interest and embrace of cockeyed ideas. But citizens' response is invariably affected by the quality of public leadership.[136] We can't move from tribal conflict to reasoned discussion unless political leaders exhibit it. When politicians fill the public sphere with partisan bombast, recrimination, and claims of moral superiority, our politics has nowhere to go but down.

The quality of leadership also affects the news media's response. We can, and should, expect more of the press, but it will disappoint us time and again if we expect it to make up for defects in our leadership. As journalist Walter Lippmann noted, the news media are not equipped to give order and direction to our politics.[137] For an institution to do that job, it must have the incentive to identify problems, propose solutions to those problems, and submit them to the voters for approval or rejection. Political parties are designed for that purpose. The press is not. The press has its role, but it is not that role. When operating at its best, the press's role is to bring to light the developments that can help citizens understand their choices. But, when political parties and leaders go haywire, the press tends to amplify it. It will highlight the chaos and magnify the disorder.[138]

Our politics has gone off the rails, and there is plenty of blame to go around—everyone from our citizens to our journalists to our activists to our interest groups. But if we can't fix our leadership problem, everything else becomes harder to fix. The quality of our leadership is an index of the quality of our democracy. The better the leadership, the more tolerant will be our society, the more restrained will be our use of power, the more likely our problems will be addressed, the more fully our extreme elements will be contained, and the more realistic will be our image of the world in which we live.[139]

NOTES

CHAPTER 1

1. Faiz Siddiqui and Susan Svrluga, "N.C. Man Told Police He Went to D.C. Pizzeria with Gun to Investigate Conspiracy Theory," *Washington Post,* December 5, 2016, www.washingtonpost.com/news/local/wp/2016/12/04/d-c-police-respond -to-report-of-a-man-with-a-gun-at-comet-ping-pong-restaurant/?utm_term= .c1b46f58145a.

2. Kathy Frankovic, "Belief in Conspiracies Depends Largely on Political Identity," *YouGov,* December, 27 2016, https://today.yougov.com/news/2016/12/27/belief -conspiracies-largely-depends-political-iden.

3. Robert D. Johnston, *The Politics of Healing* (New York: Routledge, 2004), 136.

4. David J. Garrow, "The FBI and Martin Luther King," *Atlantic,* July–August 2002, www.theatlantic.com/magazine/archive/2002/07/the-fbi-and-martin-luther -king/302537; Nicole Hemmer, *Messengers on the Right: Conservative Media and the Transformation of American Politics* (Philadelphia: University of Pennsylvania Press, 2016), 93.

5. Richard Hofstadter, "The Paranoid Style in American Politics," *Harper's Magazine,* November 1964, 77.

6. "Debunking the 9/11 Myths: Special Report—The World Trade Center," *Popular Mechanics,* August 1, 2017, www.popularmechanics.com/military/a6384/debunking -911-myths-world-trade-center.

7. "Debunking the 9/11 Myths: Special Report—Flight 93," *Popular Mechanics,* August 1, 2017, www.popularmechanics.com/military/a5688/debunking-911 -myths-flight-93.

8. Marc Fisher, John Woodrow Cox, and Peter Hermann, "Pizzagate: From Rumor, to Hashtag, to Gunfire in D.C.," *Washington Post,* December 6, 2016, www .washingtonpost.com/local/pizzagate-from-rumor-to-hashtag-to-gunfire-in

-dc/2016/12/06/4c7def50-bbd4–11e6–94ac-3d324840106c_story .html?utm_term= .fb57334cf4de.

9. Steven Kull, Clay Ramsay, and Evan Lewis, "Misperceptions, the Media, and the Iraq War," *Political Science Quarterly* 118 (Winter 2003–2004): 569–98.

10. "A Crisis in Civic Education," *American Council of Trustees and Alumni,* 2016, www.goacta.org/images/download/A_Crisis_in_Civic_Education.pdf. Respondents were college students.

11. Given the proliferation of recent polls, it could be argued that the greater incidence of misinformation in recent years is a methodological artifact. That explanation, however, ignores the recent changes in the information system and in politics and society that foster a heightened level of misinformation. These changes are discussed in this and subsequent chapters.

12. Bianca DiJulio, Jamie Firth, and Mollyann Brodie, "Data Note: Americans' Views on the U.S. Role in Global Health," *Kaiser Family Foundation,* January 23, 2015, www.kff.org/global-health-policy/poll-finding/data-note-americans-views -on-the-u-s-role-in-global-health.

13. Kathleen Hall Jamieson and Paul Waldman, *The Press Effect: Politicians, Journalists, and the Stories That Shape the Political World* (New York: Oxford University Press, 2002), 167.

14. Anthony Leiserowitz, Edward W. Maibach, Connie Roser-Renouf, and Jay D.Hmielowski, "Politics and Global Warming: Democrats, Republicans, Independents, and the Tea Party," Yale University and George Mason University, New Haven, CT: Yale Project on Climate Change Communication, 2011, http://environment.yale .edu/climate/files/PoliticsGlobalWarming2011.pdf.

15. James H. Kuklinski, Paul J. Quirk, Jennifer Jerit, David Schwieder, and Robert F. Rich, "Misinformation and the Currency of Democratic Citizenship," *Journal of Politics* 62 (2000): 790–816.

16. FBI statistics for 2005–15 compared to Gallup poll responses for 2005–15.

17. "Trump Remains Unpopular; Voters Prefer Obama on SCOTUS Pick," *Public Policy Polling,* December 2016, www.publicpolicypolling.com/pdf/2015/PPP_Release _National_120916.pdf.

18. "Trump Remains Unpopular."

19. Kull, Ramsay, and Lewis, "Misperceptions."

20. Elise Viebeck, "Poll: Four in 10 Believe in Obama Healthcare Law 'Death Panels,'" *The Hill,* September 26, 2012, http://thehill.com/policy/healthcare/258753 -poll-four-in-10-believe-in-health-law-death-panels.

21. Kathleen Frankovic, "Belief in Conspiracies Largely Depends on Political Identity," *YouGov,* December 27, 2016, https://today.yougov.com/topics/politics /articles-reports/2016/12/27/belief-conspiracies-largely-depends-political-iden.

22. Emily Swanson and Mark Blumenthal, "'Wasteful Spending' Poll: Few Agree on What Government Waste Is, Most Want to Cut It," *HuffPost,* December 6, 2017, www.huffingtonpost.com/2013/03/18/wasteful-spending-poll_n_2886081.html.

23. Glenn Kessler, "No, China Does Not Hold More Than 50 Percent of U.S. Debt," *Washington Post*, December 29, 2014, www.washingtonpost.com/news /fact-checker/wp/2014/12/29/no-china-does-not-hold-more-than-50-percent-of-u-s -debt/?utm_term=.aa091627942e.

24. Wendy Gross, Tobias H. Stark, Jon Krosnick, Josh Pasek, Gaurav Soods, Trevor Tompson, Jennifer Agiesta, and Dennis Junius, "Americans' Attitudes toward the Affordable Care Act," Stanford University, 2012, 9, https://pprg.stanford.edu /wp-content/uploads/Health-Care-2012-Knowledge-and-Favorability.pdf.

25. "Trump Remains Unpopular."

26. "Quarter Doubt Obama Born in U.S.," *CNN*, August 2010, http://politicalticker .blogs.cnn.com/2010/08/04/cnn-poll-quarter-doubt-president-was-born-in-u-s.

27. Public Policy Polling survey, April 2013, cited at www.usatoday.com/story /news/nation/2013/04/03/newser-poll-conspiracy-theories/2049073.

28. "The New Food Fights: U.S. Public Divides over Food Science," *Pew Research Center*, December 2016, www.pewinternet.org/2016/12/01/the-new-food-fights.

29. "Republicans Blame Bill, Not Trump, for Health Bill Defeat," *CBS*, March, 2017, www.cbsnews.com/news/republicans-health-care-trump-approval-russia -election-meddling-cbs-news-poll.

30. Clay Ramsay, Steven Kull, Evan Lewis, and Stefan Subias, "Misinformation and the 2010 Election," Program on International Policy Attitudes (PIPA), University of Maryland, December 10, 2010, 7, https://drum.lib.umd.edu/handle/1903/11375.

31. Kull, Ramsay, and Lewis, "Misperceptions."

32. "Social Security," *Gallup*, October 2015, http://news.gallup.com/poll/1693/social -security.aspx.

33. Ludwig Wittgenstein, *Philosophical Investigations* (Oxford, UK: Basil Black- well, 1953), 162.

34. Political scientists disagree on the severity of the information problem. Some have interpreted the evidence as indicating widespread political ignorance. Others have argued that survey questions that test respondents on their factual information are a flawed indicator of the public's political awareness. It is safe to conclude, however, that policy awareness is not the public's strong suit. For opposing views on the question of how much the public knows, see Bruce Ackerman and James Fishkin, *Deliberation Day* (New Haven, CT.: Yale University Press, 2004), 5; and Christopher Achen and Larry Bartels, *Democracy for Realists: Why Elections Do Not Produce Responsive Government* (Princeton, NJ: Princeton University Press, 2016).

35. Walter Lippmann, *Public Opinion* (New York: Free Press, 1922), 125.

36. Michael X. Delli Carpini and Scott Keeter, *What Americans Know about Politics and Why It Matters* (New Haven, CT: Yale University Press, 1996), 133. See also Achen and Bartels, *Democracy for Realists*; and Samuel DeCanio, *Democracy and the Origins of the American Regulatory State* (New Haven, CT: Yale University Press, 2015).

37. Hunter Walker, "A Shocking Number of Americans Don't Know Basic Facts about the US Government," *Business Insider*, September 19, 2014, www.busines insider.com/poll-many-americans-dont-know-basic-facts-about-government -2014-9.

38. Poll from 1952 cited in Helene Landemore, *Democratic Reason* (Princeton, NJ: Princeton University Press, 2013), 35.

39. "From ISIS to Unemployment: What Do Americans Know?" *Pew Research Center*, 2014.

40. James David Barber, "Characters in the Campaign," in James David Barber, ed., *Race for the Presidency* (Englewood Cliffs, N.J.: Prentice-Hall, 1978), 181.

41. Stephen Engelberg, "Open Your Mind," *American Journalism Review*, March 1999, http://ajrarchive.org/Article.asp?id=304.

42. See Paul Goren, *On Voter Competence* (New York: Oxford University Press, 2012).

43. For the different sides of this debate, see, for example, Philip E. Converse, "The Nature of Belief Systems in Mass Publics," in David Apter, ed., *Ideology and Discontent* (New York: Free Press, 1964.), 206–61; V. O. Key Jr., with Milton C. Cummings, *The Responsible Electorate: Rationality in Presidential Voting, 1936–1960* (New York: Vintage Books, 1964); Samuel L. Popkin, *The Reasoning Voter: Communication and Persuasion in Presidential Campaigns* (Chicago: University of Chicago Press, 1991); Benjamin I. Page and Robert Y. Shapiro, *The Rational Public: Fifty Years of Trends in Americans' Policy Preferences* (Chicago: University of Chicago Press, 1992); John R. Zaller, *The Nature and Origins of Mass Opinion* (New York: Cambridge University Press, 1992); Scott L. Althaus, *Collective Preferences in Democratic Politics: Opinion Surveys and the Will of the People* (New York: Cambridge University Press, 2003); Martin Gilens, "Two-Thirds Full? Citizen Competence and Democratic Governance," in Adam Berinsky, ed., *New Directions in Public Opinion* (New York: Routledge, 2011); and Robert Erikson, Michael MacKuen, and James Stimson, *The Macro Polity* (New York: Cambridge University Press, 2002).

44. James Surowiecki, *The Wisdom of Crowds: Why the Many Are Smarter Than the Few and How Collective Wisdom Shapes Business, Economies, Societies, and Nations* (Boston: Little Brown, 2004).

45. Scott Althaus, "Free Falls, High Dives, and the Future of Democratic Accountability," in Doris Graber, Denis McQuail, and Pippa Norris, eds., *The Politics of News/The News of Politics*, 2nd ed. (Washington, DC: Congressional Quarterly Press, 2007), 185.

46. Colby Itkowitz, "Americans Are Seriously Stressed Out about the Future of the Country, Survey Finds," *Washington Post*, February 15, 2017, www.washingtonpost .com/news/inspired-life/wp/2017/02/15/americans-are-seriously-stressed-out-about -the-future-of-the-country-survey-finds/?utm_term=.203f893f0547.

47. "The American Middle Class Is Losing Ground," *Pew Research Center*, December 9, 2015, www.pewsocialtrends.org/2015/12/09/the-american-middle-class -is-losing-ground.

48. Doug Short, "Charting the Incredible Shift from Manufacturing to Services in America," *Business Insider*, September 5, 2011, www.businessinsider.com/charting -the-incredible-shift-from-manufacturing-to-services-in-america-2011-9.

49. Julie Beck, "How Uncertainty Fuels Anxiety," *Atlantic*, March 18, 2015, www .theatlantic.com/health/archive/2015/03/how-uncertainty-fuels-anxiety/388066.

50. Daniel Kahneman, *Thinking Fast and Slow* (New York: Farrar, Straus and Giroux, 2011), 201.

51. Justin Kruger and David Dunning, "Unskilled and Unaware of It: How Difficulties in Recognizing One's Own Incompetence Lead to Inflated Self-Assessments," *Journal of Personality and Social Psychology* 77 (1999): 1121–34.

52. Charles S. Taber and Milton Lodge, "Motivated Skepticism in the Evaluation of Political Beliefs," *American Journal of Political Science* 50 (2006): 755–69, http:// onlinelibrary.wiley.com/doi/10.1111/j.1540-5907.2006.00214.x/abstract; Brendan Nyhan, Jason Reifler, and Peter A. Ubel, "The Hazards of Correcting Myths about Health Care Reform," *Medical Care* 51 (2013): 127–32; Brendan Nyhan, "Why the 'Death Panel' Myth Wouldn't Die: Misinformation in the Health Care Debate," *Forum* 8 (2010), www.dartmouth.edu/~nyhan/health-care-misinformation.pdf.

53. Taber and Lodge, "Motivated Skepticism"; Brendan Nyhan and Jason Reifler, "When Corrections Fail: The Persistence of Political Misperceptions," *Political Behavior* (2010): 303–30; Hollyn M. Johnson and Colleen M. Seifert, "Sources of the Continued Influence Effect: When Discredited Information in Memory Affects Later Inferences," *Journal of Experimental Psychology: Learning, Memory, and Cognition* 20 (1994): 1420–36; see also Derek D. Rucker and Richard E. Petty, "When Resistance Is Futile: Consequences of Failed Counterarguing for Attitude Certainty," *Journal of Personality and Social Psychology* 86 (2004): 219–35.

54. Dan M. Kahan, Ellen Peters, Erica Dawson, and Paul Slovic, "Motivated Numeracy and Enlightened Self-Government," *Behavioural Public Policy* 1 (2013): 54–86, https://ssrn.com/abstract=2319992; Dana Nucitelli, "Can the Republican Party Solve Its Science Denial Problem?" *Guardian*, April 28, 2016, www.theguardian .com/environment/climate-consensus-97-per-cent/2016/apr/28/can-the-republican -party-solve-its-science-denial-problem; see also Josh Clinton and Carrie Roush, "Poll: Persistent Partisan Divide over 'Birther' Question," *NBC News*, June 2016, www.nbcnews.com/politics/2016-election/poll-persistent-partisan-divide-over -birther-question-n627446. The "smart idiot" effect also holds when it comes to news exposure. Those who pay closer attention to news are harder to disabuse of a false belief than those who don't pay close attention because they're more likely to think their belief is well founded. See Tom Nichols, *The Death of Expertise* (New York: Oxford University Press, 2017), 143.

55. Numerous polls indicate declining trust in traditional voices of authority. The subject is addressed at length in chapter 4.

56. Hemmer, *Messengers on the Right*, 93, 103.

57. Andrew Breiner, "Pizzagate, Explained: Everything You Want to Know about the Comet Ping Pong Pizzeria Conspiracy Theory but Are Too Afraid to Search for

on Reddit," *Salon*, December 10, 2016, www.salon.com/2016/12/10/pizzagate -explained-everything-you-want-to-know-about-the-comet-ping-pong-pizzeria -conspiracy-theory-but-are-too-afraid-to-search-for-on-reddit; Fisher, Cox, and Hermann, "Pizzagate."

58. Francovic, "Belief in Conspiracies."

59. Daniel Kahneman, Amos Tversky, and Paul Slovic, *Judgment under Uncertainty: Heuristics and Biases* (Cambridge: Cambridge University Press, 1982); George Zipf, *Human Behavior and the Principle of Least Effort* (Boston: Addison-Wesley, 1949).

60. Page and Shapiro, *Rational Public*, 19.

61. Example from Ezra Klein, "Unpopular Mandate," *New Yorker*, June 25, 2012, 31.

62. "Public Attitudes toward the War in Iraq: 2003–2008," *Pew Research Center for the People and the Press*, March 19, 2008, http://pewresearch.org/pubs/770 /iraq-war-five-year-anniversary.

63. Chris Wells, Justin Reedy, John Gastil, and Carolyn Lee, "Information Distortion and Voting Choices: The Origins and Effects of Factual Beliefs in Initiative Elections," *Political Psychology* 30 (2009): 953–69.

64. Bradley Jones, "Support for Free Trade Agreements Rebounds Modestly, but Wide Partisan Differences Remain," *Pew Research Center*, April 25, 2017, www .pewresearch.org/fact-tank/2017/04/25/support-for-free-trade-agreements-rebounds -modestly-but-wide-partisan-differences-remain.

65. Toby Bolsen, James N. Druckman, and Fay Lomax Cook, "The Influence of Partisan Motivated Reasoning on Public Opinion," *Political Behavior* 36 (2014): 235.

66. Meghan McCarthy, "Republican Voters Remain Loyal to Trump in First National Poll after Video," *Morning Consult*, October 9, 2016, https://morningconsult .com/2016/10/09/republican-voters-remain-loyal-trump-first-national-poll-video.

67. Ariel Edwards-Levy, "Trump Voters Believe Sex Allegations against Weinstein, but Not against Trump," *HuffPost*, October 20, 2017, www.huffingtonpost.com /entry/trump-voters-weinstein-poll_us _59ea11c9e4b 0f9d35bca3fd9.

68. See, for example, Raymond Nickerson, "Confirmation Bias: A Ubiquitous Phenomenon in Many Guises," *Review of General Psychology* 2 (1998): 175–220.

69. Charles G. Lord, Lee Ross, and Mark R. Lepper, "Biased Assimilation and Attitude Polarization: The Effects of Prior Theories on Subsequently Considered Evidence," *Journal of Personality and Social Psychology* 11 (1979): 2098–109.

70. See, for example, Colleen Seifert, "The Continued Influence of Misinformation on Memory: What Makes a Correction Effective?" *Psychology of Learning and Motivation* 41 (2002): 265–92; Ullrich K. H. Ecker, Stephan Lewandowsky, and Joe Apai, "Terrorists Brought Down the Plane!—No, Actually It Was a Technical Fault: Processing Corrections of Emotive Information," *Quarterly Journal of Experimental Psychology* 64 (2011): 283–310.

71. Ramsay, Kull, Lewis, and Subias, "Misinformation," 18.

72. Frankovic, "Belief in Conspiracies."

73. Ben Smith, "More Than Half of Democrats Believed Bush Knew," *Politico*, April 22, 2011, www.politico.com/blogs/ben-smith/2011/04/more-than-half-of-democrats-believed-bush-knew-035224; see also "Half of New Yorkers Believe US Leaders Had Foreknowledge of Impending 9–11 Attacks and 'Consciously Failed' to Act; 66% Call for New Probe of Unanswered Questions by Congress or New York's Attorney General," *Zogby International*, August 30, 2004.

74. "In Presidential Contest, Voters Say 'Basic Facts,' Not Just Policies, Are in Dispute," *Pew Research Center*, October 14, 2016, www.people-press.org/2016/10/14/in-presidential-contest-voters-say-basic-facts-not-just-policies-are-in-dispute.

75. Lauren Griffen and Annie Niemand, "Why Each Side of the Partisan Divide Thinks the Other Is Living in an Alternate Reality," *Conversation*, January 20, 2017, https://theconversation.com/why-each-side-of-the-partisan-divide-thinks-the-other-is-living-in-an-alternate-reality-71458; Lippmann, *Public Opinion*, 82.

76. Howard G. Lavine, Christopher D. Johnston, and Marco R. Steenbergen, *The Ambivalent Partisan: How Critical Loyalty Promotes Democracy* (Oxford: Oxford University Press, 2012).

77. Taber and Lodge, "Motivated Skepticism"; Kari Edwards and Edward E. Smith, "A Disconfirmation Bias in the Evaluation of Arguments," *Journal of Personality and Social Psychology* 71 (1996): 5–24; W. Lance Bennett, "Press–Government Relations in a Changing Media Environment," in Kate Kenski and Kathleen Hall Jamieson, eds., *The Oxford Handbook of Political Communication* (New York: Oxford University Press, 2014).

78. Lydia Saad, "Republicans,' Dems' Abortion Views Grow More Polarized," *Gallup*, March 2010, http://news.gallup.com/poll/126374/republicans-dems-abortion-views-grow-polarized.aspx; Lydia Saad, "US Abortion Attitudes Stable; No Consensus on Legality," *Gallup*, May 2017, www.gallup.com/poll/211901/abortion-attitudes-stable-noconsensus-legality.aspx; Riley E. Dunlap, "Climate-Change Views: Republican-Democratic Gaps Expand," *Gallup*, May 2008, http://news.gallup.com/poll/107569/climatechange-views-republicandemocratic-gaps-expand.aspx; Lydia Saad and Jeffrey Jones, "U.S. Concern about Global Warming at Eight-Year High," *Gallup*, March 2016, http://news.gallup.com/poll/190010/concern-global-warming-eight-year-high.aspx. Earlier data point taken from Art Swift, "In U.S., Support for Assault Weapons Ban at Record Low," *Gallup*, October 2016, http://news.gallup.com/poll/196658/support-assault-weapons-ban-record-low.aspx.

79. Keith T. Poole and Howard Rosenthal, *Ideology and Congress: A Political Economic History of Roll Call Voting*, 2nd ed. (New York: Routledge, 2017).

80. Nolan McCarty, Keith T. Poole, and Howard Rosenthal, *Polarized America: The Dance of Ideology and Unequal Riches* (Cambridge, MA: MIT Press, 2008), fig. 2.9.

81. Quoted in Alice Dagnes, *Politics on Demand: The Effects of 24-Hour News on American Politics* (Santa Barbara, CA: ABC-CLIO, 2010), 111.

82. Brendan Nyhan, "The Politics of Health Care Reform," *Forum* 8 (2010): 9, www.bepress.com/forum/vo18/iss1/art5.

83. *Glenn Beck,* Fox, February 11, 2009.

84. Post on Sarah Palin's Facebook page, August 7, 2009, www.facebook.com/note .php?note_id=113851103434&ref=mf.

85. Boehner quoted in Angie Drobnic Nyhan, "PolitiFact's Lie of the Year: 'Death Panels,'" *PolitiFact*, December 18, 2009, www.politifact.com/truth-o-meter/article /2009/dec/18/politifact-lie-year-death-panels. Foxx and Grassley quoted in Nyhan, "Why the 'Death Panel' Myth," 9.

86. "Health Care Reform Closely Followed, Much Discussed," *Pew Research Center,* August 2009, www.people-press.org/2009/08/20/health-care-reform -closely-followed-much-discussed.

87. Bolsen, Druckman, and Cook, "Influence of Partisan Motivated Reasoning," 235–62.

88. Ramsay, Kull, Lewis, and Subias, "Misinformation"; Filippo Menczer, "The Spread of Misinformation in Social Media," Center for Complex Networks and Systems Research, Indiana University, September 2016, https://researchhorizons.soic.indiana .edu/files/2016/09/Menczer.pdf; "Evaluating Information," a report of the Stanford History Education Group, Stanford University, November 2016, 1–29, https://stacks. stanford.edu/file/druid :fv751yt5934/SHEG%20Evaluating%20Information%20online .pdf.

89. For a discussion of counterculture movements, see Colin Barker, "Some Reflections on Student Movements of the 1960s and Early 1970s," *Critical Review* 81 (2008): 43–91, https://journals.openedition.org/rccs/646.

90. See Paul Feyerabend, *Against Method: Outline of an Anarchist Theory of Knowledge* (New York: Humanities Press, 1975).

91. David Halperin, "Before Rubio, before Luntz: Meet a Founding Father of Climate Change Denial," *HuffPost,* March 3, 23013; Maxwell T. Boykoff and Jules G. Boykoff, "Balance as Bias: Global Warming and the U.S. Prestige Press," *Global Environmental Change* 15 (2004): 126.

92. Frederick W. Mayer, "Stories of Climate Change: Competing Narratives, the Media, and U.S. Public Opinion 2001–2010," Discussion Paper D-72, Joan Shorenstein Center on the Press, Politics, and Public Policy, Kennedy School of Government, Harvard University, February 2012, 8, www.hks.harvard.edu/presspol/publications /papers/discussion_papers/d72_mayer.pdf.

93. Dunlap, "Climate-Change Views."

94. Mark Thompson, *Enough Said: What's Gone Wrong with the Language of Politics* (New York: St. Martin's Press, 2016), 168; "Interview: Frank Luntz," *Frontline,* November 9, 2004, www.pbs.org/wgbh/pages/frontline/shows/persuaders/interviews /luntz.html.

95. Josh Pasek, Gaurav Sood, and Jon A. Krosnick, "Misinformed about the Affordable Care Act? Leveraging Certainty to Assess the Prevalence of Misperceptions," *Journal of Communication* 60 (2015): 660–73; see also Matthew Levendusky, *Clearer Cues, More Consistent Voters* (Chicago: University of Chicago Press, 2009), 111–31; and Rune Slothuus and Claes H. de Vreese, "Political Parties, Motivated Reasoning, and Issue Framing Effects," *Journal of Politics* 72, no. 3 (2009): 630–45.

96. Regina Lawrence and Matthew Schafer, "Debunking Sarah Palin: Mainstream News Coverage of 'Death Panels,'" *Journalism* 13 (2012), http://journals.sagepub. com/doi/abs/10.1177/1464884911431389?journalCode=joua.

97. Sidney Blumenthal, "Afterword," in Walter Lippmann, *Liberty and the News* (Princeton, N.J.: Princeton University Press, 2008), 80–81; Bartholomew H. Sparrow, *Uncertain Guardians* (Baltimore, MD.: Johns Hopkins University Press, 1999), 26.

98. Bennett, "Press-Government Relations." Fallows used the term to headline his blog in *Atlantic*. Jamieson and Waldman, *Press Effect*, chap. 7.

99. Lauren Carroll, "Donald Trump Says Hillary Clinton 'Slept' through Benghazi Attack," *PolitiFact*, June 23, 2016, www.politifact.com/truth-o-meter/statements/2016 /jun/23/donald-trump/donald-trump-says-hillary-clinton-slept-through-be.

100. See, for example, Karl Hulse and Kate Zernike, "Bloodshed Puts New Focus on Vitriol Politics," *New York Times*, January 8, 2011; and Jeff Zeleny and Jim Rutenberg, "In the Shock of the Moment, the Politicking Stops . . . Until It Doesn't," *New York Times*, January 9, 2011.

101. Paul Steinhauser, "CNN Poll: Palin Unfavorable Rating at All Time High," *CNN*, January 17, 2011, http://politicalticker.blogs.cnn.com/2011/01/19/cnn-poll-palin -unfavorable-rating-at-all-time-high; Nick Baumann, "Exclusive: Loughner Friend Explains Alleged Gunman's Grudge against Giffords," *Mother Jones*, January 10, 2011, www.motherjones.com/politics/2011/01/jared-lee-loughner-friend-voicemail -phone-message; see also Tom Jensen, "Poll: Majority Says Palin Not Responsible for Giffords Shooting, but Dislike Her Response," *Public Policy Polling*, January 18, 2011, www.publicpolicypolling.com/news/poll-majority-says-palin-not-responsible-for -giffords-shooting-but-dislike-her-response.

102. Thomas E. Patterson, *The Mass Media Election* (New York: Praeger, 1980), 156–59.

103. Yochai Benkler, Robert Faris, and Hal Roberts, *Network Propaganda: Manipulation, Disinformation, and Radicalization in American Politics* (New York: Oxford University Press, 2018).

104. Hemmer, *Messengers on the Right*, 99.

105. Hemmer, *Messengers on the Right*, 260. For reasons that are not fully understood, conservatives have a stronger preference for like-minded communication. According to both polling and ratings data, conservative talk show hosts dominate the partisan talk show sector.

106. "Audio and Podcasting Fact Sheet," *Pew Research Center*, June 16, 2017, www .journalism.org/fact-sheet/audio-and-podcasting.

107. Limbaugh quoted in McKay Coppins, "The Deep Republican Roots of Trump's Media Bashing," *Atlantic*, October 11, 2017, www.theatlantic.com /politics/archive/2017/10/trump-press-crackdown/542670.

108. Jason Boughton, "Rachel Maddow: Her Biased Opinion," *Blastingnews*, April 14, 2018, https://us.blastingnews.com/opinion/2018/04/rachel-maddow-her -biased-opinion-002505691.html.

109. Jeffrey Berry and Sarah Sobieraj, *The Outrage Industry* (New York: Oxford University Press, 2016).

110. Quoted in Helen Ragovin, "My Way or the Highway," *TuftsNow*, September 13, 2017, http://now.tufts.edu/articles/my-way-or-highway.

111. *Countdown with Keith Olbermann*, MSNBC, February 15, 2010.

112. See Robb Willer, Matthew Feinberg, and Rachel Wetts, "Threats to Racial Status Promote Tea Party Support among White Americans," Stanford Graduate School of Business, Working Paper No. 3422, May 4, 2016, www.gsb.stanford.edu /faculty-research/working-papers/threats-racial-status-promote-tea-party -support-among-white.

113. Farhad Manjoo, "Rumor's Reasons," *New York Times Magazine*, March 16, 2008, www.nytimes.com/2008/03/16/magazine/16wwln-idealab-t.html.

114. Gordon Pennycook, "Prior Exposure Increases Perceived Accuracy of Fake News," presentation at Combating Fake News Conference, Harvard University, Cambridge, MA, February 17, 2017.

115. "What You Know Depends on What You Watch," Farleigh Dickinson University, PublicMind Poll, May 2012, http://publicmind.fdu.edu/2012/confirmed. At the bottom in terms of knowledge were regular consumers of talk radio and cable outlets that feature talk shows.

116. See, for example, Kull, Ramsay, and Lewis, "Misperceptions."

117. Hemmer, *Messengers on the Right*, 274.

118. Reworking of a remark made by a guest on Bill Maher's HBO show, November 17, 2017. The yellow journalism of the early 1900s might be the closest comparison to partisan talk shows, but newspapers of that era delivered mostly factual accounts of the day's events, saving their fabrications for eye-catching moments.

119. Ethan Zuckerman, *Digital Cosmopolitans: Why We Think the Internet Connects Us, Why It Doesn't, and How to Rewire It* (New York: Norton, 2013).

120. Soroush Vosoughi, Deb Roy, and Sinan Aral, "The Spread of True and False News Online," *Science* 369 (2018): 1146–51, http://science.sciencemag.org /content/359/6380/1146.

121. Zach Beauchamp, "Democrats Are Falling for Fake News about Russia: Why Liberal Conspiracy Theories Are Flourishing in the Age of Trump," *Vox*, May 19, 2017, www.vox.com/world/2017/5/19/15561842/trump-russia-louise-mensch; McKay Coppins, "How the Left Lost Its Mind," *Atlantic*, July 2, 2017, www.theatlantic.com /politics/archive/2017/07/liberal-fever-swamps/530736.

122. "Megyn Kelly Faces Backlash over Interview with Alex Jones," *ABC News*, June 13, 2017, www.youtube.com/watch?v=uZlmcyVDdfc.

123. Maxwell Strachan, "A Conspiracy Theory about a Stoneman Douglas Student Reaches No. 1 on YouTube," *HuffPost*, February 21, 2018, www.huffingtonpost.com /entry/youtube-stoneman-douglas_us_5a8d9389e4b00 a30a2517348.

124. Zach Exley, "Black Pigeon Speaks: The Anatomy of the Worldview of an Alt-Right YouTuber," Shorenstein Center on Media, Politics, and Public Policy research paper, Harvard Kennedy School, Harvard University, June 28, 2017.

125. "November 2018 Overview," *SimilarWeb*, downloaded January 5, 2019, www .similarweb.com/website/breitbart.com.

126. Hemmer, *Messengers on the Right,* 93.

127. "What Aren't They Telling Us?" Chapman University survey, October 2016, https://blogs.chapman.edu/wilkinson/2016/10/11/what-arent-they-telling-us.

128. Peter Dhalgren, *Media and Political Engagement* (New York: Cambridge University Press, 2009), 165.

129. Cass Sunstein, *Republic.com* (Princeton, NJ: Princeton University Press, 2001); Matthew Hindman, *The Myth of Digital Democracy* (Princeton, NJ: Princeton University Press, 2009), 138; Klein, "Unpopular Mandate," 33.

130. Matthew Fisher, Mariel K. Goddu, and Frank C. Keil, "Searching for Explanations: How the Internet Creates an Illusion of Knowledge," *Journal of Experimental Psychology* 144 (2015): 674–87, cited in Nichols, *Death of Expertise*, 119.

131. Thomas J. Johnson and Barbara Kaye, "Believing the Blogs of War? How Blog Users Compare on Credibility and Characteristics in 2003 and 2007," *Media, War, and Conflict* 3 (2010): 315–33.

132. Stephan Lewandowsky, Ullrich K. H. Ecker, Colleen M. Seifert, Norbert Schwarz, and John Cook, "Abstract Misinformation and Its Correction: Continued Influence and Successful Debiasing," *Psychological Science in the Public Interest* 13 (2012); Heidi J. Larson, Louis Z. Cooper, Juhani Eskola, Samuel L. Katz, and Scott Ratzan, "Addressing the Vaccine Confidence Gap," *Lancet* 378 (2011): 526–35.

133. Craig Silverman, Lauren Strapagiel, Hamza Shaban, Ellie Hall, and Jeremy Singer-Vine, "Hyperpartisan Facebook Pages Are Publishing False and Misleading Information at an Alarming Rate," *BuzzFeed News*, October 20, 2016, www.buzzfeed .com/craigsilverman/partisan-fb-pages-analysis?utm _term=.cqgEYp3BX# qxRE08g2Z.

134. "Chain Email's File," *Politifact*, downloaded October 24, 2017, www.politifact .com/personalities/chain-email.

135. Andrew Guess, Brendan Nyhan, and Jason Reifler, "Selective Exposure to Misinformation: Evidence from the Consumption of Fake News during the 2016 U.S. Presidential Campaign," European Research Council, January 9, 2018, available at www.dartmouth.edu/~nyhan/fake-news-2016.pdf.

136. Lippmann, *Public Opinion*, chap. 1.

137. Lewandowsky et al., "Abstract Misinformation"; Larson et al., "Addressing the Vaccine Confidence Gap."

138. "Pertussis (Whooping Cough): Surveillance and Reporting," *Centers for Disease Control and Prevention*, www.cdc.gov/pertussis/surv-reporting.html.

139. Lawrence Lessig, "The Regulation of Social Meaning," *University of Chicago Law Review* 62 (1995): 943–1045; Steven Mufson, "Before Trump's Tax Plan, There Was 'Voodoo Economics' and 'Hyperbole,'" *Washington Post*, December 3, 2016, www.washingtonpost.com/business/economy/before-trumps-tax-plan-there-was -voodoo-economics-hyperbole/2016/12/21/c37c97ea-c3d2–11e6–8422-eac61c0ef74d _story.html?utm_term=.fc1b0658be87.

140. Quoted in George Will, "The Wisdom of Pat Moynihan," *Washington Post*, October 3, 2010, www.washingtonpost.com/wp-dyn/content/article/2010/10/01 /AR2010100105262.html.

141. Observation of Roderick Hart at the 2011 Breaux Symposium, Manship School of Mass Communication, Louisiana State University, Baton Rouge, LA, March 29, 2011.

142. Glenn Kessler, "Fact Checker," *Washington Post*, downloaded January 9, 2019, www.washingtonpost.com/news/fact-checker/?utm_term=.5f3f72715f7d; Glenn Kessler and Meg Kelly, "President Trump Made 2,140 False or Misleading Claims in His First Year," *Washington Post*, January 20, 2018, www.washingtonpost.com /news/fact-checker/wp/2018/01/20/president-trump-made-2140-false-or-misleading -claims-in-his-first-year/?utm_term=.c2f5bab7d97f; David Leonhardt and Stuart A. Thompson, "Trump's Lies," *New York Times*, July 21, 2017, www.nytimes.com /interactive/2017/06/23/opinion/trumps-lies.html; Nolan D. McCaskill, "Trump Tweet: 'Any Negative Polls Are Fake News,'" *Politico*, February 6, 2017, www.politico .com/story/2017/02/trump-tweet-americans-want-extreme-vetting-234678.

143. Harry G. Frankfurt, *On Bullshit* (Princeton, N.J.: Princeton University Press, 2005), 61.

144. Derek Thompson, "Where Did All the Workers Go? 60 Years of Economic Change in 1 Graph," *Atlantic*, January 26, 2012, www.theatlantic.com/business /archive/2012/01/where-did-all-the-workers-go-60-years-of-economic-change -in-1-graph/252018.

145. Christopher H. Achen and Larry M. Bartels, "Do Sanders Supporters Favor His Policies?" *New York Times*, May 23, 2016, www.nytimes.com/2016/05/23/opinion /campaign-stops/do-sanders-supporters-favor-his-policies.html?_r=0.

146. Steve Benen, "Trump Says His 'Gut' Is More Reliable Than Everyone Else's 'Brains,'" *MSNBC*, November 28, 2018, www.msnbc.com/rachel-maddow-show /trump-says-his-gut-more-reliable-everyone-elses-brains.

147. John Hibbing and Elizabeth Theiss-Morse, *Stealth Democracy: Americans' Beliefs about How Government Should Work* (New York: Cambridge University Press, 2002).

148. Jonathan Rauch, "How American Politics Went Insane," *Atlantic*, July–August 2016, www.theatlantic.com/magazine/archive/2016/07/how-american-politics-went-insane/485570; Trump quoted in Steve Benen, "Donald Trump Puts His Messianic Message in a New Light," *MSNBC*, October 14, 2016.

149. David Brooks, "Finding a Way to Roll Back Fanaticism," *New York Times*, August 15, 2017, A23; Hannah Arendt, *The Origins of Totalitarianism* (New York: Harcourt, 1951), 474.

150. See, for example, Tyler Anbinder, *Nativism and Slavery: The Northern Know Nothings and the Politics of the 1850s* (New York: Oxford University Press, 1992).

151. See "Scientific Racism," *Wikipedia*, downloaded August, 12, 2017, https://en.wikipedia.org/wiki/Scientific_racism.

152. One Know Nothing policy would have banned Catholics from holding government jobs or teaching in public schools.

CHAPTER 2

1. Colleen Shalby, "Newt Gingrich Says a President 'Cannot Obstruct Justice,'" *Los Angeles Times*, June 18, 2017, www.latimes.com/politics/washington/la-na-essential-washington-updates-newt-gingrich-says-president-cannot-1497636327-htmlstory.html.

2. Shalby, "Newt Gingrich."

3. "Trump Sets New Low Point for Inaugural Approval Rating," *Gallup*, January 23, 2017, http://news.gallup.com/poll/202811/trump-sets-new-low-point-inaugural-approval-rating.aspx.

4. "Obama Job Approval Ratings Most Politically Polarized by Far," *Gallup*, January 25, 2017, http://news.gallup.com/poll/203006/obama-job-approval-ratings-politically-polarized-far.aspx.

5. Sean Illing, "20 of America's Top Political Scientists Gathered to Discuss Our Democracy. They're Scared," *Vox*, October 13, 2017, www.vox.com/2017/10/13/16431502/america-democracy-decline-liberalism.

6. Michael J. Rosenfeld, Thomas J. Reuben, and Maja Falcon, "How Couples Meet and Stay Together," *Stanford University Libraries*, 2011, cited in Shanto Iyengar and Sean J. Westwood, "Fear and Loathing across Party Lines," *American Journal of Political Science* 59 (2015): 690–707.

7. Robert D. Putnam, *Bowling Alone: The Collapse and Revival of American Community* (New York: Simon and Schuster, 2000); see also Robert Putnam, "The Prosperous Community," *American Prospect*, Spring 1993, http://prospect.org/article/prosperous-community-social-capital-and-public-life.

8. Alexis de Tocqueville, *Democracy in America* (1835–1840), J. P. Mayer and A. P. Kerr, eds. (Garden City, NY: Doubleday/Anchor, 1969), bk. 2, chap. 4.

9. Theda Skocpol, *Diminished Democracy: From Membership to Management in American Civic Life* (Norman: University of Oklahoma Press, 2004).

10. NORC survey, 2017.

11. Bill Bishop, *The Big Sort: Why the Clustering of Like-Minded America Is Tearing Us Apart* (New York: Houghton Mifflin, 2008); Alan A. Abramowitz, "U.S. Senate Elections in a Polarized Era," in Burdett A. Loomis, ed., *The U.S. Senate: From Deliberation to Dysfunction* (Washington, DC: CQ Press, 2011): 27–48.

12. David Wasserman, "Purple American Has All But Disappeared," *FiveThirtyEight,* March 8, 2017, https://fivethirtyeight.com/features/purple-america -has-all-but-disappeared.

13. Craig Gilbert, "Dividing Lines: Comparing Polarization in Milwaukee to Other Big Metros," *Milwaukee Wisconsin Journal-Sentinel,* May 5, 2014, http:// archive.jsonline.com/newswatch/257952371.html.

14. Wendy K. Tam Cho, James G. Gimpel, and Iris S. Hui, "Voter Migration and the Geographic Sorting of the American Electorate," *Annals of the Association of American Geographers,* 2012, www.tandfonline.com/doi/abs/10.1080/00045608 .2012.720229. The study indicates that, although most of the partisan clustering is the result of indirect effects, some people do choose a location based on its political makeup; see also Samuel J. Abrams and Morris P. Fiorina, "'The Big Sort' That Wasn't: A Skeptical Reexamination," *PS: Political Science and Politics* 45 (2012): 203–10; and Jesse Sussell and James A. Thomson, "Are Changing Constituencies Driving Rising Polarization in the U.S. House of Representatives?" *Rand Corporation,* 2015, www.rand.org/pubs/research_reports/RR896.html.

15. Malia Jones and Kristian Knutsen, "The Political Geography of Wisconsin: Partisanship and Population Density: Voters Are Increasingly Polarized between and within Major Urban and Suburban Areas," University of Wisconsin Applied Population Laboratory, *WisContext,* November 7, 2016, www.wiscontext.org/political -geography-wisconsin-partisanship-and-population-density. Current proportions based on my examination of Wisconsin's county-by-county vote totals in the 2016 presidential election.

16. "Partisanship and Political Animosity in 2016," *Pew Research Center,* June 2016, www.people-press.org/2016/06/22/partisanship-and-political-animosity -in-2016.

17. Elisabeth Noelle-Neumann, *The Spiral of Silence* (Chicago: University of Chicago Press, 1984); see also Dietram Schuefele, "Spiral of Silence Theory," in *The Sage Handbook of Public Opinion Research* (New York: Sage, 2007), 175.

18. W. M. L. Finlay, "The Propaganda of Extreme Hostility: Denunciation and the Regulation of the Group," *British Journal of Social Psychology* 46, no. 2 (2007): 323–41.

19. Frank Newport, "In U.S., 46% Hold Creationist View of Human Origins," *Gallup News,* June 1, 2012, http://news.gallup.com/poll/155003/hold-creationist -view-human-origins.aspx.

20. Example taken from Kurt Anderson, "How America Lost Its Mind," *Atlantic,* September 2017, www.theatlantic.com/magazine/archive/2017/09/how-america -lost-its-mind/534231.

21. Joan Vennochi, "Matt Damon Is Right about Sexual Misconduct," *Boston Globe*, December 19. 2017, www.bostonglobe.com/opinion/2017/12/19 /matt-damon-right-about-sexual-misconduct/tQeemaoxJXV2283pg3TPMK /story.html.

22. John Stuart Mill, *On Liberty*, Michael B. Mathias and Daniel Kolak, eds. (New York: Longman, 2006), 35.

23. For a nuanced discussion of partisan stereotyping, see Katherine J. Cramer, *The Politics of Resentment* (Chicago: University of Chicago Press, 2016).

24. Alan I. Abramowitz and Steven Webster, "The Rise of Negative Partisanship and the Nationalization of U.S. Elections in the 21st Century," *Electoral Studies* 41 (2016): 16, 21.

25. Abramowitz and Webster, "Rise of Negative Partisanship," 18.

26. "Partisanship and Political Animosity in 2016."

27. "Partisanship and Political Animosity in 2016."

28. Sean J. Westwood, Shanto Iyengar, Stefaan Walgrave, Rafael Leonisio, Luis Miller, and Oliver Strubis, "The Tie That Divides: Cross-National Evidence of the Primacy of Partyism," *European Journal of Political Research* 57 (2018): 333–54, https://onlinelibrary.wiley.com/doi/full/10.1111/1475-6765 .12228.

29. Sarah Pulliam Bailey, "The Trump Effect? A Stunning Number of Evangelicals Will Now Accept Politicians' 'Immoral' Acts," *Washington Post*, October 19, 2016, www.washingtonpost.com/news/acts-of-faith/wp/2016/10/19/the-trump-effect -evangelicals-have-become-much-more-accepting-of-politicians-immoral -acts/?utm_term=.3953cffe4fdc; presidential election exit polls, 2000–2016.

30. Iyengar and Westwood, "Fear and Loathing," 690–707.

31. Compiled by author from UCLA's television archive database, February 2017.

32. Gregory Holyk, "Majority Disapprove of Decision Not to Charge Clinton on Emails," *ABC News*, July, 2016, http://abcnews.go.com/Politics/majority-disapproves -decision-charge-clinton-emails-poll/story?id=40445344.

33. Rich Noyes, "Study: TV News Is Obsessed with Trump-Russia Probe," *MRC*, June 27, 2017, www.newsbusters.org/blogs/nb/rich-noyes/2017/06/27study-tv -news-obsessed-trump-russia-probe.

34. "Trump Rating Holds Steady Despite Campaign's 2016 Russia Meeting," *Monmouth University Polling Institute*, July 2017, www.monmouth.edu/polling -institute/reports/MonmouthPoll_NJ_071717.

35. "Partisanship and Political Animosity in 2016."

36. David Ropeik, "How Tribalism Overrules Reason, and Makes Risky Times More Dangerous," *Big Think*, undated, http://bigthink.com/risk-reason-and-reality /how-tribalism-overrules-reason-and-makes-risky-times-more-dangerous.

37. Observation made by Jane Mansbridge at a Harvard Kennedy School conference in 2017.

38. Cary Funk and Brian Kennedy, "The Politics of Climate," *Pew Research Center*, October 4. 2016, www.pewinternet.org/2016/10/04/the-politics-of -climate.

39. Cass R. Sunstein and Richard H. Thaler, *Nudge* (London: Penguin, 2008); Milton Lodge and Charles Taber, *Three Steps toward a Theory of Motivated Political Reasoning* (New York: Cambridge University Press, 2000).

40. Nyhan and Reifler, "When Corrections Fail"; see also Dennis Chong and James N. Druckman, "Framing Public Opinion in Competitive Democracies," *American Political Science Review* 101 (2007): 641.

41. On the issue of avoidance, see John Henderson and Alexander Theodoridis, "Seeing Spots: An Experimental Examination of Voter Appetite for Partisan and Negative Campaign Ads," *SSRN,* July 2015.

42. Norbert Schwarz, "Metacognitive Experiences in Consumer Judgment and Decision Making," *Journal of Consumer Psychology* 14 (2004): 332–48, cited in Adam J. Berinsky, "Rumors and Health Care Reform: Experiments in Political Information," *British Journal of Political Science* 47 (2017): 241–62.

43. Shanto Iyengar and Kyu S. Hahn, "Red Media, Blue Media: Evidence of Ideological Selectivity in Media Use," *Journal of Communication* 59 (2009): 19–39; Natalie Jomini Stroud, "Media Use and Political Predispositions," *Political Behavior* 30 (2008): 341–66.

44. A classic study of selection perception is Albert H. Hastorf and Hadley Cantril, "They Saw a Game: A Case Study," *Journal of Abnormal and Social Psychology* 49 (1954): 129–34.

45. Leon Festinger, Henry W. Rieckman, and Stanley Shachter, *When Prophecy Fails* (New York: Harper Torchbooks, 1964), 31.

46. See Sidney Kraus, *Televised Presidential Debates and Public Policy* (New York: Routledge, 2000).

47. Gary Langer, "Clinton Trounces Trump in Debate Reactions; Trump's Unfavorability Edges Up," *ABC News,* October 2, 2016, http://abcnews.go.com /Politics/clinton-whomps-debate-reactions-trumps-unfavorability-edges-poll /story?id=42498052.

48. The study was conducted at Ohio State University, cited in Nichols, *Death of Expertise*, 69.

49. Thompson, *Enough Said*, 22.

50. "Trump Remains Unpopular," 10.

51. Ezra Klein, "4 Political Scientists Are Tracking Whether Trump Is Damaging American Democracy," *Vox,* October 5, 2017, www.vox.com/policy-and-politics /2017/10/5/16414338/trump-democracy-authoritarianism.

52. Rebecca Savransky, "Poll: Most Americans Think Russia Using Social Platforms for Targeted Ads Is 'Serious Issue,'" *The Hill,* October 30, 2017, http://thehill. com/policy/technology/357800-poll-majority-thinks-russia-using-social -platforms-for-targeted-ads-is.

53. Kevin P. Phillips, *The Emerging Republican Majority* (New Rochelle, NY: Arlington House, 1969); Joshua Green, "Birth of the Southern Strategy," *Bloomberg Businessweek,* December 4, 2014, www.bloomberg.com/news/articles/2014-12-04 /birth-of-the-southern-strategy.

54. Richard M. Scammon and Ben J. Wattenberg, *The Real Majority* (New York: Coward-McCann, 1970).

55. Poole and Rosenthal, *Ideology and Congress.*

56. Achen and Bartels, *Democracy for Realists.*

57. "Trends in Political Values and Core Attitudes: 1987–2007," *Pew Research Center,* March 22, 2007, www.people-press.org/2007/03/22/trends-in-political-values -and-core-attitudes-1987–2007.

58. Jocelyn Kiley, "In Polarized Era, Fewer Americans Hold a Mix of Conservative and Liberal Views," *Pew Research Center,* October 27, 2017, www.pewresearch.org/fact -tank/2017/10/23/in-polarized-era-fewer-americans-hold-a-mix-of-conservative-and -liberal-views/?utm_source=Pew+Research+Center&utm_campaign =0abc6f17c9 -EMAIL_CAMPAIGN_2017_10_26&utm_medium=email&utm_term=0 _3e953b9b70–0abc6f17c9–400267813.

59. Clinton Rossiter, *Parties and Politics in America* (Ithaca, NY: Cornell University Press, 1960), 11.

60. Andrew Sullivan, "America Wasn't Built for Humans," *New York Magazine,* September 19, 2017, http://nymag.com/daily/intelligencer/2017/09/can-democracy -survive-tribalism.html.

61. American National Election Studies (ANES) surveys, 1964–2016.

62. William B. Prendergast, *The Catholic Voter in American Politics* (Washington, DC: Georgetown University Press, 1999).

63. "Ku Klux Klan," *History,* undated, downloaded January 2, 2018, www.history .com/*topics*/ku-klux-klan.

64. Robert Putnam and David Campbell, *American Grace: How Religion Divides and Unites Us* (New York: Simon and Schuster, 2012).

65. 2000–2016 presidential election exit polls.

66. Edward Thorndike, "A Constant Error in Psychological Ratings," *Journal of Applied Psychology* 4, no. 1 (1920): 25–29.

67. For immigrants, see "Partisanship and Political Animosity in 2016." For feminists and gays and lesbians, see Marc Hetherington and Thomas Rudolph, "Why Don't Americans Trust the Government? Because the Other Party Is in Power," *Washington Post,* January 30, 2014, www.washingtonpost.com/news/monkey -cage/wp/2014/01/30/why-dont-americans-trust-the-government-because-the -other-party-is-in-power/?utm_term=.12789c32ff31. For Muslims, see John Sides, "Race, Religion, and Immigration in 2016: How the Debate over American Identity Shaped the Election and What It Means for a Trump Presidency," *Democracy Fund Voter Study Group,* June 2017, www.voterstudygroup.org/reports/2016-elections /race-religion-immigration-2016.

68. Paul Taylor, "The Demographic Trends Shaping American Politics in 2016 and Beyond," *Pew Research Center,* January 27, 2016, www.pewresearch.org/fact -tank/2016/01/27/the-demographic-trends-shaping-american-politics-in -2016-and-beyond.

69. Amy Chua, *Political Tribes: Group Instincts and the Fate of Nations* (New York: Penguin Press, 2018), 166.

70. Tom Jensen, "Democrats and Republicans Differ on Conspiracy Theory Beliefs," *Public Policy Polling*, April 2, 2013, www.publicpolicypolling.com /polls/democrats-and-republicans-differ-on-conspiracy-theory-beliefs.

71. "Public Expresses Mixed Views of Islam, Mormonism," *Pew Research Center*, September 25, 2007, www.people-press.org/2007/09/25/public-expresses-mixed -views-of-islam-mormonism/2/#more-familiar-more-positive.

72. Richard V. Reeves, *Dream Hoarders* (Washington, DC: Brookings Institute Press, 2017).

73. See Elena Portacolone and Jodi Halpern, "Move or Suffer: Is Age-Segregation the New Norm for Older Americans Living Alone?" *Journal of Applied Gerontology* 35 (2014): 1–21, www.researchgate.net/publication/265342155_Move_or_Suffer_Is_Age -Segregation_the_New_Norm_for_Older_Americans_Living_Alone.

74. Charles J. Sykes, *How the Right Lost Its Mind* (New York: St. Martin's Press, 2017), 14.

75. See, for example, Cramer, *Politics of Resentment*.

76. Speech of Nancy Gibbs, Harvard Kennedy School, November 15, 2017; Jasmine C. Lee and Kevin Quealy, "The 425 People, Places and Things Donald Trump Has Insulted on Twitter: A Complete List," *New York Times*, January 3, 2018, www .nytimes.com/interactive/2016/01/28/upshot/donald-trump-twitter-insults.html.

77. Quoted in Steven Levitsky and Daniel Ziblatt, *How Democracies Die* (New York: Crown, 2018), 147.

78. Michael Oreskes, "Political Memo; for G.O.P. Arsenal, 133 Words to Fire," *New York Times*, September 9, 1990.

79. Quoted in Nancy Gibbs and Michael Duffy, "The Fall of the House of Newt," *Time*, November 16, 1998, 47.

80. Andy Barr, "The GOP's No-Compromise Pledge," *Politico*, October 28, 2010, www.politico.com/story/2010/10/the-gops-no-compromise-pledge-044311.

81. Op-ed was carried on *NBC News* online on October 10, 2017, www .nbcnews.com/think/politics/democrats-must-forget-about-trump-join-gop-tax -reform-ncna808976.

82. "Former US Attorney: FBI Officials Will Likely Face Charges," *Fox News*, February 7, 2018, www.foxnews.com/transcript/former-us-attorney-fbi-officials-will -likely-face-charges.

83. Sarah Sobieraj and Jeffrey M. Berry, "From Incivility to Outrage: Political Discourse in Blogs, Talk Radio, and Cable News," *Political Communication* 28 (2011): 19–41; quotes, 29–30, with some examples inserted by author.

84. Quoted in speech by Nancy Gibbs, Harvard Kennedy School, November 15, 2017.

85. Kathleen Hall Jamieson and Joseph N. Cappella, *Echo Chamber* (New York: Oxford University Press, 2010), 195–98; Sobieraj and Berry, "From Incivility to Outrage."

86. William P. Eveland Jr. and Ivan Dylko, "Reading Political Blogs in the 2004 Election Campaign," in Mark Tremayne, *Blogging, Citizenship, and the Future of Media* (New York: Routledge, 2006), 108; see also Thomas J. Johnson and Barbara K. Kaye, "Wag the Blog," *Journalism and Mass Communication Quarterly* 81 (2004): 622–42.

87. Eytan Bakshy, Solomon Messing, and Lada A. Adamic, "Exposure to Ideologically Diverse News and Opinion on Facebook," *Science* 348 (2015): 1130–32; R. Kelly Barrett, "Echo Chambers Online? Politically Motivated Selective Exposure among Internet News Users," *Journal of Computer-Mediated Communication* 14 (2009): 266–85; Seth Stevens-Davidowitz, *Everybody Lies: Big Data, New Data, and What the Internet Can Tell Us about Who We Really Are* (New York: Dey St., 2017), 142–43.

88. Hindman, *Myth of Digital Democracy*, 138.

89. Eszter Hargittai, Jason Gallo, and Matthew Kane, "Cross-Discussions among Conservative and Liberal Bloggers," *Public Choice* 134 (2008): 67–86.

90. Matthew A. Baum and Tim Groeling, "New Media and the Polarization of American Political Discourse," *Political Communication* 25 (2008): 360; Natalie J. Stroud, "Media Use and Political Predispositions," *Political Behavior* 30 (2008): 341–66.

91. "The Post-truth World: Yes, I'd Lie to You," *Economist*, September 10, 2017, www.economist.com/news/briefing/21706498-dishonesty-politics-nothing -new-manner-which-some-politicians-now-lie-and.

92. Yochai Benchler, *Wealth of Nations* (New Haven, CT: Yale University Press, 2006); Pablo Barbara, John T. Jost, Jaonathan Nagler, Joshua A. Tucker, and Richard Bonneau, "Tweeting from Left to Right: Is Online Political Communication More Than an Echo Chamber?" *Psychological Science* 26 (2015): 1531–42, http://journals .sagepub.com/doi/abs/10.1177/0956797615 594620.

93. Joshua Gillin, "Mike Pence Did Not Say Women Would Seek Out Sexual Assault to Have Abortions," *PolitiFact*, February 2, 2017, www.politifact.com /punditfact/statements/2017/feb/02/blog-posting/mike-pence-did-not-say-women -would-seek-out-sexual.

94. Stevens-Davidowitz, *Everybody Lies*, 7–9.

95. Carmen Stavrositu, "Selective Exposure," in Kerric Harvey, ed., *Encyclopedia of Social Media and Politics* (Thousand Oaks, CA: Sage, 2014): 1117–19; Amy Mitchell, Jeffrey Gottfried, Jocelyn Kiley, and Katerina Eva Matsa, "Political Polarization and Media Habits," *Pew Research Center*, October 21, 2014, www.journalism.org/2014/10/21 /political-polarization-media-habits.

96. Michael J. Robinson, "Public Affairs Television and the Growth of Political Malaise," *American Political Science Review* 70 (1973): 409–32; Martin J. Wattenberg, *Is Voting for Young People?* (New York: Pearson Longman, 2008), 32.

97. Filipe R. Campante and Daniel A. Hojman, "Media and Polarization," *Journal of Public Economics* 100 (2013): 79–92, https://ideas.repec.org/a/eee/pubeco /v100y2013icp79-92.html.

98. Quoted in Barbara Gamarekian, "In Pursuit of the Clever Quotemaster," *New York Times,* May 12, 1989, Y10.

99. Larry J. Sabato, *Feeding Frenzy* (New York: Free Press, 1991).

100. Jonathan S. Morris and Rosalee A. Clawson, "Media Coverage of Congress in the 1990s: Scandal, Personalities, and the Prevalence of Policy and Process," *Political Communication* 22 (2005): 297–313.

101. Kathleen Hall Jamieson and Karlyn Kohrs Campbell, *The Interplay of Influence,* 5th ed. (Belmont, CA: Wadsworth, 2001), 42.

102. Eric Montpetit, *In Defense of Pluralism* (Cambridge: Cambridge University Press, 2016).

103. Center for Media and Public Affairs, *Campaign '96: The Media and the Candidates,* Final Report to the Markle Foundation, 1998. See also Erik P. Bucy and Maria Elizabeth Grabe, "Taking Television Seriously: A Sound and Image Bite Analysis of Presidential Campaign Coverage, 1992–2004," *Journal of Communication* 57 (2007): 652–75; and Bruce Buchanan, *Renewing Presidential Politics* (Lanham, MD: Rowman and Littlefield, 1996), 149.

104. Tim Groeling and Matthew A. Baum, "Journalists' Incentives and Media Coverage of Elite Foreign Policy Evaluations," *Conflict Management and Peace Science* 26 (2009): 437–70.

105. David Van Reybrouck, "Why Elections Are Bad for Democracy," *Guardian,* June 29, 2016, www.theguardian.com/politics/2016/jun/29why-elections-are -bad-for-democracy.

106. See, for example, Leonhardt and Thompson, "Trump's Lies."

107. Laurel Harbridge, "Congress Is More Bipartisan Than You Think," *Washington Post,* May 4, 2015, www.washingtonpost.com/news/monkey-cage/wp/2015/05/04 /congress-is-more-bipartisan-than-you-think/?utm_term=c499a6e23413.

108. Mary Layton Atkinson, *Combative Politics: The Media and Public Perceptions of Lawmaking* (Chicago: University of Chicago Press, 2017), 148, 30.

109. Amy Mitchell, Jeffrey Gottfried, Michael Barthel, and Elisa Shearer, "Party ID and News," *Pew Research Center,* July 7, 2016, www.journalism.org/2016/07/07 /party-id-and-news.

110. Lynn Schofield Clark and Regina Marchi, *Young People and the Future of News* (New York: Cambridge University Press, 2017), 185.

111. Meighan Stone, "Snake and Stranger: Media Coverage of Muslims and Refugee Policy," Shorenstein Center on Media, Politics and Public Policy," Harvard Kennedy School, Harvard University, Cambridge, MA, June 2017, https://shorensteincenter .org/wp-content/uploads/2017/06/Media-Coverage-Muslims-Meighan-Stone.pdf.

112. See, for example, Robert Entman and Andrew Rojecki, *The Black Image in the White Mind: Media and Race in America* (Chicago: University of Chicago Press, 2000).

113. Nuala Gathercole Lam, "Titanic's Chinese Survivors Resurface from Depths of History," *Sixth Tone,* August 23, 2017, www.sixthtone.com/news/1000733 /titanics-chinese-survivors-resurface-from-depths-of-history.

114. Sullivan, "America Wasn't Built for Humans."

115. Achen and Bartels, *Democracy for Realists.*

116. Shanto Iyengar and Masha Krupenkin, "The Strengthening of Partisan Affect," *Political Psychology* 39 (2018): 201–18; Sykes, *How the Right Lost Its Mind,* 180.

117. Sullivan, "America Wasn't Built for Humans."

118. Robert M. Entman, "Framing: Toward Clarification of a Fractured Paradigm," *Journal of Communication* 43 (1993): 51–58; Lynn Vavreck, *The Message Matters* (Princeton, NJ: Princeton University Press, 2009).

119. Francis Fukiyama, *The End of History and the Last Man* (New York: Free Press, 2006).

120. Taylor, "Demographic Trends Shaping American Politics."

121. Sullivan, "America Wasn't Built for Humans."

CHAPTER 3

1. The discussion of Drobota is drawn from Tess Townsend, "The Bizarre Truth behind the Biggest Pro-Trump Facebook Hoaxes," *Inc,* undated, www.inc.com/tess -townsend/ending-fed-trump-facebook.html.

2. Alexander Smith and Vladimir Banic, "Fake News: How a Partying Macedonian Teen Earns Thousands Publishing Lies," *NBCNews.com,* December 9, 2016, www.nbcnews.com/news/world/fake-news-how-partying-macedonian-teen-earns -thousands-publishing-lies-n692451.

3. *BuzzFeed News* analysis.

4. Hannah Roberts, "This Is What Fake News Actually Looks Like—We Ranked 11 Election Stories That Went Viral on Facebook," *Business Insider,* November 17, 2016, www.businessinsider.com/fake-presidential-election-news-viral-facebook -trump-clinton-2016–11.

5. Max Fisher, "Russia and the U.S. Election: What We Know and Don't Know," December 12, 2016, www.nytimes.com/2016/12/12/world/europe/russia-trump -election-cia-fbi.html; see also Micah L. Sifry, *WikiLeaks and the Age of Transparency* (New York: Counterpoint Press, 2011).

6. David Easton, "A Re-assessment of the Concept of Political Support," *British Journal of Political Science* 5 (1975): 447; Arthur H. Miller and Ola Listhaug, "Political Parties and Confidence in Government: A Comparison of Norway, Sweden and the United States," *ResearchGate,* July 1990, www.researchgate.netpublication/30012133.

7. Marc J. Hetherington, "The Political Relevance of Political Trust," *American Political Science Review* 92 (1998): 803.

8. Kai Ryssdal, "Poll Finds Americans' Economic Anxiety Reaches New High," *Marketplace,* October 13, 2016, www.marketplace.org/2016/10/13/economy/americans -economic-anxiety-has-reached-new-high.

9. "Beyond Distrust," *Pew Research Center,* November 23, 2015, www.people-press .org/2015/11/23/beyond-distrust-how-americans-view-their-government.

10. "Beyond Distrust."

11. Courtenay Smith, "Reader's Digest Trust Poll: The 100 Most Trusted People in America," *Reader's Digest,* undated, www.rd.com/culturereaders-digest-trust -poll-the-100-most-trusted-people-in-america.

12. Poll figures are from James Davison Hunter and Carl Desportes Bowman, "The Vanishing Center of American Democracy: The 2016 Survey of Political Culture," Institute for Advanced Studies in Culture, University of Virginia, 2016.

13. "Beyond Distrust."

14. "Beyond Distrust."

15. Hunter and Bowman, "Vanishing Center," 22.

16. "Beyond Distrust."

17. "Beyond Distrust."

18. Hunter and Bowman, "Vanishing Center," 23.

19. "Beyond Distrust."

20. "Right Direction, Wrong Track," *Rasmussen Reports,* August 7, 2017.

21. Colin Crouch, *Post-Democracy* (New York: Polity, 2004).

22. Yascha Mounk, "Yes, People Really Are Turning Away from Democracy," *Washington Post,* December 8, 2016, www.washingtonpost.com/news/wonk /wp/2016/12/08/yes-millennials-really-are-surprisingly-approving-of-dictators /?utm_term=.3e7c0f7fc8f7.

23. Hunter and Bowman, "Vanishing Center," 28.

24. Illing, "20 of America's Top Political Scientists."

25. Zach Beauchamp, "45 Percent of Republicans Want the Government to Shutter 'Biased or Inaccurate' Media," *Vox,* July 27, 2017, www.vox.com/world/2017/7/27 /16036054/poll-republicans-press-freedom-trump.

26. Cited in Ralph Volney Harlow, *The Growth of the United States,* vol. 2 (New York: Holt, 1943), 134.

27. William H. Branson, "Trends in United States International Trade and Investment since World War II," in Martin Feldstein, ed., *The American Economy in Transition* (Chicago: University of Chicago Press, 1980), 183.

28. Katie Sanders, "Rattner: Manufacturing Wages Today in America Lower Than Average Wages in the Economy as a Whole," *Punditfact,* March 30, 2014, www .politifact.com/punditfact/statements/2014/mar/30/steven-rattner/rattner -manufacturing-wages-today-america-lower-av.

29. Lawrence Mischel, "Causes of Wage Stagnation," *Economic Policy Institute,* January 6, 2015, www.epi.org/publication/causes-of-wage-stagnation.

30. "American Middle Class Is Losing Ground." Middle class is defined as people earning from two-thirds to two times the average income.

31. John Sides, "What Will Make People Trust Goverment Again?" *Monkey Cage,* February 14, 2010, http://themonkeycage.org/2010/02what_will_make_people _love_gov.

32. Illing, "20 of America's Top Political Scientists."

33. Hunter and Bowman, "Vanishing Center," 46, 22.

34. "Beyond Distrust."

35. "Beyond Distrust."

36. Jens Borchert and Jurgen Zeiss, *The Political Class in Advanced Democracies* (New York: Oxford University Press, 2004).

37. Martin Gilens and Benjamin I. Page, "Testing Theories of American Politics: Elites, Interest Groups, and Average Citizens," *Perspectives on Politics* 12 (2104): 564–81, http://citeseerx.ist.psu.edu/viewdoc/download;jsessionid=37EDA24D1D5 DA87AEB950CEFE63883FF?doi=10.1.1.668.8647&rep=rep1&type=pdf.

38. "Beyond Distrust."

39. Ronald J. Inglehart, "How Much Should We Worry?" *Journal of Democracy,* 27 (2016): 18, http://pscourses.ucsd.edu/ps200b/Inglehart%20How%20Much%20 SHould%20we%20Worry.pdf.

40. Arthur M. Schlesinger Jr., *The Vital Center* (New Brunswick, NJ: Transaction, 1998 [1949]), 42.

41. Marc J. Hetherington, *Why Trust Matters: Declining Political Trust and the Demise of American Liberalism* (Princeton, NJ: Princeton University Press, 2005).

42. Patrick Fagan and Robert Rector, "The Continuing Good News about Welfare Reform," *Heritage Foundation*, February 6, 2003, www.heritage.org/welfare/report /the-continuing-good-news-about-welfare-reform.

43. "We've Come to Take Our Government Back," *CNN,* May 18, 2010, http:// politicalticker.blogs.cnn.com/2010/05/18paul-weve-come-to-take-our -government-back.

44. "Beyond Distrust."

45. Tom Keane, "Jeb Bush's Politics of Joy," *Boston Globe,* December 30, 2014, www.bostonglobe.com/opinion/2014/12/29/jeb-bush-politics-joy/mqVQUwAizoW- gXGaBAB2QFM/story.html.

46. Quoted in Renee Jeffrey, "Beyond Banality? Ethical Responses to Evil in Post-September 11 International Relations," *International Affairs* 81 (2005): 175–86, www.jstor.org/stable/3569194?seq=1#page_scan_tab_contents.

47. Entman, "Framing"; Vavreck, *Message Matters.*

48. Robert M. Entman, "Framing and Party Competition: How Democrats Enabled the GOP's Move to the Uncompromising Right," *Issues in Governance Studies* 70 (2015), www.brookings.edu/wp-content/uploads/2016/07/party_competition.pdf.

49. Entman, "Framing and Party Competition."

50. Arlie Russell Hochschild, *Strangers in Their Own Land* (New York: New Press, 2016).

51. Robert P. Jones, Daniel Cox, E. J. Dionne Jr., William A. Galston, Betsy Cooper, and Rachel Lienesch, "How Immigration and Concerns about Cultural Changes Are Shaping the 2016 Elections: Findings from the 2016 PRRI/Brookings Immigration Survey," *PRRI,* June 23, 2016, www.prri.org/wp-content/uploads /2016/06/PRRI-Brookings-2016-Immigration-survey-report.pdf.

52. Hunter and Bowman, "Vanishing Center," 22; "Beyond Distrust."

53. Thomas B. Edsall, "The Democratic Party Is in Worse Shape Than You Thought," *New York Times,* June 8, 2017, www.nytimes.com/2017/06/08/opinion /the-democratic-party-is-in-worse-shape-than-you-thought.html.

54. Cliff Young and Chris Jackson, "The Rise of Neo-nativism," *ISPOS, Ideas Spotlight,* October 9, 2015, http://spotlight.ipsos-na.com/index.php/news /the-rise-of-neo-nativism-putting-trump-into-proper-context.

55. Thomas F. Pettigrew, "Social Psychological Perspectives on Trump Support-ers," *Journal of Social and Political Psychology* 5 (2017), https://jspp.psychopen.eu /article/view/750/html.

56. Sykes, *How the Right Lost Its Mind*, 189–90.

57. Nancy Benac, "Remember Nixon: There's History behind Trump's Attacks on the Press," *Associated Press,* February 17, 2017, https://apnews.com/8b29195631f 44033ad94d8b2b74048c0/remember-nixon-theres-history-behind-trumps-press -attacks. The quote was originally reported by the *Washington Post's* Bob Woodward and Carl Bernstein.

58. David D'Alessio and Mike Allen, "Media Bias in Presidential Elections: A Meta-analysis," *Journal of Communication* 50 (2000): 133–56.

59. Matthew Gentzkow and Jesse M. Shapiro, "What Drives Media Slant? Evi-dence from U.S. Daily Newspapers," *Econometrica* 78 (2010): 35–71, https://web .stanford.edu/~gentzkow/research/biasmeas.pdf.

60. Thomas E. Patterson, "News Coverage of Donald Trump's First 100 Days," Shorenstein Center on Media, Politics and Public Policy," Harvard Kennedy School, Harvard University, Cambridge, MA, May 18, 2017, https://shorensteincenter.org /news-coverage-donald-trumps-first-100-days; Thomas E. Patterson, "News Cover-age of the 2016 Presidential Primaries: Horse Race Reporting Has Consequences," Shorenstein Center on Media, Politics and Public Policy," Harvard Kennedy School, Harvard University, Cambridge, MA, July 11, 2016, https://shorensteincenter.org /news-coverage-2016-presidential-primaries; Thomas E. Patterson, "News Coverage of the 2016 General Election: How the Press Failed the Voters," Shorenstein Center on Media, Politics and Public Policy," Harvard Kennedy School, Harvard University, Cambridge, MA, December 7, 2016, https://shorensteincenter.org/news-coverage -2016-general-election.

61. Rob Faris, Hal Roberts, Bruce Etling, Nikki Bourassa, Ethan Zuckerman, and Yochai Benkler, "Partisanship, Propaganda, and Disinformation: Online Media and the 2016 U.S. Presidential Election," Berkman Klein Center for Internet and Society, Harvard University, August 16, 2017, https://cyber.harvard.edu/publications /2017/08/mediacloud.

62. Jonathan M. Ladd, *Why Americans Hate the Media and How It Matters* (Princeton, NJ: Princeton University Press, 2012).

63. Art Swift, "Americans' Trust in Mass Media Sinks to New Low," *Gallup News,* September 14, 2016, http://news.gallup.com/poll/195542/americans-trust-mass -media-sinks-new-low.aspx.

64. Steven Shepard, "Poll: 46 Percent Think Media Make Up Stories about Trump," *Politico*, October 18, 2017, www.politico.com/story/2017/10/18/trump-media-fake-news-poll-243884.

65. Gina Martinez, "Half of Republicans Believe the Media Is the Enemy of the People: Poll," *Time*, August 14, 2018, http://time.com/5367145/republicans-media-enemy-of-the-people-poll.

66. Ladd, *Why Americans Hate the Media*, 199.

67. Andrew Prokopandrew, "Marco Rubio vs. Ted Cruz: The Increasingly Popular Prediction about the GOP Race's Future," *Vox*, October 29, 2015, www.vox.com/2015/10/28/9633422/republican-debate-winners-cruz-rubio.

68. Thomas E. Patterson, *Out of Order* (New York: Knopf, 1993), 23.

69. Matthew A. Baum and Tim J. Groeling, *War Stories: The Causes and Consequences of Public Views of War* (Princeton, NJ: Princeton University Press, 2010).

70. Tim Groeling, *When Politicians Attack* (New York: Cambridge University Press, 2010), 9.

71. Dylan Byers, "Media Doesn't Hold Back on Obama," *Politico*, September 16, 2013, www.politico.com/story/2013/09obama-holds-fire-but-media-doesnt-096839.

72. Quoted in Thomas E. Patterson, "More Style Than Substance: Television News in U.S. National Elections," *Political Communication and Persuasion* 8 (1991): 157.

73. Joseph N. Cappella and Kathleen Hall Jamieson, *Spiral of Cynicism* (New York: Oxford University Press, 1997), 159.

74. Andrew Malcolm, "Poll Finds Americans Are Disgusted with Political Media," *Investor's Business Daily*, August 9, 2012, http://news.investors.com/politics-andrew-malcolm/080912–621566-daily-kos-poll-finds-americans-think-very-little-of-media-covering-politics.htm?p=full.

75. Sentence is modeled after a quote in David Shaw, "Beyond Skepticism: Have the Media Crossed the Line into Cynicism," *Los Angeles Times*, April 17, 1996, A1.

76. Eric Alterman, *What Liberal Media?* (New York: Basic Books, 2003).

77. See Jeffrey Katz, "Tilt?" *Washington Journalism Review*, January–February, 1993, 25.

78. See, for example, Robinson, "Public Affairs Television"; Cappella and Jamieson, *Spiral of Cynicism*; Arthur H. Miller, Edie N. Goldenberg, and Lutz Erbring, "Type-Set Politics: Impact of Newspapers on Public Confidence," *American Political Science Review* 73 (1979): 67–84; Matthew R. Kerbel, *Remote and Controlled: Media Politics in a Cynical Age*, 2nd ed. (Boulder, CO: Westview Press, 1999), 85; Kiku Adatto, "Sound Bite Democracy: Network Evening News Presidential Campaign Coverage, 1968 and 1988," Joan Shorenstein Center on the Press, Politics and Public Policy, Research Paper R-2, John F. Kennedy School of Government, Harvard University, Cambridge, MA, June 1990, 74; and Claes H. de Vreese and Matthijs Elenbaas, "Media in the Game of Politics: Effects of Strategic Metacoverage on Political Cynicism," *International Journal of Press/Politics* 13 (2008): 286.

79. John C. Merrill, Peter J. Gade, and Frederick R. Blevens, *Twilight of Press Freedom* (Malwah, NJ: Lawrence Erlbaum, 2001), 139.

80. "Top Talk Audiences," *Talkers.com*, www.talkers.com/top-talk-audiences.

81. Richard Meagher, "The 'Vast Right-Wing Conspiracy': Media and Conservative Networks," *New Political Science* 34 (2012): 469–84; Riley Dunlap and Peter Jacques, "Climate Change Denial Books and Conservative Think Tanks," *American Behavioral Science* 57 (2013): 699–731, www.ncbi.nlm.nih.gov/pmc/articles/PMC3787818.

82. W. Lance Bennett and Steven Livingston, "The Disinformation Order: Disruptive Communication and the Decline of Democratic Institutions," *European Journal of Communication* 33 (2018): 122–39, https://journals.sagepub.com/doiabs/10.1177/0267323118760317.

83. Hemmer, *Messengers on the Right*, 93.

84. Sykes, *How the Right Lost Its Mind*, 84.

85. Jackie Calmes, "They Don't Give a Damn about Governing: Conservative Media's Influence on the Republican Party," Shorenstein Center of Media, Politics and Public Policy, Harvard Kennedy School, July 27, 2015, https://shorensteincenter.org/conservative-media-influence-on-republican-party-jackie-calmes.

86. Andrew Desiderio, "Bannon to Senate GOP: I'm Gonna Mow You All Down, Save Ted Cruz," *Daily Beast*, October 9, 2017, www.thedailybeast.combannon-to-senate-gop-im-gonna-mow-you-all-down-save-ted-cruz.

87. Hemmer, *Messengers on the Right*, 267.

88. Richard Forgette and Jonathan Morris, "High-Conflict Television News and Public Opinion," *Political Research Quarterly* 59 (2006): 448.

89. See Jamieson and Cappella, *Echo Chamber*.

90. Diana Mutz, *In-Your-Face Politics* (Princeton, NJ: Princeton University Press, 2015), 89; Diana C. Mutz and Byron Reeves, "The New Videomalaise: Effects of Televised Incivility on Political Trust," *ScholarlyCommons*, Annenberg School for Communication, University of Pennsylvania, February 2005, https://repository.upenn.edu/cgi/viewcontent.cgi?article=1123&context=asc_papers.

91. David Niven, S. Robert Lichter, and David Amundson, "The Political Content of Late Night Comedy," *Harvard International Journal of Press/Politics* 8 (2003): 118–33; Geoffrey Baym, "The Daily Show: Discursive Integration and the Reinvention of Political Journalism," *Political Communication* 22 (2005): 259; Paul R. Brewer and Emily Marquardt, "Mock News and Democracy: Analyzing the Daily Show," *Atlantic Journal of Communication* 15 (2007): 249–67; Lauren Guggenheim, Nojin Kwak, and Scott W. Campbell, "Nontraditional News Negativity: The Relationship of Entertaining Political News Use to Political Cynicism and Mistrust," *International Journal of Public Opinion Research* 23 (2011): 287–314.

92. Jody Baumgartner and Jonathan S. Morris, "The Daily Show Effect: Candidate Evaluations, Efficacy, and American Youth," *American Politics Research* 34 (2006): 341–67; Yariv Tsfati, Riva Tukachinsky, and Yoram Peri, "Exposure to News, Political

Comedy, and Entertainment Talk Shows: Concern about Security and Political Mistrust," *International Journal of Public Opinion Research* 21 (2009): 399–423.

93. Guggenheim, Kwak, and Campbell, "Nontraditional News Negativity," 308.

94. See Jill Dougherty, "The Reality behind Russia's Fake News," *CNN*, December 2, 2016; Kathryn Watson, "Russian Bots Still Interfering in U.S. Politics after Election, Says Expert Witness," *CBS News,* March 30, 2017.

95. Marissa Lang, "Number of Americans Exposed to Russian Propaganda Rises, as Tech Giants Testify," *San Francisco Chronicle,* November 1, 2017, www.sfchronicle .com/business/article/Facebook-Google-Twitter-say-150-million-12323900.php; speech of Nancy Gibbs, Harvard Kennedy School, November 15, 2017.

96. Devin Coldewey, "Facebook's Generation of 'Jew Hater' and Other Advertising Categories Prompts System Inspection," *Tech Crunch,* September 14, 2017, https:// techcrunch.com/2017/09/14facebooks-generation-of-jew-hater-and-other -advertising-categories-prompts-system-inspection.

97. Bennett and Livingston, "Disinformation Order."

98. Donna Brazile, *Hacks: The Inside Story of the Break-Ins and Breakdowns That Put Donald Trump in the White House* (Boston: Hatchette Books, 2017).

99. Comment to author by Kathleen Hall Jamieson, October 2017.

100. Tim Lister, Jim Sciutto, and Mary Ilyushina, "Putin's 'Chef,' the Man behind the Troll Factory," *CNN*, October 17, 2017, www.cnn.com/2017/10/17/politics/russian -oligarch-putin-chef-troll-factory/index.html.

101. Greg Fish, "Putin's Professional Trolls Catfished and Paid Pro-Trump Activists in the US," *Politech,* October 17, 2017, https://rantt.computins-professional -trolls-catfished-and-paid-pro-trump-activists-in-the-us-b360e0b86424.

102. Sheera Frenkel and Daisuke Wakabayashi, "Shots Are Fired, and Bots Swarm to Social Divides," *New York Times,* February 20, 2018, A13.

103. See, for example, Diana Mutz, "Mass Media and the Depoliticization of Personal Experiences," *American Journal of Political Science* 36 (1992): 483–508.

104. "Pessimistic Public Doubts Effectiveness of Stimulus, TARP," *Pew Research Center,* April 28, 2010, www.people-press.org/2010/04/28pessimistic-public-doubts -effectiveness-of-stimulus-tarp.

105. Jon Greenberg, "Seth Rich: Separating Fact and Speculation," *Politifact,* August 7, 2017, www.politifact.com/truth-o-meter/article/2017/aug/07/seth-rich -separating-fact-and-speculation.

106. Quoted in Kurt Andersen, *Fantasyland: How America Went Haywire* (New York: Random House, 2017), 426; see also Anderson, "How America Lost Its Mind."

107. Quoted in Joshua Norman, "9/11 Conspiracy Theories Won't Stop," *CBS News,* September 11, 2011, www.cbsnews.comnews/9-11-conspiracy-theories -wont-stop.

108. Robert Longley, "The Deep State Theory, Explained," *ThoughtCo,* September 18, 2017, www.thoughtco.com/deep-state-definition-4142030.

109. Aaron Blake, "The 'Deep State' Is President Trump's Most Compelling Conspiracy Theory," *Washington Post,* April 27, 2017, www.washingtonpost.com /news/the-fix/wp/2017/04/27/the-deep-state-is-president-trumps-most-compelling-conspiracy-theory/?utm_term=.e6b2d07424b7.

110. Nichols, *Death of Expertise,* 55–56.

111. Bennett and Livingston, "Disinformation Order."

112. See Tom W. G. van der Meer, "Political Trust and the 'Crisis of Democracy,'" *Oxford Research Encyclopedias,* January 2017, http://politics.oxfordre.com /view/10.1093/acrefore/9780190228637.001.0001/acrefore-9780190228637-e-77.

113. Joel Slemrod and Jon M. Bakija, *Taxing Ourselves* (Cambridge, MA: MIT Press, 2004).

114. "Beyond Distrust."

115. Thomas E. Patterson, *The Vanishing Voter* (New York: Knopf, 2002).

116. David Broder, "War on Cynicism," *Washington Post,* July 6, 1994, A19.

117. Edsall, "Democratic Party Is in Worse Shape."

118. Example taken from the Salant Lecture of Jameel Jaffer, Shorenstein Center on the Media, Politics and Public Policy, Harvard Kennedy School, October 17, 2017.

119. Reid Wilson, "Pollsters Fight to Figure Out Trump Phenomenon," *The Hill,* September 1, 2016, https://thehill.com/homenewscampaign/294018-pollsters-fight-to -figure-out-the-trump-phenomenon.

CHAPTER 4

1. Brian Kahn, "We Just Breached the 410 PPM Threshold for CO_2: Carbon Dioxide Has Not Reached This Height in Millions of Years," *Scientific American,* April 21, 2017, www.scientificamerican.com/article/we-just-breached-the-410-ppm -threshold-for-co2; Andrew Freedman, "The Last Time CO_2 Was This High, Humans Didn't Exist," *Climate Central,* May 3, 2013, www.climatecentral.org/news/the-last -time-co-was-this-high-humans-didnt-exist-15938.

2. Doug Criss, "5 Things for Tuesday, April 18: North Korea, Facebook, Trump Travel," *CNN,* April 18. 2017. The climate change reading was also not on CNN's top story list for April 17 and April 19, www.cnn.com/2017/04/18/us/five-things-april-18 -trnd/index.html.

3. Michelle Ye Hee Lee, "Are President Trump's Trips to Mar-a-Lago Similar to Obama's Travels?" *Washington Post,* April 19, 2017.

4. Rebecca Harrington and Skye Gould, "Here's How Often Trump Golfed during the First 100 Days Compared to Obama, Bush, and Clinton," *Business Insider,* April 30, 2017, www.businessinsider.com/how-often-trump-golfed-during-first-100 -days-compared-to-obama-bush-and-clinton-2017-4.

5. Hunter and Bowman, "Vanishing Center," 17.

6. Quoted in Annie Linskey, "GOP Leaders Still Puzzle over President," *Boston Sunday Globe,* August 27, 2017, A6.

7. Paul H. Weaver, "Is Television News Biased?" *Public Interest* 27 (1972): 69.

8. Quoted in Michael Robinson and Margaret Sheehan, *Over the Wire and on TV* (New York: Russell Sage Foundation, 1983), 226.

9. Kiku Adatto, *Picture Perfect: Life in the Age of the Photo-Op*, rev. ed. (Princeton, NJ: Princeton University Press, 2008).

10. See, for example, Robert MacNeil, *The People Machine* (New York: Harper and Row, 1968).

11. Campaign advisor Joseph Napolitan, quoted in McNeil, *People Machine*, 139; Daniel Boorstin, *The Image: A Guide to Pseudo-events in America* (New York: Vintage, 1962), 1.

12. Timothy Crouse, *Boys on the Bus* (New York: Ballantine Books, 1972), 323.

13. *CBS Evening News*, October 9, 1972, reported in Thomas E. Patterson and Robert D. McClure, *The Unseeing Eye: The Myth of Television Power in National Elections* (New York: Putnam, 1976), 32.

14. Ben Bradlee, *A Good Life: Newspapering and Other Adventures* (New York: Simon and Schuster, 1995), 352.

15. Carl Leubsdorf, "The Reporter and the Presidential Campaign," *ANNALS* (1976): 6.

16. Michael Schudson, "What Time Means in a News Story," Occasional Paper No. 4, Gannett Center for Media Studies, Columbia University, 1986, 1.

17. Jorgen Westerstahl and Folke Johansson, "News Ideologies as Molders of Domestic News," *European Journal of Communication* 1 (1986): 126–43; Sabato, *Feeding Frenzy*.

18. Thompson, *Enough Said*, 92.

19. There were only two periods when positive coverage clearly stood out—the months after the terrorist attacks of September 11, 2001, and the Barack Obama's transition and early presidential months in late 2008 and early 2009.

20. Quoted in Marvin Kalb, "The Rise of the New News," Discussion Paper D-34, Joan Shorenstein Center on the Press, Politics, and Public Policy, John F. Kennedy School of Government, Harvard University, October 1998, 13.

21. Daniel C. Hallin, "Sound Bite News: Television Coverage of Elections, 1968–1988," *Journal of Communication*, 42 (1992): 6.

22. Adatto, "Sound Bite Democracy," 4.

23. Mark J. Rozell, "Press Coverage of Congress, 1946–92," in Thomas E. Mann and Norman J. Ornstein, eds., *Congress, the Press, and the Public* (Washington, DC: American Enterprise Institute and Brookings Institution, 1994), 110.

24. See, for example, Patterson, *Out of Order*, 53–93; Buchanan, *Renewing Presidential Politics*, 149; Regina G. Lawrence and Melody Rose, *Hillary Clinton's Race for the White House: Gender Politics and the Media on the Campaign Trail* (Boulder, CO: Lynne Rienner, 2009), 183; and Jeffrey Cohen, *The Presidency in the Era of 24-Hour News* (Princeton, NJ: Princeton University Press, 2008), 119.

25. U.S. Congressman Jack Brooks, quoted in Carol Matlack, "Crossing the Line," *National Journal* 21 (1989): 724–29.

26. Paul Taylor, *See How They Run* (New York: Knopf, 1991), 6.

27. Fox Butterfield, "Dukakis Says Race Was Harmed by TV," *New York Times,* April 22, 1990, quoted in Philip Wander and David McNeil, "The Coming Crisis in American Politics," *Political Communication Review* 16 (1991): 38.

28. Jamieson and Waldman, *Press Effect,* 93–94; see also Nicholas A. Valentino, Thomas A. Buhr, and Matthew N. Beckmann, "When the Frame Is the Game: Revisiting the Impact of 'Strategic' Campaign Coverage on Citizens' Information Retention," *Journalism and Mass Communication Quarterly* 78 (2001): 105.

29. Cappella and Jamieson, *Spiral of Cynicism,* 208.

30. Atkinson, *Combative Politics,* 153.

31. Statement of John Carroll while a fellow at the Harvard Kennedy School's Shorenstein Center on Media, Politics, and Public Policy, 2006.

32. See Jamieson and Cappella, *Echo Chamber,* 244–47.

33. Rush Limbaugh, "RUSH: Ask the Clintons How Many People Do You Know in Your Life That Have Been MURDERED?" *Daily Rushbo,* August 16, 2010, http://dailyrushbo.comrush-ask-the-clintons-how-many-people-do-you-know-in-your-life-that-have-been-murdered.

34. Limbaugh's TV show ran for four years. It was produced by Roger Ailes.

35. Said by Donna Brazile to the author, September 11, 2017.

36. "All False Statements Involving Rachel Maddow," *PolitiFact,* undated, downloaded on January 8, 2019, www.politifact.com/personalities/rachel-maddow/statements/byruling/false.

37. "Fox News Used Fake Security Expert to 'Validate' Presidential Attack on Sweden Immigration," *Newshound,* February 26, 2017, www.newshounds.us/fox_news_used_fake_security_expert_to_validate_presidential_attack_on_sweden_immigration_022617#Y7u0JfEZyDmh1SAF.99www.newshounds.us/fox_news_used_fake_security_expert_to_validate_presidential_attack_on_sweden_immigration_022617.

38. "Fox News Used Fake Security Expert."

39. George Orwell, "Politics and the English Language," *eBooks@Adelaide,* University of Adelaide Library, University of Adelaide, originally published in 1946, https://ebooks.adelaide.edu.au/o/orwell/george/o79p.

40. Joshua Green, "Meet Mr. Death," *American Prospect,* December 19, 2001, http://prospect.org/article/meet-mr-death.

41. Ashlea Ebeling, "Final Tax Bill Includes Huge Estate Tax Win for the Rich: The $22.4 Million Exemption," *Forbes,* December 21, 2017, www.forbes.com/sites/ashleaebeling/2017/12/21final-tax-bill-includes-huge-estate-tax-win-for-the-rich-the-22-4-million-exemption/#46384201d541.

42. Matt Bai, "The Framing Wars," *New York Times Magazine,* July 17, 2005, www.nytimes.com/2005/07/17/magazine/the-framing-wars.html.

43. Edward L. Bernays, *Propaganda* (New York: Horace Liveright, 1928), 27.

44. Kate Sullivan, "Trump Says Troops on US Border Can Use 'Lethal Force,' Threatens to Close Border," *CNN,* November 22, 2018, www.cnn.com/2018/11/22/politics/trump-us-troops-lethal-force-closing-border/index.html.

45. John E. Miller, *Democracy and the Informed Citizen* (Brookings, SD: Prairie View Press, 2018), 123.

46. Amy Gutmann and Dennis Thompson, *The Spirit of Compromise: Why Governing Demands It and Campaigning Undermines It,* updated ed. (Princeton, NJ: Princeton University Press, 2014).

47. Frances E. Lee, *Insecure Majorities: Congress and the Perpetual Campaign* (Chicago: University of Chicago Press, 2016), 140.

48. Frances E. Lee, *Beyond Ideology: Politics, Principles, and Partisanship in the U.S. Senate* (Chicago: University of Chicago Press, 2009); Lee, *Insecure Majorities,* 200–204.

49. Marc Hetherington and Thomas Rudolph, *Why Washington Won't Work: Polarization, Political Trust, and the Governing* (Chicago: University of Chicago Press, 2015).

50. "Osama Bin Laden's Death Continues to Dominate the News," *Pew Research Center,* May 9, 2011, www.journalism.org/index_reportpej_news_coverage _index_may_2_8_2011.

51. Thomas E. Patterson, "Of Polls, Mountains: U.S. Journalists and Their Use of Election Surveys," *Public Opinion Quarterly* 69 (2005): 716–24.

52. Quoted in Peter Hamby, "Did Twitter Kill the Boys on the Bus," Shorenstein Center on Media, Politics and Public Policy," Harvard Kennedy School, Harvard University, Cambridge, MA, September 2013, 26, https://shorensteincenter.org /wp-content/uploads/2013/08/d80_hamby.pdf.

53. "The Invisible Primary—Invisible No Longer," *Pew Research Center,* October 29, 2007, 8, www.journalism.org/node/8187.

54. Duncan J. Watts and David M. Rothschild, "Don't Blame the Election on Fake News. Blame It on the Media," *Columbia Journalism Review,* December 5, 2017, www.cjr.org/analysis/fake-news-media-election-trump.php.

55. Shanto Iyengar, Helmut Norpath, and Kyu S. Hahn, "Consumer Demand for News: Horserace Sells," *Journal of Politics* 66 (2004): 157–75; Jacquielynn Floyd, "When Horse Races Go Too Far Astray," *Dallas Morning News,* August 30, 2004, 1B.

56. Jamieson and Waldman, *Press Effect,* 93–94. On the question of framing and voter response, see Martin Gilens, Lynn Vavreck, and Martin Cohen, "The Mass Media and the Public's Assessments of Presidential Candidates, 1952–2000," *Journal of Politics* 69 (2007): 1160–75.

57. Taylor, *See How They Run,* 22–23.

58. "Rum, Romanism, and Rebellion—And the Election That Got Away," *In the Past Lane,* October 29, 2012, http://inthepastlane.comrum-romanism-and-rebellion -october-29-2012.

59. Patterson, "News Coverage of the 2016 General Election."

60. John G. Geer, "Fanning the Flames: The News Media's Role in the Rise of Negativity in Presidential Campaigns," Joan Shorenstein Center on the Press, Politics

and Public Policy, Harvard Kennedy School, Cambridge, MA., February 2010, 6, 9, https://shorensteincenter.org/wp-content/uploads/2012/03/d55_geer.pdf?x78124.

61. "Campaign 2000 Final: How TV News Covered the General Election Campaign," *Media Monitor* 14, no. 6 (November–December 2000), 2.

62. Richard Davis, "News Coverage of National Political Institutions," Ph.D. dissertation, Syracuse University, 1984; Hugh Heclo and Lester M. Salamon, *The Illusion of Presidential Government* (Boulder, CO: Westview Press, 1981).

63. Thomas P. O'Neill Jr., "Congress: The First 200 Years," *National Forum* 64 (Fall 1984): 20–21.

64. Patterson, "News Coverage of Donald Trump's First 100 Days."

65. See, for example, Jon Greenberg, "George Will: We Spend More on Lobbying Than on Campaigns," *PolitiFact,* June 1, 2015, www.politifact.com/punditfact /statements/2015/jun/01/george-will/george-will-we-spend-more-lobbying -campaigns.

66. A. Trevor Thrall, "The Myth of the Outside Strategy: Mass Media News Coverage of Interest Groups," *Journal of Political Communication* 23 (2006): 407–20; Daniel Indiviglio, "5 Ways Lobbyists Influenced the Dodd-Frank Bill," *Atlantic,* July 5, 2010, www.theatlantic.com/businessarchive/2010/07/5-ways-lobbyists -influenced-the-dodd-frank-bill/59137.

67. Alison Dagnes, *Politics on Demand: The Effects of 24-Hour News on American Politics* (Santa Barbara, CA: Praeger, 2010), 30.

68. Based on the cable networks' ratings before Trump entered presidential politics in June 2015.

69. James Fallows, "Did You Have a Good Week?" *Atlantic Monthly,* December 1994, 32–33.

70. Karl Deutsch, *Nerves of Government* (New York: Free Press, 1963).

71. Quoted in Eli Watkings, "Conway: Do Falsehoods Matter as Much as What We Get Right?" *CNN,* February 7, 2017, www.cnn.com/2017/02/07/politics/kellyanne -conway-donald-trump-falsehoods/index.html.

72. Quoted in "Communication as a Fermenting Agent—a Keynote View," *SDC Magazine,* May 1967, 4, as cited in Jay W. Stein, *Mass Media, Education, and a Better Society* (Chicago: Nelson-Hall, 1979), 40.

CHAPTER 5

1. See, for example, Tom Huddleston Jr., "The New York Times Has 132,000 Reasons to Thank Donald Trump," *Fortune,* November 29, 2016, http://fortune .com/2016/11/29/new-york-times-subscribers-donald-trump.

2. Patterson, "News Coverage of the 2016 General Election."

3. Quoted in Andrew Gripp, "Is Television Ruining Our Political Discourse?" September 26, 2015, https://andrewgripp.wordpress.com/2015/09/26/is-television -ruining-our-political-discourse.

4. See, for example, Shelley Hepworth, Vanessa Gezari, Kyle Pope, Cory Schouten, Carlett Spike, David Uberti, and Pete Vernon, "Covering Trump: An Oral History of an Unforgettable Campaign," *Columbia Journalism Review,* November 22, 2016, www.cjr.org/special_report/trump_media_press_journalists.php.

5. Statement of CBS's CEO Les Moonves on February 29, 2016; Paul Farhi, "One Billion Dollars Profit? Yes, the Campaign Has Been a Gusher for CNN," *Washington Post,* October 27, 2016, www.washingtonpost.com/lifestyle/style/one-billion-dollars -profit-yes-the-campaign-has-been-a-gusher-for-cnn/2016/10/27/1fc879e6–9c6f -11e6–9980–50913d68eacb_story.html?utm_term=.f27fd77cb055.

6. "CNN President Jeff Zucker Defends Network's 'Heavy Focus' on Trump and Hiring of Trump Boosters," *Media Matters,* March 31, 2016, www.mediamatters .org/blog/2016/03/31/cnn-president-jeff-zucker-defends-networks-heav/209655.

7. Sasha Issenberg, *The Victory Lab: The Secret Science of Winning Campaigns* (New York: Broadway Books, 2013).

8. Nick Thompson, "International Campaign Finance: How Do Countries Compare?" *CNN,* March 5, 2012, www.cnn.com/2012/01/24/world/global-campaign -finance/index.html.

9. *Citizens United v. Federal Election Commission* 558 U.S. 310 (2010).

10. See Michael Schudson, *The Power of News* (Cambridge, MA: Harvard University Press, 1995), 199.

11. Matthew Gentzkow, Edward L. Glaeser, and Claudia Goldin, "The Rise of the Fourth Estate," in Edward L. Glaeser and Claudia Goldin, *Corruption and Reform: Lessons from America's Economic History* (Chicago: University of Chicago Press, 2008), 187–230.

12. V. O. Key Jr., *Public Opinion and American Democracy* (New York: Knopf, 1961), 388; see also Paul Starr, *The Creation of the Media* (New York: Basic Books, 2004).

13. See Richard T. LeGates and Frederic Stout, eds., *The City Reader* (New York: Routledge, 2011).

14. Robert W. McChesney, *Rich Media, Poor Democracy* (Urbana: University of Illinois Press, 1999).

15. Quoted in Marc Gunther, "The Transformation of Network News: How Profitability Has Moved Networks Out of Hard News," *Nieman Reports,* June 15, 1999, http://niemanreports.org/articles/the-transformation-of-network-news.

16. Tom Rosentiel and Amy Mitchell, "The State of the News Media 2011," Pew Research Center's Project for Excellence in Journalism, March 14, 2011, http:// stateofthemedia.org/2011/overview-2.

17. See William A. Hachten, *The Troubles of Journalism* (New York: Routledge, 2005).

18. See, for example, John Maltby, Liza Day, Lynn E. McCutcheon, Raphael Gillett, James Houran, and Diane D. Ashe, "Personality and Coping: A Context for

Examining Celebrity Worship and Mental Health," *British Journal of Psychology* 95 (2004): 411–29.

19. Thomas E. Patterson, "Doing Well and Doing Good," Report of the Joan Shorenstein Center on the Press, Politics, and Public Policy, Kennedy School of Government, Harvard University, December 2000, 3, www.hks.harvard.edu /presspol/publications/reports/soft_news_and_critical_journalism_2000.pdf; Minow quoted in James McCartney, "News Lite," *American Journalism Review,* June 1977, 19–21.

20. W. Russell Nueman, *The Future of the Mass Audience* (New York: Cambridge University Press, 1991).

21. Patterson, "Doing Well and Doing Good," 3–5. See also Michele Weldon, *Everyman News: The Changing American Front Page* (Columbus: University of Missouri Press, 2007), 37; Weldon found in a study of twenty daily newspapers that soft news increased by a third during the 2001–4 period.

22. Walter C. Dean and Atiba Pertilla, "I-teams and 'Eye Candy': The Reality of Local TV News," in Tom Rosensteil, Marion Just, Todd L. Belt, Atiba Pertilla, Walter Dean, and Dante Chinni, *We Interrupt This Newscast* (New York: Cambridge University Press, 2007), 31–35; see also Matthew Robert Kerbel, *If It Bleeds It Leads* (New York: Basic Books, 2000).

23. Although studies show that these outlets increased their soft news coverage, they did so less substantially and through features rather than by shifting front-page coverage.

24. Franklin Foer, *World without Mind: The Existential Threat of Big Tech* (New York: Penguin Press, 2017), 147. Reference to the number of users is from Crowd-Tangle's website.

25. Thompson, *Enough Said*, 106.

26. Foer, *World without Mind*, 139.

27. The example was inspired by one in Foer, *World without Mind*, 151.

28. Quoted in Eli Pariser, *The Filter Bubble: What the Internet Is Hiding from You* (New York: Penguin Books, 2012), 14.

29. Patterson, "Doing Well and Doing Good," 4–6.

30. Patterson, "News Coverage of Donald Trump's First 100 Days." Coverage of earlier presidents estimated from data in Jeffrey E. Cohen, *The Presidency in the Era of 24-Hour News* (Princeton, NJ: Princeton University Press, 2008), 33.

31. Tom Brokow, statement made at a Kennedy School Forum, Harvard University, May 9, 1997.

32. E-poll, 2010, http://blog.epollresearch.com/tag/lindsay-lohan.

33. Neil Postman, *Amusing Ourselves to Death: Public Discourse in the Age of Show Business* (New York: Viking, 1985), 106.

34. This paragraph in its content is modeled after Barber, "Characters in the Campaign."

35. Content in this paragraph derived from Clive Irving, "The Secret of CNN's Turnaround Flight: MH 370," *Daily Beast,* March 6, 2016, www.thedailybeast.com /the-secret-of-cnns-turnaround-flight-mh370.

36. Douglas Mataconis, "Casey Anthony Trial Got More News Coverage Than GOP Candidates," *Outside the Beltway,* July 6, 2011, www.outsidethebeltway.com /casey-anthony-trial-got-more-news-coverage-than-gop-candidates; "Casey Anthony Murder Trial Garners Extensive Media Coverage," *Los Angeles Times,* July 6, 2011, http://articles.latimes.com/2011/jul/06/entertainmentla-et-casey-anthony -trial-sidebar-20110706.

37. Elizabeth Cohen, "Ebola in the Air? A Nightmare That Could Happen," *CNN,* October 6, 2014, www.cnn.com/2014/09/12/health/ebola-airborne/index.html.

38. Tulip Mazumdar, "Ebola Outbreak," *BBC News,* January 29, 2015, www.bbc .com/news/health-31019097.

39. "Ebola Worries Rise, but Most Are 'Fairly' Confident in Government, Hospitals to Deal with Disease," *Pew Research Center,* October 21, 2014, www.people -press.org/2014/10/21/ebola-worries-rise-but-most-are-fairly-confident-in -government-hospitals-to-deal-with-disease.

40. Bill Kovach and Tom Rosenstiel, *Warp Speed* (New York: Century Foundation), 99.

41. The content of this paragraph owes to Bennett, "Press-Government Relations," 258.

42. Bennett, "Press-Government Relations."

43. Quoted in Ken Auletta, "Non-stop News," *New Yorker,* January 25, 2010, 42.

44. "Trump: I'll Release My Tax Returns If Obama Releases Birth Certificate," *USA Today,* April 19, 2011.

45. John McQuaid, "He Said, She Said," *John McQuaide's Science, Globalization, Politics, Media Blog,* April 13, 2009.

46. Denis McQuail, *Mass Communication Theory* (London: Sage, 1994), 145.

47. Mayer, "Stories of Climate Change," 11.

48. Lauren Feldman, Edward W. Maibach, Connie Roser-Renouf, and Anthony Leiserowitz, "Climate on Cable: The Nature and Impact of Global Warming Coverage on Fox News, CNN, and MSNBC, *International Journal of Press/Politics* 20 (2011): 1–29, http://climateshiftproject.org/wp-content/uploads/2011/11/FeldmanStudy.pdf.

49. Postman, *Amusing Ourselves.*

50. Lars Willnat and David H. Weaver, "The American Journalist in the Digital Age," School of Journalism, Indiana University, Bloomington, IN, 2014, http:// archive.news.indiana.edu/releases/iu/2014/05/2013-american-journalist-key-findings .pdf. Poll was conducted in 2013.

51. Steve Salerno, "Journalist-Bites-Reality!" *eSkeptic,* online release, February 12, 2008; John H. McManus, *Market-Driven Journalism* (Thousand Oaks, CA: Sage, 1994), 162–63; Eric Jensen, "Scientific Sensationalism in American and British Press

Coverage of Therapeutic Cloning," *Journalism and Mass Communication Quarterly* 89 (2012): 40–54; Richard Davis, *The Press and American Politics* (Upper Saddle River, NJ: Prentice-Hall, 2000), 24–27.

52. Quoted in Stephen Bates, "Realigning Journalism with Democracy: The Hutchins Commission, Its Times, and Ours," Annenberg Washington Program of Northwestern University, Washington, DC, 1995, 11.

53. Meg Greenfield, "Chronic Political Amnesia," *Newsweek*, Sept. 22, 1980, 96.

54. Greg Prince, "Trump's Tweets Are Seen by Less Than One Percent of His Followers, Social Media Expert Claims," *Newsweek*, January 3, 2018, www.newsweek .com/trump-tweets-one-percent-mainstream-media-769207.

55. See Kevin G. Barnhurst and Catherine A. Steele, "Image Bite News: The Coverage of Elections on U.S. Television, 1968–1992," *Harvard International Journal of Press/Politics* 2 (1997): 40–58.

56. Stephanie Brown, *Speed: Facing Our Addiction to Fast and Faster—and Overcoming Our Fear of Slowing Down* (Boston, MA: Berkeley, 2014).

57. Paul Starr, "Governing in the Age of Fox News," *Atlantic*, January–February 2010, www.theatlantic.com/magazine/archive/2010/01/governing-in-the-age-of-fox -news/307838.

58. Sobieraj and Berry, "From Incivility to Outrage," 27–30.

59. "The Smothers Brothers Comedy Hour," *Wikipedia*, https://en.wikipedia .org/wiki/The_Smothers_Brothers_Comedy_Hour.

60. Joe Concha, "Hannity Tops Media 'Rich List' with $29 Million Salary," *The Hill*, November 17, 2016, http://thehill.com/media/306579-hannity-tops-media -rich-list-with-29-million-salary.

61. Derived from speech by Nancy Gibbs, Harvard Kennedy School, November 15, 2017; see Dan Kahan, "Donald Trump: Science Communication Environment Polluter-in-Chief," Cultural Cognition Project at Yale Law School, January 11, 2017, www.culturalcognition.net/blog/2017/1/11/donald-trump-science-communication -environment-polluter-in-c.html.

62. Sobieraj and Berry, "From Incivility to Outrage," 34.

63. Deborah Jordon Brooks and John G. Geer, "Beyond Negativity: The Effects of Incivility on the Electorate," *American Journal of Political Science* 52 (2007): 1–16; Jamieson and Cappella, *Echo Chamber*.

64. Mutz, *In-Your-Face Politics*.

65. Hindman, *Myth of Digital Democracy*, 90–91.

66. "ComScore Releases February 2016 U.S. Desktop Search Engine Rankings," *ComScore*, March 16, 2016, www.comscore.com/Insights/Rankings/comScore -Releases-February-2016-US-Desktop-Search-Engine-Rankings; Shannon Gree- wood, Andrew Perrin, and Maeve Duggan, "Social Media Update 2016, *Pew Research Center*, November 11, 2016, www.pewinternet.org/2016/11/11/social-media-update -2016.

67. Pamela Shoemaker, Timothy Vos, and Stephen Reese, "Journalists as Gate-keepers," in K. Wahl-Jorgensen and T. Hanitzsch, eds., *Handbook of Journalism Studies* (London: Routledge/Lawrence Erlbaum, 2009).

68. Alex S. Jones, *Losing the News* (New York: Oxford University Press, 2009), 2–3.

69. Wael Ghonim, "Transparency: Towards a Responsible Social Media," unpublished draft paper, Shorenstein Center on the Media, Politics and Public Policy, October 2017.

70. Ghonim, "Transparency."

71. Clark and Marchi, *Young People*, 29.

72. Oliver Darcy, "Google and Facebook Help Spread Bad Information after Las Vegas Attack," *CNN,* October 3, 2017, http://money.cnn.com/2017/10/02/media/facebook-google-misinformation-las-vegas/index.html.

73. Maksym Gabielkov, Arthi Ramachandran, Augustin Chaintreau, and Arnaud Legout, "Social Clicks: What and Who Gets Read on Twitter?" presented at ACM SIGMETRICS/IFIP Performance 2016, France, June 2016, available at https://hal.inria.fr/hal-01281190.

74. Vosoughi, Roy, and Aral, "Spread of True and False News Online."

75. "Biography of Nikita Khrushchev," *National Cold War Exhibition,* www.nationalcoldwarexhibition.org/explore/biography.cfm?name=Khrushchev,%20Nikita, accessed July 14, 2012.

76. "Donald Trump's Presidential Announcement Speech," *Time,* June 16, 2015, http://time.com/3923128/donald-trump-announcement-speech.

77. Quoted by Nancy Gibbs in speech at Harvard Kennedy School, November 15, 2017.

78. See Alan I. Abramowitz, "Economic Conditions, Presidential Popularity, and Voting Behavior in Midterm Congressional Elections," *Journal of Politics* 47 (1985): 31–43.

79. D. Sunshine Hillygus and Todd G. Shields, *The Persuadable Voter: Wedge Issues in Presidential Campaigns* (Princeton, NJ: Princeton University Press, 2008).

80. "When Considering 2016 Candidates, the Biggest Litmus Tests for GOP Voters: ISIS and Abortion," *Washington Times,* March 30, 2016, www.washingtontimes.com/news/2015/mar/30/2016-election-when-considering-candidates-biggest-.

81. "Abortion," *Gallup News,* In Depth: Topics A to Z, undated, downloaded October 28, 2017, http://news.gallup.com/poll/1576/abortion.aspx.

82. E. J. Dionne Jr., *Why Americans Hate Politics* (New York: Simon and Schuster, 1991).

83. Geer, "Fanning the Flames," 4.

84. Wesleyan Media Project data, http://mediaproject.wesleyan.edu/dataaccess, except for 1996, which is from Geer, "Fanning the Flames," 4.

85. Erika Franklin Fowler, Travis Ridout, and Michael M. Franz, "Political Advertising in 2016: The Presidential Election as Outlier?" *Forum* 14 (2016): 458, 462.

86. Ted Barder, "Striking a Responsive Chord: How Political Ads Motivate and Persuade Voters by Appealing to Emotions," *American Journal of Political Science* 49 (2005): 388–405.

87. Arne Öhman and Susan Fears, "Phobias, and Preparedness: Toward an Evolved Module of Fear and Fear Learning," *Psychological Review* 108 (2001): 483–522.

88. Heather Savigny and Mick Temple, "Political Marketing Models: The Curious Incident of the Dog That Doesn't Bark," *Political Studies* 58 (2010): 1049–69.

89. Geer, "Fanning the Flames," 5.

90. Brian Cogan and Tony Kelso, *Encyclopedia of Politics, the Media, and Popular Culture* (Santa Barbara, CA: Greenwood, 2009), 155, 187, 335.

91. "Campaign 2004: The Summer," *Media Monitor* 18, no. 5 (September–October 2004): 3.

92. Geer, "Fanning the Flames," 6, 9.

93. Travis N. Ridout and Michael M. Franz, *The Persuasive Power of Campaign Advertising* (Philadelphia: Temple University Press, 2011), 79–102. Quote from Thomas Edsall, "What Motivates Voters More Than Loyalty? Loathing," *New York Times*, March 1, 2018.

94. Shekhar Misra, "Deceptive Political Advertising: Some New Dimensions," *Journal of Legal, Ethical and Regulatory Issues* 18 (2015): 71–78; Byron Tau, "Judge Strikes Down Ohio Law on Election Lies," *Politico*, September 11, 2014, www.politico .com/blogs/under-the-radar/2014/09/judge-strikes-down-ohio-law-on-election -lies-1953330.

95. A litany of deceptive ads can be found in Brooks Jackson and Kathleen Hall Jamieson, *Un-spun: Finding Facts in a World of Disinformation* (New York: Random House, 2007); see also Lynda Lee Kaid and Anne Johnston, *Videostyle in Presidential Campaigns: Style and Content of Televised Political Advertising* (Westport, CT: Praeger, 2000). On ads from outside groups, see "Stations: Stand by Your Ad—Fact Sheet," a project of Flackcheck.org of the Annenberg Public Policy Center of the University of Pennsylvania, May 2012.

96. Patterson and McClure, *Unseeing Eye*; John Geer, *In Defense of Negativity* (Chicago: University of Chicago Press, 2006); Kyle Mattes and David P. Redlawsk, *The Positive Case for Negative Campaigning* (Chicago: University of Chicago Press, 2015).

97. Linda Qiu, "10 Most Aired Political Ads, Fact-Checked," *PolitiFact*, November 3, 2016, www.politifact.com/truth-o-meter/article/2016/nov/03/10-most-aired -political-ads-fact-checked.

98. Brooks and Geer, "Beyond Negativity," 1–16; Paul Freedman and Kenneth M. Goldstein, "Measuring Media Exposure and the Effects of Negative Campaign Ads," *American Journal of Political Science* 43 (1999): 1189–208; James D. King and Jason B. McConnell, "The Effect of Negative Campaign Advertising on Vote Choice,"

Social Science Quarterly 84 (2003): 843–57: Glenn Leshner and Esther Thorson, "Overreporting Voting: Campaign Media Public Mood, and the Vote," *Political Communication* 17 (2000): 263–78; Fuyuan Shen and H. Denis Wu, "Effects of Soft-Money Issue Advertisements on Candidate Evaluation and Voting Preference," *Mass Communication and Society* 5 (2002): 395–410.

99. Richard R. Lau, Lee Sigelman, and Ivy Brown Rovner, "The Effects of Negative Political Campaigns: A Meta-Analytic Assessment," *Journal of Politics* 69 (2007): 1180–83, 1186.

100. Lippmann, *Public Opinion*, 73.

101. Lippmann, *Liberty and the News*, 47.

102. Quoted in Jennifer Senior, "Review: 'The Attention Merchants' Dissects the Battle for Clicks and Eyeballs," *New York Times,* November 2, 2016, www.nytimes.com/2016/11/03/books/review-attention-merchants-tim-wu.html.

103. Herbert A. Simon, "Designing Organizations for an Information-Rich World," in Martin Greenberger, *Computers, Communication, and the Public Interest* (Baltimore, MD: Johns Hopkins University Press, 1971), 40–41.

104. Kevin McSpadden, "You Now Have a Shorter Attention Span Than a Goldfish," *Time,* May 14, 2015, http://time.com/3858309/attention-spans-goldfish.

105. Patterson, *Mass Media Election*, 159–65.

106. Mark Bauerlein, *The Dumbest Generation* (New York: Penguin Books, 2008), 45; "Daily Time Spent Reading Newspapers per Capita in the United States from 2010 to 2018 (in minutes)," *Statista,* downloaded October 24, 2017, www.statista.com/statistics/186934/us-newspaper-reading-habits-since-2002. On print vs. online, see Ryan Chittum, "Print Newspapers Still Dominate Readers' Attention: Another Look at How Much Time Is Spent Reading Newspapers Online and in Print," *Columbia Journalism Review,* undated, downloaded October 31, 2017, http://archives.cjr.org/the_audit/newspapers_time_spent.php.

107. Rolf Dobelli, *The Art of Thinking Clearly* (New York, Harper, 2014).

108. Marshall McLuhan, *Understanding Media* (Cambridge, MA: MIT Press, 1964), xi.

109. Quoted in Steve Lohr, "The Smartphone's Rapid Rise from Gadget to Tool to Necessity," *New York Times,* June 10, 2009, B1.

110. Quoted in Cara Feinberg, "The Mediatrician," *Harvard Magazine,* November–December 2011, 52.

111. Kenneth Burke, "How Many Texts Do People Send Every Day?" *Text Request,* May 18, 2016, www.textrequest.com/blog/many-texts-people-send-per-day.

112. Samantha Murphy, "Afraid of Losing Your Cell Phone? You May Have Nomophobia Like Half the Population," *Mashable Tech,* February 21, 2012, http://mashable.com/2012/02/21/nomophobia.

113. Kurt Vonnegut, *The Cat's Cradle* (New York: Dell, 1998), 11.

CHAPTER 6

1. Washington Post/University of Maryland poll, September 27–October 5, 2017, www.washingtonpost.com/politics/polling/washington-postuniversity-maryland democracy-poll-sept/2017/10/28/103b9f34-bbd7-11e7-9b93-b97043e57a22_page.html.

2. Albert Camus, "Rules of Engagement," *Harper's Magazine,* July 2011, 16. Originally written in 1939, the article was censored by French authorities and went unpublished until discovered in an archive.

3. Illing, "20 of America's Top Political Scientists."

4. Chua, *Political Tribes,* 172–73.

5. Quoted in Clark and Marchi, *Young People,* 193.

6. Daniel Boorstin, *The Genius of American Politics* (Chicago: University of Chicago Press, 1953).

7. Boorstin, *Genius of American Politics.*

8. Frank Newport, "Americans Favor Compromise to Get Things Done in Washington," *Gallup,* October 9, 2017, https://news.gallup.com/poll/220265/americans-favor -compromise-things-done-washington.aspx.

9. Lee, *Insecure Majorities.*

10. Quoted in Louis Galambos and Daun van Ee, "A President's First Term: Eisenhower's Pursuit of 'The Middle Way,'" *Humanities* 22 (2001), www.neh.gov /humanities/2001/januaryfebruary/feature/presidents-first-term.

11. Lee, *Insecure Majorities.*

12. Kristi Andersen, *The Creation of a Democratic Majority, 1928–1936* (Chicago: University of Chicago Press, 1979).

13. President Harry Truman pushed for comprehensive health care reform in the late 1940s, and President Bill Clinton did so in the early 1990s. Both efforts failed.

14. Tevi Troy, "The Democrats and Health Care: An Account of Political Self-Destruction," *Wall Street Journal,* December 22, 2010, www.wsj.com/articles/SB10 001424052748704851204576034070250138538.

15. See, for example, Theda Skocpol and Vanessa Williams, *The Tea Party and the Remaking of Republican Conservatism,* updated ed. (New York: Oxford University Press, 2016).

16. John Judis and Ruy Teixeira, *The Emerging Democratic Majority,* reprint ed. (New York: Scribner, 2004); James Carville and Rebecca Buckwalter-Poza, *40 More Years: How the Democrats Will Rule the Next Generation* (New York: Simon and Schuster, 2011).

17. Sykes, *How the Right Lost Its Mind,* 229.

18. See, for example, Cramer, *Politics of Resentment;* Hochschild, *Strangers;* and Thomas Frank, *What's the Matter with Kansas* (New York: Holt, 2005).

19. Joel A. Brown, "The Struggle Is Real: Understanding the American 'Culture War,'" *Religion and Culture Forum,* July 11, 2017, https://voices.uchicago.edu/religion culture/2017/07/11/the-struggle-is-real-understanding-the-american-culture -war-by-russell-d.

20. Speech by Nancy Gibbs at the Harvard Kennedy School, November 15, 2017.

21. Levitsky and Ziblatt, *How Democracies Die.*

22. Mickey Edwards, *The Parties versus the People* (New Haven, CT: Yale University Press, 2013).

23. Chua, *Political Tribes,* 177.

24. Chua, *Political Tribes,* 191.

25. Chua, *Political Tribes,* 191. Attributed to an interview of Newt Gingrich by the *Washington Post*'s Michael Scherer.

26. Examples include Pew Research Center poll, August 2017; Wall Street Journal/ABC poll, September 2017; Washington Post/University of Maryland poll, October 2017.

27. Levitsky and Ziblatt, *How Democracies Die,* 8–9.

28. Thomas E. Mann and Norman J. Ornstein, *It's Even Worse Than It Looks: How the American Constitutional System Collided with the New Politics of Extremism,* expanded ed. (New York: Basic Books, 2016).

29. Karen Stenner, *The Authoritarian Dynamic* (New York: Cambridge University Press, 2005).

30. Ron Elvin, "What Is the 'Regular Order' John McCain Longs to Return to on Health Care?" *NPR,* July 26, 2017, www.npr.org/2017/07/26/539358654/what-is-the-regular-order-john-mccain-longs-to-return-to-on-health-care.

31. Luke Johnson, "Dennis Hastert Warns John Boehner about Leadership after Fiscal Cliff Deal," *HuffPost,* January 3, 2013, www.huffingtonpost.com/2013/01/03/dennis-hastert-john-boehner_n_2403108.html.

32. Carl Hulse, "Now, Dennis Hastert Seems an Architect of Dysfunction as Speaker," *New York Times,* May 2, 2016, www.nytimes.com/2016/05/03/us/politics/now-dennis-hastert-seems-an-architect-of-dysfunction-as-speaker.html.

33. Burr quoted in Sabrina Siddiqui, "Richard Burr: Mike Lee Government Shutdown Threat 'Dumbest Idea I've Ever Heard Of," *HuffPost,* September 25, 2013, www.huffingtonpost.com/2013/07/25/richard-burr-mike-lee_n_3653870.html. McCain quoted in "John McCain: Defund Effort 'Not Rational,'" *Politico,* September 19, 2013, www.politico.com/video/2013/09/john-mccain-defund-effort-not-rational-006151. Bohener quoted in E. J. Dionne Jr., "Boehner Climbs Off the Tiger," *Washington Post,* September 27, 2015, www.washingtonpost.com/opinions/boehner-climbs-off-the-tiger/2015/09/27/9ead1890-6488-11e5-8e9e-dce8a2a2a679_story.html?utm_term=.7638c1e60038.

34. U.S. Senate data archive, www.senate.gov/pagelayout/reference/cloture_motions/clotureCounts.htm.

35. Adams wrote those words into the Massachusetts state constitution, which he drafted in 1780.

36. Quoted in Lee, *Insecure Majorities,* 204.

37. Thomas R. Pickering and James Stoutenberg, "Did Washington Predict Trump?" *New York Times,* February 19, 2018, A21.

38. Quoted in Lee, *Insecure Majorities*, 139.

39. Orrin Hatch, "The Ted Kennedy I Knew," *Politico*, August 26, 2009, www .politico.com/story/2009/08/the-ted-kennedy-i-knew-026482.

40. Charles Gibson, "Restoring Comity to Congress," Shorenstein Center on Media, Politics and Public Policy," Harvard Kennedy School, Harvard University, Cambridge, MA, January 1, 2011, https://shorensteincenter.org/restoring-comity-to -congress.

41. Justin Grimmer and Gary King, "General Purpose Computer-Assisted Clustering and Conceptualization," *Proceedings of the National Academy of Sciences* 108 (2011): 2649.

42. Joanne B. Freeman, *The Field of Blood: Violence in Congress and the Road to Civil War* (New York: Farrar, Straus, and Giroux, 2018); U.S. House of Representatives, "The Most Infamous Floor Brawl in the History of the U.S. House of Representatives," http://history.house.gov/Historical-Highlights/1851-1900/The-most-infamous-floor -brawl-in-the-history-of-the-U-S--House-of-Representatives.

43. Miller, *Democracy and the Informed Citizen*, 139.

44. Matt Compton, "We Can't Wait: President Obama in Nevada," *White House*, October 24, 2011, https://obamawhitehouse.archives.gov/blog/2011/10/24 /we-cant-wait-president-obama-nevada.

45. Gibson, "Restoring Comity."

46. James Madison, Federalist No. 10.

47. Rauch, "How American Politics Went Insane."

48. See Key, *Responsible Electorate*.

49. Poole and Rosenthal, *Ideology and Congress*.

50. See Gary W. Cox and Matthew McCubbins, *Setting the Agenda: Responsible Party Government in the U.S. House of Representatives* (New York: Cambridge University Press, 2005).

51. Danielle Thomsen, *Opting Out of Congress* (New York: Cambridge University Press, 2017); Jack Fresquez, "Charlie Dent and the Death of the Moderate in Congress," *The Politic*, November 1, 2017, http://thepolitic.org/charlie-dent-and-the-death -of-the-moderate-in-congress.

52. Paul Kane, "Sen. Jeff Flake Relishes His Role As Republican Trump Critic: He Can't Help Himself," *Washington Post*, August 25, 2016, www.washingtonpost .com/news/powerpost/wp/2016/08/25/sen-jeff-flake-relishes-role-as-republican -trump-critic-he-cant-help-himself/?utm_term=.169d5f7d6b94.

53. Robert G. Boatright, *Getting Primaried: The Changing Politics of Congressional Primary Challenges* (Ann Arbor: University of Michigan Press, 2013); Darrell M. West, "Broken Politics," Brookings Institution, *Issues in Governance Studies*, no. 33 (March 2010): 4. See, for example, Alan I. Abramowitz, Brad Alexander, and Matthew Gunning, "Incumbency, Redistricting, and the Decline of Competition in U.S. House Elections," *Journal of Politics* 68 (2006): 75–88.

54. Pew Research Center poll, 2014, www.people-press.org/2014/06/12/political -compromise-in-principle.

55. Eyder Peralta, "Sen. Lugar Loses Primary to Tea Party Challenger, Ending 36-Year Career," *NPR,* May 8, 2012, www.npr.org/sections/itsallpolitics/2012/05/08 /152292025/facing-a-tough-primary-lugar-encourages-everyone-to-vote; David A. Fahrenthold, Rosalind S. Helderman, and Jenna Portnoy, "What Went Wrong for Eric Cantor," *Washington Post,* June 11, 2014, www.washingtonpost.com/politics /what-went-wrong-for-eric-cantor/2014/06/11/0be7c02c-f180-11e3-914c-1fbd0614e2d4 _story.html?utm_term=.96180f942434.

56. Sean M. Theriault, *Party Polarization in Congress* (New York: Cambridge University Press, 2008); Barry C. Burden, "Candidate Positions in U.S. Congressional Elections," *British Journal of Political Science* 34 (2004): 211–27.

57. Anthony King, *Running Scared* (New York: Free Press, 1997); Calmes, "They Don't Give a Damn."

58. Calmes, "They Don't Give a Damn"; Eliana Johnson, "Ingraham's Insurrection," *National Review,* June 12, 2014, www.nationalreview.com/2014/06/ingrahams -insurrection-eliana-johnson.

59. *Citizens United v. Federal Election Commission* (2104). A subsequent Supreme Court decision, *McCutcheon v. FEC,* could be one of the few recent developments that works to the advantage of moderates. The Court ruled that, whereas Congress can limit the amount a donor can contribute to a particular candidate or party organization, it cannot limit the total amount of such contributions. A donor could, for example, contribute to a party's national organization and all fifty of its state organizations. Several donors took that approach in 2016. The party organizations then channeled most of the money to their more moderate candidates. See Carrie Levine, "Soft Money Is Back—and Both Parties Are Cashing In," *Politico,* August 4, 2017. For a view of where *Citizens United* fits in the longer arc of American history, see Zephyr Teachout, *Corruption in America: From Benjamin Franklin's Snuff Box to Citizens United,* reprint ed. (Cambridge, MA: Harvard University Press, 2018).

60. Boatright, *Getting Primaried,* 55.

61. Mann and Ornstein, *It's Even Worse.*

62. Quoted in James W. Ceasar, *Presidential Selection* (Princeton, NJ: Princeton University Press, 1979), 11.

63. L. Sandy Maisel and Walter Stone, "Determinants of Candidate Emergence in U.S. House Elections," *Legislative Studies Quarterly* 22 (1997): 17–96.

64. Stephen Ansalebehere, James Snyder Jr., and Charles Stewart III, "Old Voters, New Voters, and the Personal Vote," *American Journal of Political Science* 44 (2000): 17–34.

65. Michael P. McDonald, "Redistricting and Competitive Districts," in Michael P. McDonald and John Samples, eds., *The Marketplace of Democracy* (Washington, DC: Brookings Institution Press, 206), 222–24.

66. Bishop, *Big Sort.*

67. On gerrymandering, see Nolan McCarty, Keith T. Poole, and Howard Rosenthal, "Does Gerrymandering Cause Polarization?" *American Journal of Political Science* 53, no. 2 (July 2009); and Thomas E. Mann, "Polarizing the House of Representatives: How Much Does Gerrymandering Matter?" in Pietro S. Nivola and David W. Brady, eds., *Red and Blue Nation? Characteristics and Causes of America's Polarized Politics* (Washington, DC: Brookings Institution Press, 2006). On geographical sorting, see Sussell and Thomson, "Are Changing Constituencies."

68. Thomas F. Schaller, "Multi-member Districts: Just a Thing of the Past," *Sabato's Crystal Ball*, March 21, 2013, www.centerforpolitics.org/crystalball/articles/multi-member-legislative-districts-just-a-thing-of-the-past.

69. Gary C. Jacobson, "The Electoral Origins of Polarized Politics: Evidence from the 2010 Cooperative Congressional Election Study," *American Behavioral Scientist* 56 (2012): 1612–30, https://journals.sagepub.com/doi/abs/10.1177/0002764212463352.

70. Elaine C. Kamarck," Increasing Turnout in Congressional Primaries," *Brookings Institution,* July 2014, 10, www.brookings.edu/wp-content/uploads/2016/06/KamarckIncreasing-Turnout-in-Congressional-Primaries72614.pdf.

71. "Top-two" primaries are another possible way to lure moderate voters into participating at a higher rate. Instituted recently in the states of California and Washington, a top-two primary is open to all registered voters, and the two candidates who receive the most votes, regardless of party, advance to the general election. In lopsided districts where two candidates of the same party prevail, one of them is usually more moderate than the other. Top-two primaries are new enough that they haven't been studied closely, but they appear to increase the odds only slightly that a moderate will win. Voters in the weaker party typically support a candidate of their own party rather than voting for a moderate candidate of the stronger party, even though doing so would improve that candidate's chances of finishing in the top two. Turnout is also a problem. In California and Washington, turnout has not greatly increased since the adoption of the top-two primary. See Eric McGhee and Boris Shor, "Has the Top Two Primary Elected More Moderates?" Public Policy Institute of California, CDDRL Working Papers, June 2016, 7, https://cddrl.fsi.stanford.edu/sites/default/files/amdem-_1.pdf; Jack Nagler, "Voter Behavior in California's Top Two Primary," *California Journal of Politics and Policy* 7 (2015), https://escholarship.org/uc/item/89g5x6vn; and Eric McGhee, with research support from Daniel Krimm, "Voter Turnout in Primary Elections," *Public Policy Institute of California,* May 2014, www.ppic.org/content/pubs/report/R_514EMR.pdf.

72. A few closed-primary states give parties the option at each election of conducting an open primary if they think it advantageous.

73. Quoted in "Open Primary," *Ballotpedia*, undated, downloaded February 16, 2018, https://ballotpedia.org/Open_primary.

74. See, for example, Stephen Ansolabehere, John Mark Hansen, Shigeo Hirano, and James M. Snyder, "More Democracy: The Direct Primary and Competition in

U.S. Elections," *Studies in American Political Development* 24 (2010): 190–205, www
.cambridge.org/core/journals/studies-in-american-political-development/article
/more-democracy-the-direct-primary-and-competition-in-us-elections/3F7CAE9
8F5D1FB88A6FBC76C948482CE.

75. See R. Michael Alvarez and Jonathan Nagler, "Should I Stay or Should I Go?
Sincere and Strategic Crossover Voting in California Assembly Races," and Anthony
M. Salvanto and Martin P. Wattenberg, "Peeking under the Blanket: A Direct Look
at Crossover Voting in the 1998 Primary," in *Voting at the Political Fault Line: California's Experiment with the Blanket Primary,* Bruce E. Cain and Elisabeth R. Gerber,
eds. (Berkeley: University of California Press, 2002).

76. Elaine C. Kamarck, *Primary Politics,* 2nd ed. (Washington, DC: Brookings
Institution Press, 2016); Elaine C. Kamarck, "Increasing Turnout in Congressional
Primaries," *Brookings Institution,* July 2014, 14, www.brookings.edu/wp-content
/uploads/2016/06/KamarckIncreasing-Turnout-in-Congressional-Primaries72614
.pdf.

77. Kamarck, "Increasing Turnout," 16.

78. Andy Barr, "O'Donnell Questions Separation of Church, State," *Politico,*
October 19, 2010, www.politico.com/story/2010/10/odonnell-questions-separation
-of-church-state-043826. Polls taken early in O'Donnell's campaign showed her up
by about ten percentage points. She lost by seventeen percentage points.

79. McGhee, "Voter Turnout in Primary Elections."

80. Patterson, *Vanishing Voter,* 178–81.

81. Jasmine C. Lee, "How States Moved toward Stricter Voter ID Laws," *New
York Times,* November 3, 2016, www.nytimes.com/interactive/2016/11/03/us/elections
/how-states-moved-toward-stricter-voter-id-laws.html. Substantial research on
voter ID laws has been done by NYU's Brennan Center for Justice, headed by Michael
Waldman.

82. See, for example, Kenneth R. Mayer, "Voter ID Study Shows Turnout Effects
in 2016 Wisconsin Presidential Election," *University of Wisconsin,* September 25,
2017, https://elections.wisc.edu/news/voter-id-study/Voter-ID-Study-Release.pdf.

83. Keesha Gaskins and Sundeep Iyer, "The Challenge of Obtaining Voter Identification," *Brennan Center for Justice,* July 18, 2012, www.brennancenter.org/publication
/challenge-obtaining-voter-identification.

84. Rough calculation by author based on 1980 and 2016 exit polls and census
data from the same years.

85. Miller, *Democracy and the Informed Citizen,* 150.

86. Andersen, *Fantasyland.*

87. Campante and Hojman, "Media and Polarization."

88. Nichols, *Death of Expertise,* 147–48.

89. Anderson, "How America Lost Its Mind."

90. "In Changing News Landscape, Even Television Is Vulnerable," *Pew Research
Center,* September 27, 2012, www.people-press.org/2012/09/27/in-changing-news
-landscape-even-television-is-vulnerable.

91. Nicholas Confessore and Daisuke Wakabayashi, "Russians Spun American Rage into a Weapon," *New York Times*, October 10, 2017.

92. Ghonim, "Transparency"; Jeff Jarvis, *What Would Google Do?* (New York: HarperCollins, 2009).

93. Hayley Tsukayama, "Facebook Must Confront the Responsibilities of Being a Media Company," *Washington Post*, November 15, 2016, www.washingtonpost .com/news/the-switch/wp/2016/11/15/facebook-must-confront-the-responsibilities -of-being-a-media-company/?utm_term=.c443039a4fc8.

94. Zuckerman, *Digital Cosmopolitans.*

95. Ghonim, "Transparency."

96. *Internet Live Stats*, downloaded January 1, 2018, www.internetlivestats.com /total-number-of-websites.

97. Kim Fridkin, Patrick J. Kenney, and Amanda Wintersieck, "Liar, Liar, Pants on Fire: How Fact-Checking Influences Citizens' Reactions to Negative Advertising," *Political Communication* 32 (2015): 127–51.

98. Brendan Nyhan and Jason Reifler, "Misinformation and Fact-Checking: Research Findings from Social Science," *New America Foundation,* February 2012, 19, www.dartmouth.edu/~nyhan/Misinformation_and_Fact-checking.pdf; see also Kelly R. Garrett, Erik C. Nisbet, and Emily K. Lynch, "Undermining the Corrective Effects of Media-Based Political Fact Checking? The Role of Contextual Cues and Naive Theory," *Journal of Communication* 63 (2013): 617–37.

99. Nichols, *Death of Expertise*, 132.

100. Janna Anderson and Lee Rainie, "The Future of Truth and Misinformation Online," *Pew Research Center,* October 19, 2017, www.pewinternet.org/2017/10/19 /the-future-of-truth-and-misinformation-online.

101. Peter Dahlgren, *Television and the Public Sphere* (London: Sage, 1995).

102. Markus Prior, *Post-broadcast Democracy: How Media Choice Increases Inequality in Political Involvement and Polarizes Elections* (New York: Cambridge University Press, 2007).

103. Campante and Hojman, "Media and Polarization."

104. Thomas E. Patterson, "Young People and News," Report of the Joan Shorenstein Center on the Press, Politics, and Public Policy, Kennedy School of Government, Harvard University, July 2007, 19–21, www.hks.harvard.edu/presspol/research /carnegie-knight/young_people_and_news_2007.pdf.

105. Nic Newman, "Mainstream Media and the Distribution of News in the Age of Social Discovery," Report of the Reuters Institute for the Study of Journalism, Oxford University, September 2011, https://reutersinstitute.politics.ox.ac.uk/risj -review/mainstream-media-and-distribution-news-age-social-discovery.

106. Matthew B. Crawford, *The World beyond Your Head: On Becoming an Individual in an Age of Distraction* (New York: Farrar, Straus and Giroux, 2015), 11; see also Tim Wu, *The Attention Merchants: The Epic Scramble to Get inside Our Heads* (New York: Knopf, 2016).

107. Jamieson and Waldman, *Press Effect*, 12.

108. Silverman et al., "Hyperpartisan Facebook Pages."

109. Craig Silverman, "Lies, Damn Lies and Viral Content: How News Websites Spread (and Debunk) Online Rumors, Unverified Claims and Misinformation," *Tow Center for Digital Journalism,* February 10, 2015, http://towcenter.org/research /lies-damn-lies-and-viral-content; see also Alice Marwick and Rebecca Lewis, "Media Manipulation and Disinformation Online," *Data and Society,* 2017, https:// datasociety .net/pubs/oh/DataAndSociety_MediaManipulationAndDisinformation Online.pdf.

110. Jamieson and Waldman, *Press Effect*, 12.

111. Benkler, Faris, and Roberts, *Network Propaganda.*

112. Lippmann, *Liberty and the News*, 6.

113. Jay Rosen, *What Are Journalists For?* (New Haven, CT: Yale University Press, 1999), 295.

114. *Journalism's Crisis of Confidence* (New York: Carnegie Corporation of New York, 2007), 3.

115. Postman, *Amusing Ourselves*, 106.

116. Quoted in Neil Hickey, "Money Lust: How Pressure for Profit Is Perverting Journalism," *Columbia Journalism Review,* July–August, 1998, 4.

117. Martin Gilens, "Political Ignorance and Collective Policy Preferences," *American Political Science Review* 95 (2001): 379–96.

118. Michael Schudson, *The Sociology of News* (New York: Norton, 2003), 50.

119. Cappella and Jamieson, *Spiral of Cynicism.*

120. Quoted in David Shaw, "Beyond Skepticism." White quoted in speech of Nancy Gibbs, Harvard Kennedy School, November 15, 2017.

121. Daniel W. Drezner, *The Ideas Industry* (New York: Oxford University Press, 2017), 69.

122. Sabato, *Feeding Frenzy.*

123. Stone, "Snake and Stranger."

124. Franklin D. Gilliam Jr., Shanto Iyengar, Adam Simon, and Oliver Wright Oliver, "Crime in Black and White: The Violent, Scary World of Local News," *Harvard International Journal of Press/Politics* 1 (1996): 6–23; Entman and Rojecki, *Black Image.*

125. Based on a survey of journalists conducted by the author and Wolfgang Donsbach that asked respondents whether their responsibility extended beyond a story's publication.

126. "Covering the Great Recession," *Pew Research Center,* October 5, 2009, www.journalism.org/2009/10/05/covering-great-recession; Ramsay et al., "Misinformation and the 2010 Election."

127. Speech of Nancy Gibbs, Harvard Kennedy School, November 15, 2017.

128. Todd Gitlin, *Media Unlimited* (New York: Henry Holt, 2002), 5–6. Lanzon quoted in David Brooks, "The Essential John McCain," *New York Times*, October 19, 2017, www.nytimes.com/2017/10/19/opinion/the-essential-john-mccain.html.

129. Mike Maciag, "Voter Turnout Plummeting in Local Elections," *Governing*, October 2014, www.governing.com/topics/politics/gov-voter-turnout-municipal -elections.html.

130. Maciag, "Voter Turnout Plummeting."

131. See, for example, David A. Moss, "Fixing What's Wrong with U.S. Politics," *Harvard Business Review*, March 2012, https://hbr.org/2012/03/fixing-whats-wrong -with-us-politics; and Diane Ravitch, *The Death and Life of the Great American School System* (New York: Basic Books, 2011).

132. Key, *Responsible Electorate*, 2.

133. Marc J. Hetherington, "Resurgent Mass Partisanship: The Role of Elite Polarization," *American Political Science Review* 95 (2001): 619–31; Geoffrey C. Layman and Thomas M. Carsey, "Party Polarization and 'Conflict Extension' in the American Electorate," *American Journal of Political Science* 46 (2002): 324–46; Gabriel S. Lenz, *Follow the Leader?* (Chicago: University of Chicago Press, 2013).

134. NPR news story, February 12, 2018; Brett Barrouquere, "FBI: Hate Crimes Reach 5-Year High in 2016, Jumped as Trump Rolled toward Presidency," *Southern Poverty Law Center*, November 13, 2017, www.splcenter.org/hatewatch/2017/11/13 /fbi-hate-crimes-reach-5-year-high-2016-jumped-trump-rolled-toward-presidency-0.

135. Lippmann, *Public Opinion*, 178–79.

136. E. E. Schattschneider, *The Semi-sovereign People*, revised ed. (Belmont, CA: Wadsworth, 1975); Joseph Schumpeter, *Capitalism, Socialism and Democracy* (New York: Harper, 1942); Achen and Bartels, *Democracy for Realists*.

137. Patterson, *Out of Order*.

138. Lippmann, *Public Opinion*, 358–68.

139. Modeled after an argument about journalism in Lippmann, *Public Opinion*, 229.

SELECTED BIBLIOGRAPHY

Abramowitz, Alan. "The Rise of Negative Partisanship and the Nationalization of U.S. Elections in the 21st Century." *Electoral Studies* 41 (2016): 12–22.

Abramowitz, Alan I., Brad Alexander, and Matthew Gunning. "Incumbency, Redistricting, and the Decline of Competition in U.S. House Elections." *Journal of Politics* 68 (2006): 75–88.

Achen, Christopher, and Larry Bartels. *Democracy for Realists: Why Elections Do Not Produce Responsive Government.* Princeton, NJ: Princeton University Press, 2016.

Andersen, Kurt. *Fantasyland: How America Went Haywire.* New York: Random House, 2017.

Atkinson, Mary Layton. *Combative Politics: The Media and Public Perceptions of Lawmaking.* Chicago: University of Chicago Press, 2017.

Baum, Matthew A., and Tim Groeling. "New Media and the Polarization of American Political Discourse." *Political Communication* 25 (2008).

Benckler, Yochai, Robert Faris, and Hal Roberts. *Network Propaganda: Manipulation, Disinformation, and Radicalization in American Politics.* New York: Oxford University Press, 2018.

Bennett. W. Lance, and Steven Livingston. "The Disinformation Order: Disruptive Communication and the Decline of Democratic Institutions." *European Journal of Communication* 33 (2018): 122–39.

Berry, Jeffrey, and Sarah Sobieraj. *The Outrage Industry.* New York: Oxford University Press, 2016.

Bishop, Bill. *The Big Sort: Why the Clustering of Like-Minded America Is Tearing Us Apart.* New York: Houghton Mifflin, 2008.

Boatright, Robert G. *Getting Primaried: The Changing Politics of Congressional Primary Challenges.* Ann Arbor: University of Michigan Press, 2013.

Boorstin, Daniel. *The Genius of American Politics.* Chicago: University of Chicago Press, 1953.

———. *The Image: A Guide to Pseudo-events in America.* New York: Vintage, 1962.

Chua, Amy. *Political Tribes: Group Instincts and the Fate of Nations.* New York: Penguin Press, 2018.

Clark, Lynn Schofield, and Regina Marchi. *Young People and the Future of News.* New York: Cambridge University Press, 2017.

Cramer, Katherine J. *The Politics of Resentment: Rural Consciousness in Wisconsin and the Rise of Scott Walker.* Chicago: University of Chicago Press, 2016.

Gilens, Martin, and Benjamin I. Page. "Testing Theories of American Politics: Elites, Interest Groups, and Average Citizens." *Perspectives on Politics* 12 (2104): 564–81.

Groeling, Tim. *When Politicians Attack.* New York: Cambridge University Press, 2010.

Hacker, Jacob S., and Paul Pierson. *Off Center: The Republican Revolution and the Erosion of American Democracy.* New Haven, CT: Yale University Press, 2005.

Hemmer, Nicole. *Messengers on the Right: Conservative Media and the Transformation of American Politics.* Philadelphia, PA: University of Pennsylvania Press, 2016.

Hetherington, Marc J. *Why Trust Matters: Declining Political Trust and the Demise of American Liberalism.* Princeton, NJ: Princeton University Press, 2005.

Hetherington, Marc, and Thomas Rudolph. *Why Washington Won't Work: Polarization, Political Trust, and the Governing.* Chicago: University of Chicago Press, 2015.

Hibbing, John, and Elizabeth Theiss-Morse. *Stealth Democracy: Americans' Beliefs about How Government Should Work.* New York: Cambridge University Press, 2002.

Hindman, Matthew. *The Internet Trap: How the Digital Economy Builds Monopolies and Undermines Democracy.* Princeton, NJ: Princeton University Press, 2018.

Hochschild, Arlie Russell. *Strangers in Their Own Land.* New York: New Press, 2016.

Iyengar, Shanto, and Sean J. Westwood. "Fear and Loathing across Party Lines." *American Journal of Political Science* 59 (2015): 690–707.

Jamieson, Kathleen Hall. *Cyberwar: How Russian Hackers and Trolls Helped Elect a President.* New York: Oxford University Press, 2018.

Jamieson, Kathleen Hall, and Joseph N. Cappella. *Echo Chamber.* New York: Oxford University Press, 2010.

Jamieson, Kathleen Hall, and Paul Waldman. *The Press Effect.* New York: Oxford University Press, 2003.

Jones, Alex S. *Losing the News.* New York: Oxford University Press, 2009.

Kahneman, Daniel. *Thinking Fast and Slow.* New York: Farrar, Straus and Giroux, 2011.

Kamarck, Elaine C. *Primary Politics,* 2nd ed. Washington, DC: Brookings Institution Press, 2016.

Ladd, Jonathan M. *Why Americans Hate the Media and How It Matters.* Princeton, NJ: Princeton University Press, 2012.

Lee, Frances E. *Beyond Ideology: Politics, Principles, and Partisanship in the U.S. Senate.* Chicago: University of Chicago Press, 2009.

———. *Insecure Majorities: Congress and the Perpetual Campaign.* Chicago: University of Chicago Press, 2016.

Levitsky, Steven, and Daniel Ziblatt. *How Democracies Die.* New York: Crown, 2018.

Mann, Thomas E., and Norman J. Ornstein. *It's Even Worse Than It Looks: How the American Constitutional System Collided with the New Politics of Extremism,* expanded ed. New York: Basic Books, 2016.

McCarty, Nolan, Keith T. Poole, and Howard Rosenthal. *Polarized America: The Dance of Ideology and Unequal Riches.* Cambridge, MA: MIT Press, 2008.

Mutz, Diana. *In-Your-Face Politics.* Princeton, NJ: Princeton University Press, 2015.

Nichols, Tom. *The Death of Expertise.* New York: Oxford University Press, 2017.

Nyhan, Brendan, and Jason Reifler. "When Corrections Fail: The Persistence of Political Misperception." *Political Behavior* 32 (2010): 303–30.

Pariser, Eli. *The Filter Bubble: What the Internet Is Hiding from You.* New York: Penguin Books, 2012.

Patterson, Thomas E. *Informing the News.* New York: Vintage, 2013.

———. *Out of Order,* New York: Knopf, 1993.

Postman, Neil. *Amusing Ourselves to Death: Public Discourse in the Age of Show Business.* New York: Viking, 1985.

Prior, Markus. *Post-broadcast Democracy: How Media Choice Increases Inequality in Political Involvement and Polarizes Elections.* New York: Cambridge University Press, 2007.

Putnam, Robert D. *Bowling Alone. The Collapse and Revival of American Community.* New York: Simon and Schuster, 2000.

Putnam, Robert, and David Campbell. *American Grace: How Religion Divides and Unites Us.* New York: Simon and Schuster, 2012.

Rosen, Jay. *What Are Journalists For?* New Haven, CT: Yale University Press, 2001.

Shirky, Clay. *Cognitive Surplus: Creativity and Generosity in a Connected Age.* New York: Penguin Books, 2010.

Skocpol, Theda, and Vanessa Williams. *The Tea Party and the Remaking of Republican Conservatism,* updated ed. New York: Oxford University Press, 2016.

Sykes, Charles J. *How the Right Lost Its Mind.* New York: St. Martin's Press, 2017.

Thompson, Mark. *Enough Said: What's Gone Wrong with the Language of Politics.* New York: St. Martin's Press, 2016.

Thomsen, Danielle. *Opting Out of Congress.* New York: Cambridge University Press, 2017.

Zittrain, Jonathan. *The Future of the Internet—And How to Stop It.* New Haven, CT: Yale University Press, 2008.

INDEX

abortion issue, 13, 37, 42, 95–96
Abramowitz, Alan, 30
Access Hollywood, 11
Achen, Christopher, 23
Adams, John, 110
advertising and media marketing:
deception in, 97; evolution of
modern model, 99–100; and
gatekeeping algorithms, 93–94;
information overload in, 98–99;
market leverage, historical profile,
84–87; political ads, 96–98. *See also*
marketing of news
age and party affiliation, 38, 39, 47, 106,
122
Ailes, Roger, 17, 75
Albright, Madeleine, 51
algorithms and gatekeeping strategies,
42, 93–94, 122
alt-right, web presence of, 19–20
American prosperity, historical
profile, 52–54
American Psychological Association,
9
"Americans for Bush," 73

Amusing Ourselves to Death
(Postman), 87
Arendt, Hannah, 24
Asian Americans, 37, 106
Atkinson, Mary Layton, 74
attack journalism: destructive power
of and need for reform, 126–27;
evolution of, 43–45, 71–73, 85–87,
125; and political strategies, 73–74,
96–97. *See also* media
misinformation, evolution of; talk
shows, partisan
attention spans, 98, 98–99
automation and job loss, 23, 24, 47, 53

Baez, Joan, 91–92
Baker, Peter, 89
balloting reforms, 119–20
Balz, Dan, 79
Bannon, Steve, 63
Barber, James David, 7
Bartels, Larry, 23
Baum, Matthew, 44
Beck, Glenn, 13, 74
Benghazi incident, 16